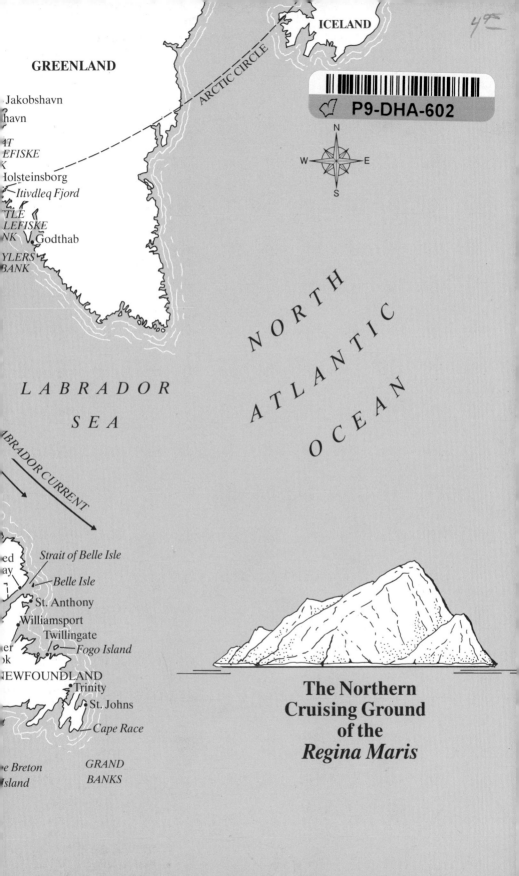

GREENLAND

Jakobshavn

havn

AT
EFISKE

Holsteinsborg

Itivdleq Fjord

TLE
LEFISKE
NK Godthab

YLERS
BANK

ARCTIC CIRCLE

ICELAND

N
W — E
S

N O R T H

A T L A N T I C

O C E A N

L A B R A D O R

S E A

LABRADOR CURRENT

Strait of Belle Isle

Belle Isle

St. Anthony

Williamsport

Twillingate

Fogo Island

NEWFOUNDLAND
Trinity

St. Johns

Cape Race

e Breton
sland

GRAND
BANKS

**The Northern
Cruising Ground
of the
*Regina Maris***

TUNING THE RIG

TUNING THE RIG

A Journey to the Arctic

HARVEY OXENHORN

1817
HARPER & ROW, PUBLISHERS, New York
Grand Rapids, Philadelphia, St. Louis, San Francisco
London, Singapore, Sydney, Tokyo, Toronto

"Ibis" originally appeared in the July 1983 issue of *The Atlantic*.
Parts of this book appeared as "Newfoundland: Tuning the Rig" in the September 1989 issue of *The Atlantic*.
"Lookin' for the Heart of Saturday Night" by Tom Waits/Fifth Floor Music, Inc. Copyright © 1974 Fifth Floor Music, Inc.
"Summer in the City" (John Sebastian, Stevens Boone, Mark Sebastian) copyright © 1966 Alley Music Corp. and Trio Music Co.,Inc. Used by permission. All rights reserved.

FIRST EDITION

Designed by Alma Orenstein

Map by Paul Pugliese

Line drawings by Kim Llewellyn

Library of Congress Cataloging-in-Publication Data
Oxenhorn, Harvey.
  Tuning the rig: a journey to the Arctic / Harvey Oxenhorn.—1st ed.
    p. cm.
  ISBN 0-06-016351-8
  1. Arctic regions—Description and travel. 2. Oxenhorn, Harvey.
3. *Regina Maris* (ship) 4. Humpback whale. I. Title.
G627.084 1990
919.804—dc20   89-46111

90 91 92 93 94 CC/HC 10 9 8 7 6 5 4 3 2 1

To the memory of my father,

JOSEPH M. OXENHORN,

with love and gratitude

CONTENTS

ACKNOWLEDGMENTS

This book sought to interweave a half dozen types of new experience for which I was unprepared with a dozen subjects about which I was equally ignorant when I started writing. I therefore relied on a wide variety of books and teachings to augment my knowledge and to help me synthesize what I had learned. In the latter category, some of the most helpful were Gregory Bateson, *Mind and Nature;* Bruce Chatwin, *The Songlines;* James Gleick, *Chaos;* Roland Huntford, *The Last Place on Earth;* Lewis Hyde, *The Gift;* David S. Landes, *Revolution in Time;* Farley Mowat, *Sea of Slaughter;* Samuel Eliot Morison, *The European Discovery of America;* Peter S. Stevens, *Patterns in Nature.* The references to Buddhism reflect, but do not claim to represent, the teachings of Chogyam Trungpa, Rinpoche, and Maurine Stuart of the Cambridge Buddhist Association. My longstanding interest in the sources of communal values, solidarity, and what might be called the "social bond" bears the lasting influence of two former teachers, Derek Traversi and Ian Watt.

I am grateful to the captains and crews with whom I've subsequently served aboard *Regina Maris, Bowdoin, When and If, Clearwater,* and *Te Vega* for sharing their seamanship and understanding. While writing, I consulted Kenneth C. Balcomb III and Peter Tyack on marine mammal biology, and Judith Perkins and J. Perran Ross on questions of ecology and ocean resource management. Captain Stephen J. Wedlock checked the manuscript for accuracy in nautical matters, and has offered invaluable insights about life at sea in a running conversation that has gone on for three years.

For editorial suggestions regarding sections of the manuscript or the work as a whole, I am grateful to Peter Davison, Seamus Heaney, Cullen Murphy, Virginia Reiser, and William Shawn, and especially to Robert Cohen, who read the book in three different drafts and gave superbly rigorous advice in matters large and small.

This book took years to complete, and like any extended project had its ups and downs. For their practical advice when it lost steerageway, I thank Jay Cantor, Christine Coffin, Hendrik Hertzberg and Phil Zuckerman. For their personal support through assorted gales and doldrums, I am grateful to Fay Baird, Susan Belfiore, Mark Breibart, Peter Canby, William Chace, Alice Hoffman, Larry Lane, Kathryn Lubar, Kim Pedersen, Stuart Pizer, Ann Parson, Ann Putnam, Stewart Reiser, Bud and Christine Ruf, Gregg Swanzey, Emma Sears, Sheryl White—and finally, as always, to my family.

Words cannot capture my full feeling for the MacDowell Colony, where I spent four of the past eight summers and where, in an atmosphere of peace, respect and limitless kindness, this work transformed itself from a simple travel article into its final form. My thanks as well to the Massachusetts Artists Foundation, Virginia Center for the Creative Arts, and the Corporation of Yaddo.

I am particularly grateful to my agent, Eric Ashworth, for his friendship, professional integrity, and navigational skills in guiding me to the right editor. I thank Terry Karten for being that editor and responding to my work on so many levels; for her good cheer, thoughtful judgment, and unflagging energy. Finally, I thank William Shinker, Christine Schillig, and the staff at Harper & Row for the personal interest they have demonstrated in this book, and the extra pains they took to make their House its home.

HARVEY OXENHORN

Knowledge the shade of a shade,
Yet must thou sail after knowledge
Knowing less than drugged beasts.

Ezra Pound,
Canto 47

The object of knowledge is relation.

James Clerk Maxwell

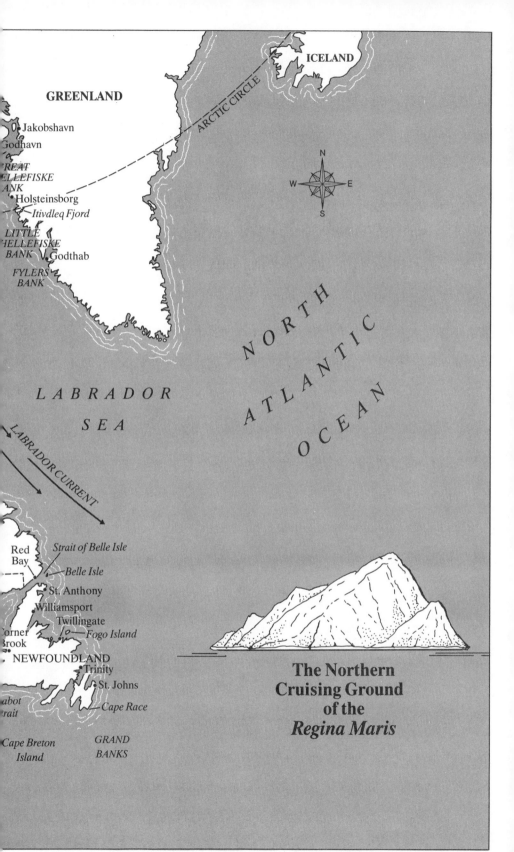

GREENLAND

Jakobshavn
Godhavn

GREAT
HELLEFISKE
BANK
Holsteinsborg
Itivdleq Fjord

LITTLE
HELLEFISKE
BANK
Godthab

FYLERS
BANK

ICELAND

ARCTIC CIRCLE

N
W   E
S

NORTH

ATLANTIC

OCEAN

LABRADOR

SEA

LABRADOR CURRENT

Red
Bay
Strait of Belle Isle

Belle Isle

St. Anthony
Williamsport
Twillingate
Fogo Island

Corner
Brook

NEWFOUNDLAND
Trinity
St. Johns

Cabot
Strait
Cape Race

Cape Breton
Island
GRAND
BANKS

**The Northern
Cruising Ground
of the
*Regina Maris***

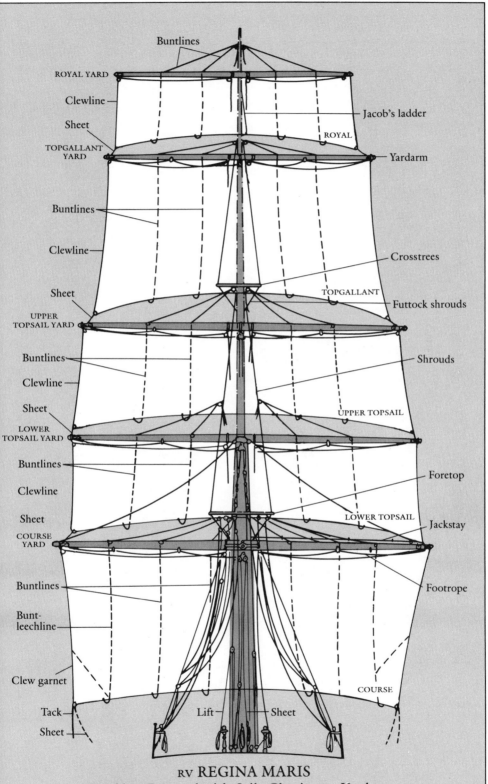

Buntlines

ROYAL YARD

Clewline

Sheet

Jacob's ladder

ROYAL

TOPGALLANT
YARD

Yardarm

Buntlines

Clewline

Crosstrees

Sheet

TOPGALLANT

Futtock shrouds

UPPER
TOPSAIL YARD

Buntlines

Shrouds

Clewline

Sheet

UPPER TOPSAIL

LOWER
TOPSAIL YARD

Buntlines

Clewline

Foretop

Sheet

LOWER TOPSAIL

Jackstay

COURSE
YARD

Buntlines

Footrope

Bunt-
leechline

Clew garnet

COURSE

Tack

Lift — Sheet

Sheet

RV REGINA MARIS
Looking Forward with Sails Clewing to Yardarms

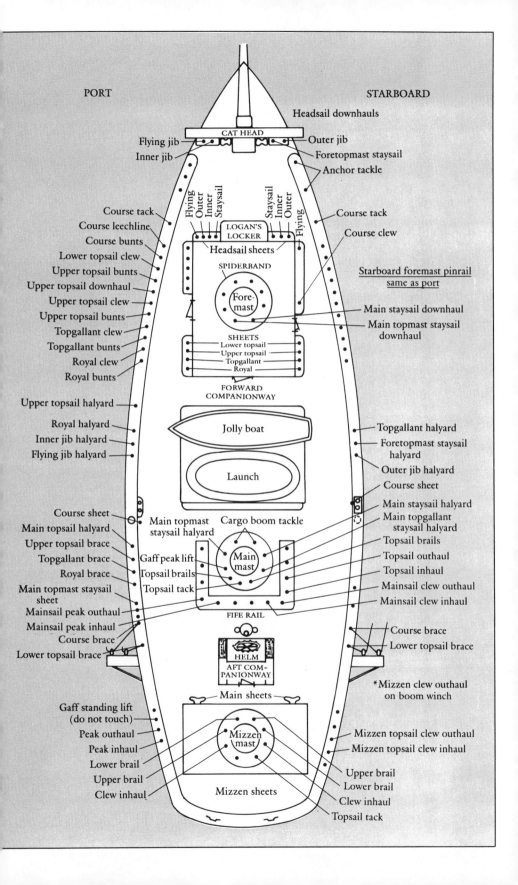

LOOKOUT

26 June. Boston, Aquarium Wharf.

On a hot June night on the Boston waterfront, I stood alone beneath the Central Artery, looking outward, east, at dusk, to the quiet harbor. Above me, traffic rumbled. At my back glowed Quincy Market, cobblestone and granite, rough hewn, now accommodating teddy bear boutiques and singles bars. Ahead, in the highway's shadow, slumbered wharves that had been the New World's first front door. And at one of these lay moored the old tall ship on which I'd sail, come morning, for the Arctic.

My knowledge of boats was not extensive. I had taught Conrad, read Melville, once swamped a sunfish in the lake at summer camp. I was no athlete and as a child had dreaded ropes and jungle gyms. Yet within the week I'd be asked to lay aloft like a true jack-tar, to "work by day, watch by night," to "hand, reef, and steer" in any weather. As my gaze moved up the ship's three masts—each seven stories high—it struck me that my preparation could have been more thorough. But there I was, bound by my own choice to "stand watch at 2000 hours." Twenty hundred hours! I swallowed hard. Then crossed Atlantic Avenue and climbed aboard.

Regina Maris is a white oak barkentine with more than three miles of line and sixteen canvas sails. Launched from the Danish isle of Fyn in the year 1908, she has carried cargo on the Baltic, transshipped nitrates from Chile, and seen service on four oceans; known two mutinies; been reduced to a hulk by fire, abandoned at sea, and dismasted in a Roaring Forties gale. The ship has been registered in London, Los Angeles, and Malta, involved in lawsuits from Panama to Piraeus, received by the queen of England one bright afternoon—and impounded the next morning. Since 1975 she has found a new life as a full-time ocean research vessel,

3

used to study and protect the animals her sister ships once slaughtered, humpback whales. In the months to come they would lead, and we would follow, from the Gulf of Maine to Newfoundland, from Labrador to Greenland, then north up an iceberg-laden coast into polar seas.

This expedition's crew was not a seasoned task force, hardly the type, from first appearances, to thrive on danger. Nine women and twenty-one men, they ranged in age from seventeen to sixty and fell into three groups. One group was professional crew: the captain, three mates and three deckhands, the engineer, the cook, and the bosun, who takes care of the ropes and sails. The second group consisted of four scientists who were excused from ship's work in order to do research and teach classes. Finally, there were the sixteen students who would help conduct the research and work as apprentice seamen. Most of them were in graduate school or college. But one was an artist, another a dentist and avid sailor who had moved, lock, stock, and drills, from a London suburb to Goose Bay, Labrador. And there was me. On shore I teach. My interests tend to wander.

Ten months earlier, I had come to the docks to meet a friend who was then the ship's biologist. He took me aboard and mentioned casually that there was talk of a sail to Greenland the following summer. I did nothing to pursue it at the time. But over the course of a long, hard, hectic winter, the image of that ship in arctic waters kept popping up in my mind and beckoning. By the time spring arrived, I had a proposal ready for George Nichols, the captain: I would be assigned to a working watch and earn my keep as a full-time apprentice seaman. In addition, I would write an account of the experience and the ship's activity, which would provide publicity and help obtain support for future operations.

Just what I would write about, and how my two responsibilities (to the ship's work and to my own) would fit together, was not clear. Based on our brief acquaintance, Nichols had seemed content to leave it undefined. That was fine with me. The key thing was to get myself on board, cast off, and work out the rest when the time came. Which was now.

Earlier in the day we'd been assigned to watches. Stepping across *Regina*'s rail, I found the five other members of the fore watch gathered around our deckhand, Joan. My new boss was a jaunty woman of twenty-three with a friendly brusqueness, a wholesome expression, and the dirtiest hands and jeans I'd ever seen.

"Knots," she was saying in a flat midwestern twang, "knots are . . . important. Anyone here can't tie a square knot?" If so, they weren't saying. "Good. How 'bout a bow-line?" Four hands went up. "OK, let's get some line."

Stepping over an inverted toilet bowl, a disassembled generator, and three crates of acorn squash, Joan raised the hinged seat of the port settee and pulled out some rope from inside. "OK," she said, "the bowline is a fixed loop at the bitter end. It's good for tethers, designed to slip over one thing, like a piling, and secure it to another, like the ship's bow. Here's how it's tied." On my fourth attempt, I successfully secured my right index finger to my left hand. That was about as far as Joan's kind talk of rabbits coming in and out of holes could get me.

Next came the "slippery clove hitch," required to "gasket the squares," that is, tie the rolled-up square sails to their yards so that they can be "let fall" quickly. Here I got help from David Oldach. A tall young man with sandy curls, chipped teeth, and a wrestler's build, he seemed at once hesitant and eager, physically strong yet with a shyness bordering on weakness in his eyes. As if to excuse my fumbling, he remarked that he'd "crewed on skipjacks" and "done some climbing" and then showed me a trick. It worked. I tied the knot three times in succession, feeling saltier by the second. "Great," said Joan over my shoulder. "Of course, when it's rough aloft, you'll want to do that with one hand."

We were joined by the first mate, Gregg Swanzey. Gregg is a stocky man of twenty-eight with rounded shoulders, large pale eyes, still hands, and a gaze so steady it would be unnerving if it weren't also kind. He had heard Joan's last comment to me and now looked amused. Gazing off tolerantly and smiling to himself, he exuded quietness, like an old-time baseball catcher, ready to leap from his pool of calm and fire a strike if anyone tried to steal.

The French call a sailing ship's chief mate the *deuxième capi-taine,* or second captain. By tradition he is also in charge of the front of the boat, its bow and anchors, and head of the fore watch (one of the three working watches, each named for a mast). The mate directs maintenance in port, assigns all work at sea, and bears responsibility for the condition of the vessel. Watching Gregg as he led us from stem to stern, I thought I had never seen a man so in possession of—or possessed by—his surroundings. You could see it in the way his hands found switches that he hadn't even looked for. As he led us up and down companion-ways, stooping here, twisting there, he never changed speed. I stumbled on behind, trying not to slip on the practically vertical stairs or bang my head on the bulkheads at every turn.

Meanwhile, I missed most of what Gregg was saying. Not that he wasn't patient, and thorough to a fault. But I just could not receive his words in the literal, instructive way he spoke them. Fife rail? Martingale? When bracing the royal yard . . . ? The next thing you knew, he'd be telling us how to drive a chariot or storm a moat!

If the language seemed out of a storybook or a history game called Frigate, what it described looked less like a functioning ship than a maritime museum after its funds had been cut. Whatever images I'd brought of white sails sweeping bright horizons were immediately dimmed, to put it mildly, by the atmosphere on board. Torn buckets and iron tools were scattered on deck beside disassembled hardware. Greasy cables crisscrossed the hatches. Clumps of damp hemp hung tied forlornly to the stays like worn-out mops; they had surely outlived whatever purpose they once had. Ropes had burned inch-deep grooves in the old oak bannis-ter that ran around the deck. Cracked straight through in places, it seemed never to have known varnish. Rust tracks bled into soot on the deckhouse walls.

"Never mind pretty," I worried, "what about *safe?*" We were not setting off for Nantucket, after all. Such things should have been taken care of by someone. If not now, when?

Below decks, the lights were dim, and the space was even tighter. The mingled stench of bilges, diesel fumes, and the two out of three heads that didn't work could make you seasick without leaving port.

"Odors," I heard Gregg say, as if sharing a cherished secret, "amazing smells. And light, and wind. [We were back on deck.] Ships are a very sensual environment. Their movement is a conversation. If you listen, they will tell you things—" He caught himself and smiled down at his wide feet, embarrassed. "Well. You'll see."

It was now past eleven. Some of us had spent the whole day on planes, none had yet unpacked, and all were due up at five. Joan dismissed the watch so we could get "a full night's sleep"; she and Gregg still had things to do and would stay on deck awhile. We said good night. The others went below. I went by myself to the bow.

Regina lay moored at Aquarium Wharf. Twenty yards from the bowsprit, which I now straddled, three harbor seals swam laps in their outdoor pool. One was the famous talking seal named Hoover. Every few minutes I could hear him bark, "How *are* you?"

I was not so well. A week before, I had mailed off a doctoral dissertation and been granted a degree three thousand miles away; after six years' effort, there was no reward, and the only rite of passage was a clerk's stamp in the office of the dean. Two weeks before, I'd completed my year's teaching—three college courses—for less than half my students' yearly fees, much less than I had earned ten years before, straight out of school. The provost had said, *"Of course* you are exploited; you really should move on."

Move on? In the past three years I had applied for forty jobs, been brought out for final talks at a half dozen places, only to find out later that interview A had been a setup; that college B had to have a woman; that department C could not agree on anyone, so they simply abolished the job. Et cetera. And as one part of things failed to come together, the others began to come apart. "One must learn to respect the detours," I had said. "Your whole life is a detour," she replied.

All right, then. Feeling marginal, I would head out to the margins. I would go beyond encumbrances, the calibrations of success sought or bestowed, and relocate myself in whatever I could find, and feel, and hold in my own hand.

Hoover was not impressed. "How *are* you?" he repeated, smacking his flippers like some stern Zen master's paddle, seeking a simpler answer to a simple question, posed in that ludicrous garbled voice from beneath the sea: How *are* you?

The *Dolley Madison* pulled in across the pier. With its bright stack of dance floors, flashing spotlights, and battery of five-foot speakers fore and aft, it looked like a floating jukebox. When the last drunk passenger had been discharged, the throb of disco halted in midphrase. Crewmen hosed down the decks, shut off the lights, locked up, and went ashore.

I kicked off my shoes and stood on the cool oak deck. A whiff of the bilges rose through the hawsehole, mingling with the highway's fumes. Then a puff of sea breeze cleared the air. Through my naked feet I felt *Regina* feel it, stretching, sighing, stirring in her mooring, like a great bud in the calyx of its sails, about to bloom.

27 June. 42°N/69°W.

A bright afternoon in the Gulf of Maine, heading northeast in a gentle breeze. Off duty, second mate Bill Cowan, age twenty-five, stands amidships, a belaying bin in one hand and a toothpick in the other. Sunlight bouncing off the water halos his thick blond hair. With his head tipped back, he scans the rig as the watch he leads, the main watch, gathers. It is time to learn the ropes.

All told, *Regina* has 140 of them, paired like flexor and extensor muscles to set, trim, hoist, and lower 5200 square feet of sail. These lines are thick and heavy; the one that hauls up the smallest jib, for example, is 195 feet long. Each works in combination with up to a dozen others. We will be required to know them all and locate each one, even in the dark.

We've been given diagrams to study. Thus to distinguish the fore topgallant staysail downhauls, mainsail peak inhauls, or mizzen clew outhauls from the gaff vang just behind (I mean *aft of*) the mizzen topsail brails, you need only memorize where each one is "coiled down" along the pinrail. Or the "taffrail." "Fife rail." "Catheads." Or the "spiderband." I've been walking the deck, chart in hand, naming each pin I pass and remembering the name for about as long as it takes to mispronounce it. It would be easier to learn these terms if I knew what they mean, what functions they describe. So in an effort to find out, I sidle up to the main watch, now assembled.

"Aaah you ready?" Bill asks, displaying his perfect teeth and sea-green eyes. "This heah's the uppa tops'l halyed. Pawt side, all by itself just aft of the royal bunts. Three-quartah-inch manilla. Jack, what does a halyed do?"

"Hauls the yard."

"Meaning what?"

"Got me!"

"How do you find out?" Silence. "You *figya* it out. Look: Staat wayuh the line comes off the pin. Now follow it up with yaw eyes." I try. Within thirty feet I've lost it.

"If youah having trouble, give it a pull." He yanks the line sideways; sixty feet up, one of two dozen tackles bounces gently. "See?" (No, not at all.) "This line is led all the way up to that block, then back down heah"—he points to an eight-inch-wide, triple-sheaved block at the height of his head—"back up to gain purchase, back down again, through heah a second time, a third, then down around the pin.

"Got that? Now. Look at the yahd. Third one. One, course. Two, lowah. Three, uppah. Fowah, t'gallant. Five, royal. OK? Numbah three, uppah tops'l. See the steel lines that run in from each end to the yahd? Right now there is no slack, 'cause the yahd is down in its lifts. When we all pull down on this, it will haul the whole yahd up along the mast. OK, let's do it."

Bill lifts the coiled portion of the line—three turns remain around the pin—and tosses it aft. It lands on deck, straight out, with a heavy thump. We line up along it, three on a side.

"Hold on. Sid, Jack, Helene, always stand inbawd of a running line. All right, now listen. When we take the line off its pin, you guys will be holding up the yahd. Nevah let go until I give the awdah. When I say, 'Haul away,' we haul. When I say, 'Hold,' you stop—but don't let go. Then I'll ask, 'Ready?' When you ansah, 'Ready,' I then call out, 'Up behind!' Immediately throw down the line, away from you, with both hands. All right. Stand by youah uppah tops'l halyed! Ready?"

"Ready!"

"Haul away!"

At the front of our line, Bill reaches overhead with both hands, pulling down on the vertical rope like a bell ringer, using his whole body. Scott Cordes, the main watch deckhand, bends behind Bill, keeping the slack against the pin. In a row behind Scott we all haul in unison. The brass sheaves squeak in their blocks. A rhythm takes hold. On the fourth heave, Bill sings out, "King Louis was the king of France before the revolu-shy-on" . . . "Away, haul away," sings Scott, "A haul away, Joe!"

"But then he got his head chopped off, which spoiled the con-sti-tu-shy-on . . ." "Away, haul away," (all) "We'll haul away Joe!"

It's corny, all right, but like magic, the rhythm of hauling falls into the beat of the music; with each call and response, the yard rises. So do my stomach muscles. Only when I'm absolutely *sure* I've got a hernia does Bill say, "Hold!" Then, squinting upward at the yard, "One maw . . . and anothah . . . and anothah . . . one maw good one . . . hold."

Letting go of the line below the block, he reaches above, to where it is looped in six parallel strands between the upper and lower tackles. Spreading his fingers wide, he takes all six lines in his hands and twists them tight against one another, using the friction to counter slippage. His wrist muscles strobe and quiver like the line that he is holding; the veins in his forearms bulge.

"Ready?"

"Ready!"

"Up behind!"

We hurl down the rope. For one split second, as Scott snakes three figure eights around the pin, Bill controls the entire line. If it slips, the yard it holds up could come crashing down like a tree felled fifty feet above our heads. But nothing happens. A moment later the line is fast, and Bill is wiping his hands on his jeans nonchalantly. Panting, looking up, I see that the yard is two feet higher than before. Around the mast, a leather sleeve that it rides on is now visible; underneath the yard, the topsail billows taut.

"OK," says Bill. "You got it? Uppah tops'l halyed, pawt side, all by itself, just aft of the royal bunts."

Sid and Craig are whispering to each other, smirking. "What's up?" Bill asks.

"Up behind!" Sid squeals, with a glance at his Turkish watchmate, named Canan. She blushes. By the rail, Helene, an extremely pretty Princeton junior, sprouts like a jonquil from her cutoffs. "Up behind?" asks Craig. She winks. They laugh.

This morning when I woke in port, rain drummed fiercely overhead, and sheets of water flowed across the small glass "deck light" just above my pillow. There was still half an hour until breakfast, so I struggled into boots and weather gear and headed up the stairs.

On deck the sky was blue as a robin's egg, the early morning sun like melted butter; my fierce storm turned out to be the mizzen watch, hard at work with a fire hose and brushes. They'd been busy while we slept. Gear that had lain scattered everywhere last night was now securely stowed. All lines hung neatly coiled on their pins, our small boats sat stacked in front of the mainmast, and the decks were cleared. Their raw wet planks glowed cocoa brown, with puddles in the worn spots steaming.

Departure was delayed while we waited for the innards of a bilge pump to return. Before I could brush my teeth after breakfast, I was hustled along by Joan at 7:50: "We *arrive* on deck *before* our watch begins." There seemed precious little cause to hurry, nothing much to do. But she had decided to take us aloft.

"What, now?" I asked, in a tone of voice not heard since Isaac spoke to Abraham. One of my watchmates named "Root" Liebman grinned and spat tobacco juice. It didn't clear the rail.

Going aloft involves two separate stages: climbing the shrouds and then slithering out along the yardarms to tend sails. Joan's plan was to have us try only the first today and go up halfway. At the foot of the foremast shroud, she advised us to maintain three points of contact, just in case our feet should slip or a line we were holding on to parted. Always climb on the windward side, she added. If you fall, it is better to land on deck than be blown off and drown. Without further ado, she handed out climbing harnesses and, not putting one on herself, said, "Follow me."

I paused for a minute to tie my left shoe, and then my right. Then my left. And then my right, again. Meanwhile, one by one, my watchmates faced outboard, stepped onto the rail, then pivoted to face the shroud, grabbed hold, and began to climb.

I gulped and followed. Five rungs . . . fifteen . . . twenty. Pausing for breath at the twenty-fifth, I glanced down, wondering: If you fell from here, would you simply break your neck, or would you splatter? Onward. At the top of the lower mast, my heart began to beat absurdly fast, my right calf cramped, my palms grew sweaty on the stays. We hadn't left dockside, but for me the whole deck was heaving. "One slip," I kept thinking, too scared now to look down, "one misstep in sixty-five nights and days . . ."

Almost as bad as this private panic on top of a very tall pole was the sight of my watchmates (including two college coeds five feet tall) forging outward overhead on the lower topsail yard. True, they were not exactly whistling while they worked, but at least they *tried*. I couldn't. Last up and first down, I descended very slowly, pausing at every other step to "clip on," then getting tangled in my tether on the next step down. When I reached the deck at last, I was rubber-legged and dizzy.

The rest of the day became an assault of small details: Do this, lift that, come here, watch out, fetch things you cannot recognize in places you can't name, as if it were all so obvious that only a fool would delay. There's a right way, of course, to do even the simplest task, and nine times out of ten, you discover later, it's the way you didn't choose.

"There is not so helpless and pitiable an object in the world," wrote Richard Henry Dana in *Two Years Before the Mast,* "as a landsman beginning a sailor's life." Nor, he might have added, can that object find a moment's respite from its own incompetence. Today we were up at six, on watch until noon. After lunch I was told that the watch coming off does dishes, and within the fore watch it was Guess Whose turn. So I filled two ten-gallon pots with salt water; heated it; washed thirty-one sets of dishes; switched to the freshwater pump for rinsing; hand-pumped the drain; and carried three forty-gallon garbage cans on deck and scrubbed them clean with water drawn in buckets from the sea. That done, I used my whole day's freshwater ration (one quart) to wash *myself* and went aft to lie down.

My berth is an upper in the port side passageway. Not "off" the passageway (through a door) but actually in it, like the luggage shelf over seats in a railroad car. It's six feet long, two wide, two high, and five off the floor. After a few failed efforts, I figured out how to get in (head first, face down, turn over *after* you're inside). I had hoped to share a cabin; I don't see how anyone could really sleep in a hall, with a constant stream of people brushing by. But I lay down anyway, pulled the curtain shut, and closed my eyes.

I had remained that way for a full three minutes, maybe even four, when I was jolted by the less than sweet sound of third mate Patrick Wadden: *"Anyone got a flashlight?"* Anything to quiet him. I opened the curtain and offered mine. He accepted it and took me in the bargain. The next hour was spent hauling ten-gallon cans up from the bilges. While setting the last on deck, I realized, to my amazement, that in the ten hours since we'd left Boston, I had not once just stood still and looked out at the sea.

✳✳✳

In his welcoming talk this morning, Captain Nichols told us, "What you do on shore is your own business; what you do on board is everyone's." He said this in reference to "special relationships," adding that he cared less about the people in a couple than the jealousies and conflicts their relationship might spawn. Later in his talk, he used the same phrase—"everybody's business"—again, this time in regard to courtesy and the quality of the work we do.

I now realize it referred to quantity of work as well. If today is typical, the notion of limits, of what it is reasonable to ask, seems never to have crossed these people's minds. If you're asleep, they wake you; when you're awake, they work you. There is no time—none at all—to get hold of yourself, to make sense of what goes on. I feel wiped out after fourteen hours! Can we keep this up, around the clock, for sixty days?

I suppose we'll have to; that's what makes the voyage possible.

Did I say "possible"? It's evening now. The wind just changed. Our square sails were unrolled against the dimming sky, and I felt the ship surge forward slightly as each new sail filled. The machinery has been shut off. Now the only sound is water on our bow and the wind against sixteen sails. We are sixty miles out to sea in a tall ship *we* are sailing. I feel like I've passed through an airlock, or a time warp, into another world.

28 June. 43°N/68°W. Gulf of Maine.

At 3:45 in the morning, a strange voice whispered in my berth, and hands reached through the curtain. Dawn watch. Minutes later I was up on deck, feeling dopey, seasick, cold. We were heading east. An orange crescent moon hung dead ahead on the horizon. I took up my lookout position on the bow.

An hour passed. As the sea gave up its blackness and the sky grew gray, the soft shapes swooping through our rig turned into birds with damp wings and bright eyes.

Another hour. At dawn, an object floated into view.

"On deck!" I shouted back, as we'd been taught. A voice from the helm called, "Yo!"

"There's something in the water."

"What?"

"Don't know."

"How far?"

"Can't tell. On our right side. Off the bow."

Gregg joined me, took a quick glance, ordered some sails struck and a change of course, and walked off to wake up George.

Our course change put the object dead ahead. At a thousand yards, it became an oblong; at five hundred yards, a dory. What were they doing out here? Were we near a fishing boat that had problems with its trawl? Were they survivors of a sinking?

Gregg said nothing in answer to my questions. At five hundred yards, we could see a single oar hanging limply in one oarlock, floating blade-up on the surface. Probably just a boat adrift, I thought, or maybe there *was* someone inside, someone who could not sit up, or . . . Suddenly I understood Gregg's silence. We stood waiting, braced ourselves for the worst, and drew abeam.

The dory was half swamped, full of gear, and plastered with seagull droppings—but unoccupied. Lawrence Schuster, our bosun, had come on deck. He jumped down into it and handed up a brass Old Timer knife, some flares, a peacoat with feathers stuck to its sleeves, and a life ring marked "INVADER." Two weeks before, the fishing boat *Invader* had been hauled out in the same East Gloucester shipyard as *Regina*. Its crew had dropped by, bringing squid and a case of beer.

A boat adrift is a hazard to navigation. Looking down, George said in a carefully controlled voice, "Sink her." Lawrence nodded but didn't speak. He pulled the stern plug and stepped over onto our channels. The little boat filled quickly, silently. As it went under, sunrise lit the sky.

Gregg stared at the spot where the boat had been. Then he

turned away, deliberately, and sang out, "Stand by your lower topsail gear."

We all leapt into action. Nobody paused again until ten to eight, when with all sails set and the deck scrubbed clean, we laid below for breakfast.

Here everything becomes procedure; even disaster has its own routines. After lunch, all hands were called for safety drills. The first one was for fire. As with everything else so far, the methods were almost the opposite of what I would have guessed. For example, once a fire gets going below, the first step is to attack it, right? Wrong; the first step is to get away from it, up on deck. Only when all hands are accounted for does a "fire party" headed by the engineer return below. Of course, as many crew as possible should assist them, right? Wrong again. To contain a blaze at sea, you must control the breeze that fans it, steering upwind if the fire's back aft, and downwind if it's forward. Thus most of the crew fight fire not with extinguishers and hoses but by handling sail. My fire station is alongside the headsail gear.

Our next drill was "Man Overboard." Underway, *Regina* takes fifteen minutes just to turn around, given all the clewing up and bracing that's required. In the meantime, the cook is preparing sugar and hot water, the second and third mates are lowering boats, and a deckhand fetches bandages and blankets. My own job, with all the sail work going on, would be conscientiously to ignore it. I am to climb up the forward deckhouse, stand on its roof with my eyes fixed on the person in the water, and not look away for *anything*. Moreover, I am to point at him constantly; this eliminates extra talk, and if I should lose sight of him in the trough of a wave, my arm might still guide someone else's vision.

Though well thought out, this is mostly a gesture, in more ways than one. In the seas to which we're bound, the surface temperature will be under thirty-two degrees; you could last, at most, two minutes. "So remember, people," George concluded, "please be very careful when you lay aloft. The real way to survive Man Overboard is, *don't . . . fall . . . in!*"

What happens if you are forced to? This led to a final drill:

"Abandon Ship." For that, my special task would be to reach the aft salon no matter what, collect a thermos-sized EPIRB (emergency-position-indicating radio beacon), and not let go of it until I am off the ship and secure inside the number two raft. EPIRBs emit a signal recognized by any passing plane, and it's on them, more than anything else, that long-range survival might depend.

As we worked through the various drills, my mind was awash, so to speak, with baroque, unpleasant images: the rig in flames like a giant candelabra; stiff blue bodies, rafts pinned underneath the surface, tangled in the rig as they attempt to rise. Clearly, what each of us does at such times matters. Yet I couldn't help but notice that spontaneous "initiatives" were not merely discouraged but forbidden. In each case, the rule seemed to be first to get all hands involved and then to fulfill your role in the collective plan. And for that, it was stressed repeatedly, you need to concentrate and listen.

Everyone had been quiet and subdued while practicing the drills, and when someone on the main watch made a joke, his mate Bill Cowan, who seemed oddly tense, immediately dressed him down. But then came survival suits. Bright orange; these are a cross between spacesuits and children's pajamas with feet. They are coldproof, waterproof, and buoyant. They have light bulbs and whistles in their sleeves, check valves in their toes, and instructions stamped in mistranslated Swedish on their arms. Imagine it: You're up in the Arctic, your ship's gone down, but you keep up the backfloat, in between the icebergs. Staring skyward, you are swaddled in orange plastic, sealed in your bright cocoon. Minutes creep by. Then hours. Days. Growing restless (never cold), you raise your arms toward heaven (just to pass the time) and discover this message stenciled on the sleeve:

> ZIPPED UPTIGHT?
> JUST RELAX YOU
> CANNOT SINK

Regina was built for cargo, not passengers. Except for the forecastle, most of the space in which we now live was once a dank hold filled with guano. Ten feet deep, roughly twenty by forty long, it is crossed overhead by foot-square timbers. Windowless, it is topped by two steel-barred skylights that can open in fair weather and is ringed on three sides by tiers of "pilot berths." At one end, near the galley, a coconut swings from the handrail overhead, above the scuttle; it has a smile painted on and wears a straw sombrero. The wall at the other end holds bookshelves and a bulletin board.

Converted into the ship's major public space and rechristened the "main salon," this hold serves as library, dormitory, clubhouse, classroom, and mess. Everything anyone does there seems to depend, around the clock, on what twenty-nine other people are doing. Tonight, for example, the dinner dishes suddenly inspired the person washing them to rush up on deck. For as long as he "lost his cookies" over the rail, our tables remained uncleared. Class couldn't start, and my own time for sleep (before watch at twelve) dwindled to three hours.

At long last, however, the dishes went back on one set of shelves as the students came down from another; the deckhands and mates went on watch as a group, and our chief scientist, Peter Bryant, started his introductory class. A geneticist by training, Peter directs the Developmental Biology Center at the University of California at Irvine and is president of the American Cetacean Society. He's a whimsical, thick-legged man of forty-five with a swirly gray beard and a Dorset accent, given to sharing complex ideas in disarmingly simple ways.

Between 1909 and 1965, he began, roughly 150,000 humpback whales were killed worldwide. Only four or five thousand now remain, scattered widely across all oceans. In order to protect cetaceans and predict their future, one has to know just how many there are. To know how many there are, you must know whether those seen off of Newfoundland or Greenland in July are the same ones as those seen off of Puerto Rico in December. And the only way to do that is by resighting individual whales.

How do you tell one from another? Peter asked. You can't tag a whale the way you would a sparrow, and since whales are sensitive and endangered, you don't want to harm or disturb them in any way. Luckily, the animals themselves provide a nonintrusive method. On the underside of every humpback's flukes is a pigment pattern as unique to that whale as fingerprints to a human being. The whales display this pattern just before they dive. So by taking thousands of high-speed "fluke shots" and comparing them to others in a catalog, we may begin to discover overlaps.

For this purpose *Regina* is equipped with a darkroom, specialized cameras, and a computer. The plan for Greenland is to guess, through oceanographic sampling, where whales would be most likely to feed, and then sail back and forth on a survey of those waters. While seeking out and photographing individuals, Peter said, we will undertake a general census. We will seek to form a picture of the humpbacks' diet up there, which determines patterns of migration, and to understand how those patterns cross, and possibly conflict with, human uses of the sea.

Judith Perkins now took over. Though still enrolled, more or less, in the Graduate School of Forestry at Yale, she is one of those polymath idealists whose practical experience consistently precedes (and interrupts) their formal training and who often know more about their field than the folks from whom they seek credentials. A cocreator of the humpback catalog, she's a veteran of fieldwork in the Maritimes, a naturalist, an oceanographer, and an expert birder too.

"Whales are terrific," she began. "They are beautiful, and it's exciting—fun—to watch them. But it may be more meaningful to think not of *single species* but of *community.* In this sense, humpbacks are what we call an 'indicator species.' Because they are at the top of the food chain, and so sensitive and complex, their activity reflects the health of less visible forms which they depend on. So by studying whales we can learn about the whole niche they inhabit—which we, incidentally, share.

"The best way to learn about something very big is to start out small. So besides watching whales, we'll be looking at seabirds who share the same prey. We'll be trawling for fish and plankton. We'll be sampling water temperature. Salinity. The profile of the ocean floor.

"In practical terms, this means three things. First of all, we will want someone aloft on whale watch eighteen hours a day—longer when we've got more daylight. Second, we will be keeping an environmental log, with entries every four hours by the watch that's going off. Finally, each of you should choose a special research project of your own.

"A lot of these will involve observations that are tedious. And our methods may seem crude compared to fields where a whole lot more is known. A lot of people, for example, have been studying humpbacks off Silver Bank, Navidad, or Maui. But where we are bound, almost nothing has been done. We are still asking basic questions. That is terribly exciting, don't you think? We don't know what we'll find there. Just by going, and observing carefully, you guys will be doing fundamental science. You will all be pioneers."

29 June. 43°N/66°W.

Having stood watch from midnight to four, I was roused at half past seven for breakfast and morning meeting, where George Nichols, fresh from his seven hours' sleep, looked maddeningly cheerful. "Good *mawning,* everyone," he grinned, part imp and all patrician. "Thank you for coming to this meeting. I'm delighted you could make it. Scott, will you please ask Miss Kelly if she cares to join us?"

Redheaded, six foot two, the main watch deckhand reached out toward the corner bunk with an arm like a derrick, swept open its curtain from end to end, and sang out, "Mor-ning mee-ting!" Inside, the delicate head of my watchmate, Kathryn Kelly, rose into view; bewildered eyes peeped out like a sparrow chick's at a marsh hawk.

"Well now, people," George began. "One of the really swell things about life at sea is that you are never much more than falling distance from your berth. Of course, a *dry* berth is generally cozier than a wet one. *Regina's* a great old lady, but as you've probably discovered by now, she works considerably, and when she works she sweats—"

"George, you don't mean she *leaks?*" The bosun, deep-voiced, barrel-chested, mugged shock through a beard like groomed sargassum.

"You could say that, Lawrence, yes." The crew all burst out laughing. The students looked confused. "So I strongly suggest that you plasticize your berths as you see fit. You can find the materials—uh—Lawrence?"

"Under the chain locker."

"Fine. Any questions?"

Lisa: "Where is the chain locker?"

"Fo'c'sle. Opposite the reefer. Next to the bucket of fids."

"Speakin' of leaks," said a voice like carborundum, "I'm gettin' pretty tired of uncloggin' the numbah one head." Fran Grost, the engineer. "Someone's not pumpin' when they get through. It's twenty strokes."

"Twenty-five," said Joan. "Twenty-five strokes *after* it leaves the bowl."

"And nothin' but toilet paper. Got it? No floss, no Q-Tips, no Tampax. I find shit like that I'm not fixin' it again. No kiddin'. If it don't go in through your mouth, it don't belong in the toilet."

On that note we finished eating and adjourned.

My bunk is back aft, near the mates and scientists. As an upper, on the centerline, it's reputed to be dry. "What about the rust stains on my walls?" I asked when I first saw it.

"That's *nothing,*" I was told, "just deck leaks."

Using polyethylene and duct tape from the fo'c'sle ("forecastle" on my diagrams, a-ha!), I rigged up a sort of tent inside my berth and lined the whole enclosure. The next step was to organize. I divided my things among four plastic bags—heavy clothes, light clothes, dirty clothes, and miscellaneous—and crammed all four bags into the eight-inch storage trough. Then hammered in nails on which to hang my knife and marlin spike.

Now all that remained on the mattress (two feet wide) were my safety harness, pillow and blankets, life preserver, and survival suit. I rigged a small fishnet hammock overhead and stuffed in the bulkier items. This left the mattress bare but with only an eight-inch clearance to the roof. Now, when I lie on my back, I can't see my feet. It's a small price to pay for comfort. And given the way they've begun to smell, it may be a blessing.

Today we crossed into a new time zone. At noon, now 1300 hours, I tried my luck aloft again. I began at the leeward rail but was reminded to switch to the windward; also to tie my marlin spike and knife to my belt, for the safety of those below.

The shrouds are less like a ladder than an inward-angled net. They tremble as you climb and magnify the motion of the ship beneath you—rolling, dipping, bouncing side to side. It is thirty-five rungs (or "battens") to the top of the lower mast. With each step, the angle seems steeper, the motion is more pronounced, and the battens themselves grow narrower, dwindling to six inches across at the "top," where you step off.

What you step onto is a tarred rope four feet long that stretches from the the vertical shroud to the horizontal yard. With my harness hook "clipped in," I set out but discovered that the safety line wasn't long enough to reach across. What now?

What was called for, clearly, was to clamber across with all four limbs at once, like a monkey through the treetops. Timing my move to *Regina*'s roll, I unclipped, stepped onto the footrope (noticing how its tacky wrapping gripped my soles), let go, and made my weight fall forward. As my upper body neared the yard, I reached for the iron bar called a jackstay that runs along its length, grabbed hold, and pulled until the lower half of me caught up and my feet stepped onto another rope slung below.

I was now "out on the yard," clipped in, face forward, holding the jackstay with both hands, with my chest against the yard (a full-grown spruce) and my feet (which I couldn't see) on a loosely fastened rope that swung them forward and backward, out from under me.

If there was work to be done, I would soon have heard the warning "Laying on!" from the others coming up behind me. Each time that someone new steps over from the shroud, the footrope he steps onto sinks in the middle beneath his weight and rises elsewhere, threatening to bounce the other people off. To make room for the new arrival and to handle sail, they keep on sliding outboard down the jackstay, like beads along an abacus. On the biggest yard, the course, there can be seven on each side. First up goes farthest out—the traditional place of honor in a storm. So far I had only watched from below. But as long as I was up, I decided to give it a try at my own pace in this calm weather.

Clutching the jackstay for dear life, I sidled outward slowly, with my knees locked and my hamstrings quivering. The farther I went, the closer the footrope rose toward the yard itself, until that yard was on a level not with my chest but with my thighs. All the way out, at the yardarm, I clipped in, took hold of a stout iron hoop, and then looked down.

There was nothing underneath my feet but water, masses of it, great humps churning, eddying, fifty feet below, heaving upward toward me every time *Regina* rolled and the yard tilted downward.

I have always found it easy to commune with nature. Now, before you could say "Jean-Jacques Rousseau," the contents of my stomach started welling upward, synchronized with the waves below and subsiding on each counterroll. A neat effect, but as the overall progress was definitely in an undesirable direction, I all at once wanted very badly to come down; in fact, I wanted it more than I'd ever wanted anything in my whole life.

By the time I made it back to the shrouds, they had come to feel like terra firma. For a long time I remained with my chin against a batten, seeing nothing, holding on with my fingers stiff as claws, the harness tether dangling down between cramped thighs like a long prehensile tail. And there I might have clung for hours, a treed racoon, had someone not looked up at me and cried, "Whale ho!"

The ship began a lazy swing to starboard. Were they serious?

Forgetting to be afraid, I started down, continuing until all at once, not more than a dozen feet below me, there *it* was: the great square head out of Ahab's nightmares; a jaw the size of our bowsprit; a body half as long as the ship itself, in which the only thing that moved was a watchful eye; and glistening, cellophane-like skin the color of café au lait. "Sperm whale! A bull," called Peter Bryant. "Where is Don?"

Don Patten was below, as usual. Curator of mammals at the Los Angeles Museum and our anatomist, Don has taken to ship life less well, perhaps, than anyone else on board. He is more than a little overweight, and when wedged into bed, which is much of the time, is reluctant to be shoehorned out of it. Now, viewed from above, emerging slowly through the aft companionway, he himself looked a lot like a breaching whale.

But he grew more animated quickly. "It's a bull, all right," Don said, "and he's pretty old." Everyone was listening, looking down across the rail. "Notice his scarring? Squid tracks. See the external nares? Look where the blowhole is, on his left side. He is . . . depressed, I think. Or drowsy. Maybe we woke him up. He shouldn't be on a bank like this. Sperm whales—the solitary bulls—like deeper water. Funny . . . I think he's ill. He's breathing hard. Might have a cold."

As if in response, the whale let off a snort and blow. On the shroud just overhead I caught an oily shower, a hot one, too, my first in several days. By the time I had wiped my face, the whale had sounded, leaving behind the fragment of a rainbow in the remnant of a sneeze.

> —*Emergency, emergency, calling Halifax Coast Guard! Emergency!*

It's three P.M. Wind moderate, southeasterly, considerable spray. I am entering the engine logs in the aft salon when our radio crackles on.

—This is Halifax Coast Guard radio. On two six. Over.
—This is Morning Star, out of Yarmouth. I have a man

overboard. I say again, man overboard.
—Man overboard, Roger. This is Halifax Coast Guard
Station ordering: Emergency. All other vessels clear
this channel.
—Halifax, this is Morning Star. He's in the water. He
can't—I can't hold him.
—Give us your position. Over.
—Roger.

Silence follows. It seems to go on forever. I am alone in the
aft salon. I look out the porthole at sunny water. On deck there
are playful shouts, then laughter.

—Morning Star. Calling Morning Star. This is Halifax.
Come in, please.

More exchanges follow. Position given and confirmed.
Search aircraft sent. The calm sea sparkles here, as it does over
there on George's Bank. The pauses grow longer. It's hard to
believe that this isn't a radio drama, that I am listening as a real
man drowns.

At length the skipper of the *Morning Star* returns. It's over
now. The man, who was hauling nets, slipped off their rail. The
mate went after him and held him up. A life ring was thrown
toward them, landing fifteen feet away. In the time the mate took
to grab it and swim back to the other man, that man, in shock,
went down.

That's what the skipper says. What he doesn't say is that the
mate jumped over, willingly; that the water temperature is 58
degrees; that the man they lost is probably a nephew, cousin,
son-in-law. The grief, unspeakable, remains unspoken. Instead,
there are now just facts, coordinates and numbers, and the self-
control in the captain's voice is enough to break your heart. Fair
weather, pleasant skies . . . and death has come calling twice in
our first three days.

It's eleven P.M.—I mean 2300 hours. We have stood watch today
for eleven hours. On lookout last hour I watched, as in a dream,

as dark shapes—dolphins—leapt across our bow. Now, staring through the porthole of the forward deckhouse, I can see the Cape Sable Light and pinpoints of lesser lights along the coast of Nova Scotia. Above me on the drylab wall, the skull of a goose beaked whale grins quietly, a whiff of formalin drifts over from the wetlab side. Things are calm, for once. I have my journal open, and the fountain pen I love, but I don't feel at all like writing. What I feel is alienated—from this journal, from the obligation to "make something" of what I am seeing. Alienated from myself.

Last week I had a personality. I had knowledge that others valued. I had dinner conversations. Thoughts. Ideas. That, in part, is why I'm aboard—to write up the expedition. With this goal in mind, I had planned to pursue twin schedules, one set by ship's work and one set by mine. When not on watch, I would seek out some quiet nook for an hour each day—after supper would be nice—to step back from the ship's activities and set down my thoughts.

My plan presumed that a ship serves those who sail her. I am learning that the opposite is true.

Once inserted into this perpetual motion machine, you become an interchangeable part of it, waking, sleeping, eating, even crapping only when the scheduled work allows. What *Regina* wants, *Regina* gets. I may not know where we will be, under what conditions, forty days from now. But I know that on August 9, at 0700 hours, I'll be due on helm and will be sure to be there on time. That is all that seems to matter here, the basis on which people judge you.

Compared to the way I live on shore, it all seems topsy-turvy. There, the practical stuff is what I get *through,* in order that I can do the "real" work—thinking, talking. Here, by contrast, it almost seems as if people relate to each other only because they have to for purely functional ends. If you think of the rig and lines as *Regina*'s sinews and the keel and timbers as her spine, then the people aboard become her nerve cells, fibers keeping the ship in touch with the various parts of herself, transmitting the messages that flex and unflex those parts to keep her going. Except for the science talks, I have yet to hear an idea discussed for its own sake, a thought that isn't present tense. Or should I say present terse? Among the crew especially, what passes for talk is just the exchange of information, relentlessly banal.

But it's not just them; it's me, it's us, it's the whole routine. I feel so disoriented, tired, sleep-deprived, doing weird things at weird hours, that the more I feel the need to compose my thoughts, the less able I am to do so. For the first time in my whole life, it seems, ideas are a luxury I can't afford. Is it that here, in the Realm of the Practical, I don't know *why* I am writing? Or is it just exhaustion? I can concentrate; I can get chores done. But I can't get any distance from them, can't interpret anything or organize my thoughts.

For that there is no time, no energy to spare, no space. Clearly, if I'm to deliver on what I promised, some relief from the watch routine must be allowed. I'll bring this up tomorrow with the captain.

30 June. 44°N/63°W. Cape Roseway, Nova Scotia.

Captain George Nichols, Jr., sailed before he walked. So did his four-year-old son, whom we left waving on India Wharf. So did his father, who won the America's Cup, and his father's father's father. At the age of seventeen, George became the youngest man ever to take part in a major Atlantic sailing race. He won it.

Born to great privilege, George has struck me, in our talks on shore, as not a rebel from his class but a maverick within it. A doctor by training, he spent most of his professional life in research and administration. At Harvard Medical School his efforts to devise a cancer diagnosis based on bone marrow extracts were considered controversial, and as a dean in the sixties he fought institutional battles to restructure medical education and transform its emphasis from treatment to prevention. During this period, the man whose parents had thought FDR a wild radical became a Democrat and an early critic of the war in Vietnam. Soon after, in his early fifties, he left medicine to cofound a program called Sea Education Association (SEA), out of Woods Hole, Massachusetts, and to skipper their research ship, the schooner *Westward*.

As a medical officer in the Navy, Nichols had once been part of a project on respiration in submarines. Through subsequent work at SEA and the New England Aquarium, he continued to study the physiology of diving. That increased his interest in marine mammals, which in turn led him to leave SEA and found the Ocean Research and Education Society (ORES).

Whereas SEA stressed oceanography and introductory education, ORES planned to concentrate on new research and field observation of mammals, especially humpback whales, and acquired the *Regina Maris* in 1975. Nichols bought the ship in Greece and sailed her home in time for the U.S. Bicentennial Tall Ships Parade, then had her reconfigured to support her new role. He has served as *Regina*'s master and the president of ORES ever since.

George Nichols is now sixty. His white, square-cut beard frames a face that is private, deliberate, and willful, handsome yet slightly acerbic, a face through which moods pass like weather at sea. When George laughs, which is often, his blue eyes ignite. His narrow cheeks grow dimpled, and he suddenly resembles someone in a pageant miscast as the sea dog, a young man made up, unconvincingly, to look old. But when faced with unwelcome requests or hard decisions, he concentrates intensely, almost glowers, and his clean-shaven, parsimonious upper lip, slightly aquiline nose, and sunken cheeks express distaste. Today that look was unmistakable as he turned away from me, stared out the window, and said, *"Absolutely not."*

We were standing in the pilot house. It was midmorning, breeze from the southeast at fourteen knots, a little bit of spray, skies clear. I had sought him out to discuss my need for writing time and found him calibrating some equipment. After a pleasant greeting and a couple of shared chuckles, I explained my situation. I was careful to say that I still wanted very much to stand regular watches, that I only needed some occasional relief, an hour here or there.

When Nichols talks, he normally faces you; when he listens, he looks sideways. He was facing sideways now, and I had the impression that he was miles away, or hearing something I had not intended. He said nothing until I was done; then, "I can see you have a problem." I waited. He didn't go on.

"Could I be excused from a watch now and then or given a free hour every several watches?" I meant it as a choice between the two.

"Absolutely not." More staring out the window. "You could write at night when the students are in class."

"But I need to learn that material too."

"Then I am afraid I can't help you, Harvey."

"Well, it doesn't seem very fair to take me on board for a specific purpose and then make it impossible for me to carry it out."

"It's not a good idea to give anybody special status on a boat."

"What about the scientists?"

"They didn't agree to stand watches. You did."

"How could I agree to do something if I had never done it before?"

He raised his eyebrows. His entire forehead wrinkled and then grew smooth. He turned back to the machine he had been working on.

"You know that I like to stand watch; it's part of the experience and I wouldn't *not* do it. But the fore watch has one more member than the others. I assume that was deliberate. So it wouldn't affect the safety of the ship. I am not looking to goof off or—"

"I believe that. I have no objection to what you say. I am not concerned with its effect on *you*. I am thinking of the others."

Old mule.

"George," I said, "don't you think you're being kind of rigid?" Silence. "There is no way I can do my own job and do all the rest as well."

He thought of something and decided not to say it.

"Is there any adjustment you can make?"

"That *I* can make?" He tightened a screw on the depth finder, wiped its glass face, and switched it on. "I'm sorry, Harvey. No."

A spectacular afternoon: seas four feet high, sky sapphire, piles of clouds far off to port above the Nova Scotia shore. Every now and then there's a sharp pop as from a firecracker or a cork when Lawrence shuts off his acetylene torch. As bosun, he is responsible for maintaining the deck as well as the rigging. While we've all been lining our bunks with plastic, he has been seeking out overhead leaks at their source. Today he is taking advantage of dry weather to recaulk a forward section of deck, using the welding equipment to melt tar. I offer to help and am set to work rolling oakum.

Oakum is shredded hemp fiber soaked with pitch distilled from pine tar and spun in flat rolls that resemble insulation. As instructed, I cut off three-foot lengths with my rigging knife and roll them into wads along my thighs. This process releases an intoxicating turpentiny smell and adds resin to the dirt that coats my jeans. Ahead of me, Root reams out rotten caulking from between the planks with a large iron claw; behind, our watchmate Clay forces the bights of oakum that I hand him into the seams that Root has cleaned. Clay's hair is tied back in a ponytail. His four-inch long beard is tucked into his drab flannel shirt to keep it away from the hot tar and hammers, and the visual effect accentuates his pallor and the gauntness of his jaw. Root, by contrast, is freckle-faced and slightly overweight; he works methodically and calmly, pausing only long enough to spit tobacco juice across the leeward rail.

As we find our rhythm, talk gives way to the musical ring of the caulking irons. The odors of pitch and pine swirl aft on the crisp salt air. Smoke and spray surround us. The afternoon sun beats down.

As soon as each seam is finished, Lawrence follows up behind us, surefooted on the moving deck, holding a number ten can full of boiling tar between gloved hands. He moves along slowly, half bent over, ladling it on. In places, the pitch runs over the seams, congealing on the planks like batter on a griddle. When it hardens he will trim it clean and throw the scraps back in a can, to be melted and poured, trimmed and recovered, and melted and poured again.

The freshwater pump on the generator has gone bad. All through the night, the watches had dutifully recorded rising temperatures each hour but didn't pay attention to what the numbers meant. So we are forced to make an unexpected stop in Halifax. The coast here is fogbound an average of twenty-four days in July, and approaching the harbor entrance at five P.M., we pass in a matter of minutes from brilliant sunshine into a false dusk.

On lookout up forward, I am anticipating dangers so intensely that I'm not sure if what I think I've seen is real. I'm embarrassed to report illusions but afraid to say nothing, just in case. Out of nowhere, all at once, a freighter towers above us, great horn blasting. Farther on, *Regina* bucks across the wake of a ship that we never even see. Farther still, the ferry bears down on us, alarmingly close, then suddenly veers off.

Dave Oldach materializes through the mist. He is hunched over, bearing a square wooden box with a crank on top, like an antique coffee grinder. To get a better view ahead, I am standing on the Logan's Locker, a five-foot-high box just forward of the deckhouse in which docking lines are stowed. Dave climbs up to stand next to me, looking purposeful as ever. "Foghorn," he explains, and begins to wind. It sounds like my nephew's toy called Cow in a Can.

"That's *it?*" I ask.

"Neat, huh? It's original equipment!"

✳✳✳

Four more lookouts are sent to the bow. Lawrence, who normally works as a scalloper out of New Bedford, has put on some jet-black oilskins. Joan is standing outboard on the cathead, carefully not holding on. I am grateful to have them share my responsibility, but I doubt that they can see any better. How do you sight a channel marker, let alone a buoy, in this mess?

Apparently third mate Patrick has given up trying. He is looking off sideways instead of ahead, rubbing his ear and repeatedly wiping the face of his watch. "I've got it," he suddenly announces, and walks aft. What can he possibly have sighted? I still can't see anything at all.

"Double horn on the starboard quartah?" asks Bill's voice amidships.

"No, past that," says Pat, "the number four. A whistle, every sixty seconds, three hundred yards to port."

We keep on, blind, until I also hear it. A sharp turn to port, a half mile more, and the powerful strobe of the Halifax light appears high on a cliff to starboard, saying "Welcome. Welcome. Welcome. Follow me."

Halifax sits several miles inland at the head of a long, narrow bay. Halfway up, on a craggy island, are a fort from the War of 1812 and a second lighthouse. As we drew near, George ordered all sails set again. And minutes later, as we glided past, the fog quite suddenly disappeared.

The temperature instantly rose ten degrees. Sunset nuzzled the cliffs on either side and turned our canvas the color of maize, against which a line of short ropes on the mainsail beat and rippled in the wind, like tassels. Emerging from out of the fogbank, we must have been like an apparition, and a flotilla of small craft flocked around.

They were joined, from behind the fort, by the schooner *Bluenose II*. Elegant, graceful, built for speed, she rapidly drew abeam, and the two ships sailed in side by side. Her passengers snapped our picture. We took theirs. Their captain, in Canadian Navy dress blues and gold braid, hailed *Regina* by loudspeaker. George replied through a speaking trumpet. *Bluenose* fired her cannon in our honor. We gave her a thirty-smile salute and a toot of the aerosol horn.

After five straight days pent up among college kids, I was ready to choose my company for once and tried to get Gregg or Dave to slip off with me. But Gregg insisted that I wait so that our whole watch could go together.

We wound up at last in a place that might have been a Howard Johnson's if the service had been faster and the food less bland. Kathy Kelly tried a light beer ("Maybe just one") while Joan drank diet Pepsi and described *real fun* stuffing stockings in Ohio. As a sailors' crawl, it left something to be desired.

So did the discotheque. Picture a hundred and fifty singles with haircuts like wet mops and lobster-trap jaws, all wrapped up in polyester, all pudgy, rotating earnestly beneath red spotlights like kabobs on a spit. Add a handful of *real* freaks, Americans clad in musty flannel with rope belts, dancing in a circle. As I sat in a corner watching, I grew increasingly embarrassed by my shipmates; I wanted them—wanted everything—to be rougher, more authentic. Authentic what, I wasn't sure. But I felt that I didn't belong.

Then something funny happened. Lisa, the youngest member of our watch, motioned to me to come dance. At nineteen, she is short, stout, bright-eyed, bosomy, and frizzy-haired, and with a paisley kerchief wrapped around her head, she looked like a cross between Grandma Moses and Eydie Gormé. When I said no, she came after me, pulling on my arm. When I tried to shake her off, Clay took the other arm. Dave was there too, and Joan, and the next thing I knew, I was in the circle, all of us weaving around woozily together. "This is the *fore watch,*" said Gregg, as if by explanation. And in spite of myself, I suddenly felt glad.

For the rest of the night, the club's other dancers kept their distance, watching us suspiciously. But on trips to the men's room, various men kept banging into me in the narrow corridor. My attempt to account for this sent Lawrence into fits of laughter. It was *I* who was hitting *them,* he explained; I'd developed a "sailor's roll."

We all rolled out at half past one, with Lawrence telling the two women whom he was trying to pick up simultaneously that he was bosun on a barkentine. They thought it was a clever line.

It was nice to return to the creak of masts and mooring lines and the shadow of the piers. I took it upon myself to belt out the "Vatican Rag" while dancing down a row of bollards. Gene Kelly Oxenhorn. It was the first time, I guess, that I'd really let go. I hadn't realized what a milquetoast I had been (or seemed) until I saw the others' mouths fall open. Joan and Lisa followed up with chanties. Then Lawrence sang song after song, in filthy English and in Portuguese, in one of the richest baritones I've ever heard. He's a fisherman out of New Bedford, right? So where the hell, I asked, did he get that voice?

Before studying anthropology, he replied—anthropology?—he was into music. Our bosun is conservatory trained.

1 July. Docked, Halifax

"Gotcha covahed, buddy." It's Al Stearns, the cook. Seven-ten A.M. While using his left hand to shift four pots of coffee to a cooler spot atop the diesel stove, he's stooping to open its cast-iron oven with a wood stick in his right hand, to check on five dozen biscuits. It is already hot in the galley; his glasses are smeared with fog. His T-shirt, turning from white to yellow (or vice versa, maybe) sweats up beneath his arms as he coils his six-foot frame between the oven door and the sink pump, moving like a manatee in shallow water. In the act of bending, he notices over his shoulder that I'm taking butter from the "reefer" and calls out to let me know that he's already done that: "Gotcha covahed, buddy."

I know for a fact that Al stayed out last night at least as late as I did and probably drank a whole lot more. Yet as usual, he has been up since six-fifteen preparing food for thirty people in a space eighteen feet square. He is assisted each day by a "galley slave" chosen in rotation from all who stand watches. Today is my first stint; after forty-five minutes, I understand why tugboat cooks draw up to $175 per day and am sure that Al, who earns less than one-fourth that amount, is worth double.

Ship's cook is not a class act like mate or bosun. The cook does not have their authority throughout the ship but rather has absolute authority in one essential part of it. For that reason, cooks are frequently tyrannical, the sort of satraps you don't want to cross.

Ours hails from Camden, Maine, next door to Bill Cowan's Rockport. The two men have known each other a long time and have a shared affection for their waterfront working-class roots and boats. They have packed a set of golf clubs and hope to tee off from an iceberg, memorializing the spot with a pink flamingo they have brought along. Of the two men, Al is the less attractive and the more endearing: big, slouchy, with the remnant of a stutter and a long, loose jaw that often hangs half open, like a whale's. His Down East accent is considerably thicker than his stews.

An only son and the middle child of five, Al left school early and took on odd jobs at restaurants. Now twenty-five, he has worked his way up from salad boy to chef. In addition, aboard *Regina,* he serves as purser. In Boston he had ordered and on-loaded 263 crates of food; he alone knows what is where and when it will be eaten.

Within the pseudofamily of a ship's crew, a cook implicitly accepts the role of mother. And despite his swollen forearms and the pinups in his cabin, there *is* something maternal about Al. In the same breath with which he will discuss being offered drugs or getting laid in Puerto Plata, he will turn to Judy as she scrapes her plate to ask, "Was your supper good, dear? Did you enjoy it?" Now Judy is a strong professional woman in her midthirties, and if anyone called her "dear" in that tone of voice in New Haven, she might lop his head off. But coming from Al, its expression of concern and total lack of irony are welcome.

When we are in port, all hands eat together at one sitting.

This morning, as directed, I have set thirty places, mixed orange juice, and pumped fuel for the stove. But I still feel like a child given make-work, being made to feel more necessary than I am. Until this moment, Al has been serious, all business. But now I sense that he has things under control, that the meal will cook itself from here on. The caffeine is just hitting when he asks, in a mossy, conspiratorial voice, "Hey Haavy. What's small and white and crawls up your leg?"

"Got me."

"Uncle Ben's per-vuh-ted rice!" He squints for a second through his steamy glasses to make sure I get it. Then, wiping his hands on his dishwater-colored cutoffs, he begins to giggle. His head bobs up and down like a doll's head on a dashboard. After we've laughed at this one—"Get it? Per-vuh-ted rice?!"—his head motions subside, like waves, to a stillness. He looks at the galley clock—7:45—and says, "OK, buddy, call it."

I step aft into the main salon. The tables I have set run most of its thirty-five-foot length, port and starboard. On three sides of the cabin, people are sleeping in built-in, double-decker pilot berths, each two feet wide by six-and-a-half feet long. Snores trickle and blow from behind their red cloth curtains. How do you wake twenty-two hung-over people, most of whom, after less than four hours in their bunks, are sleeping the sleep of the dead? I settle, with my penny whistle, on the morning song from the *Peer Gynt Suite.*

First phrase: nothing. Repetition: moans and stirrings. Third phrase, modulating upward: naked limbs fall out from under curtains: heads pop up, hair wild, eyes squinting, something out of *Marat/Sade*. Fourth phrase: voices.

Lisa: "That is wonderful."

Root: "Ya'll take that flute an' shove—"

"Anotha' lousy day in Paradise," Bill proclaims from his cabin aft.

Three minutes later, they are all present, in various stages of undress and waking, like a John Belushi diptych of the Resurrection, elbows on tables, heads on hands.

Enter Al, with a flourish, bearing sixty home-baked muffins

topped with ham and capped with poached eggs: "Heah they come, gang. Al McMuffins. Grab an' growl!"

Halifax is a stolid city of clean cobblestones, high curbs, and nineteenth-century public buildings, handsome but perhaps too ponderous for the spaces they frame. The rugged quality of a maritime and mercantile fort extends from the granite wharves to the iron fencing of the very green, English-style parks. While the scientists and watches that were off went exploring, the fore watch remained on board.

During breaks from the galley, I reorganized my bunk for the umpteenth time. Up on deck again, I studied the ropes some more and was delighted to find out that the stout oak bannister around the mainmast, where I like to hang out and play my fife, is called, of all things, the fife rail. That's where a warship's fifer stood and played whenever they raised the anchor.

While learning to distinguish vangs from brails, it was interesting to watch the steady stream of viewers. People's faces change as they approach *Regina*. The expressions of men in business suits and the boys whose hands they hold converge. They ask a hundred questions: "Do you actually climb up there?" "Do you go offshore?" "To Greenland?!" And most frequently of all, "What is the fuzzy stuff?"

The fuzzy stuff, hanging in moplike clumps throughout the rig, prevents the ropes and sails from chafing on the stays. The fact that its only job in life is to be worn down may explain its forlorn appearance, as well as its appeal for sailors. "What is it called?" is the question I like most to answer, because it lets me look people in the eye and whisper, "Baggywrinkle." This makes me feel quite salty. It reminds me that someone, somewhere, knows less about ships than I.

After supper, crowds came to watch fireworks in the harbor, in honor of Canada Day. The younger students had climbed up the foremast and spread out along the yards. What swaggering dudes they had suddenly become! There was Jack from the main watch, an insurance magnate's son, age eighteen, with an earring, a kerchief tied around his head, and a pipe sticking out of his unlived-in face. There was Rob from the mizzen watch, age seventeen, who kept checking, ostentatiously, the tension on the lines. Were they so elaborately nonchalant for the benefit of all those upturned faces on the pier, or were they posing for themselves? Both, I'd guess.

You could sense in their excitement a hunger for something larger, more demanding, and perhaps more meaningful than urban life on shore provides—a myth of themselves to believe in and to serve. And why not? Was it anything different that had brought me here?

The fireworks began at ten, shot up from an island in the harbor into fog. The explosions were invisible. But with each ka-boom the world felt large and free, and the clouds glowed from within, at first an incandescent pink, then blue, then green.

I watched for an hour, then laid below to clean up the last dozen pots and pans, and fell into bed exhausted, just past twelve. When the new galley slave woke me up at seven, there were pancakes, eggs, and oatmeal on the table. The air below deck was fresh again. We were eight miles out to sea.

2 July. 44°N/62°W.

Fair skies today, seas four feet, the wind northwesterly at twelve. Air temperature is fifty-six. We've broken out hats, wool pants, and heavy sweaters, and the portholes in the deckhouse have been sealed.

Off Egg Island just before lunch, we met large flocks of seabirds. Judy Perkins pointed out that these were northern species: fulmars, shearwaters, petrels. Also two sleek whales called minkes who were feeding in a zigzag pattern.

Like minkes, humpbacks are mysticetes, or "mustached" whales, so named for the plates of baleen that hang from the roofs of their mouths. Also called "gulpers," they feed by swimming through swarms of prey with their jaws hanging down, their grooved throats bulging out like pelicans' pouches.

When its throat has reached full distension (roughly the size of a fishing dory loaded to the gunwales), the whale clamps its jaw shut. Then, using its tongue like a piston, it forces the water out through the plates of baleen and swallows the solid food that remains behind, as in a sieve. Blue whales, the largest gulpers, process up to seventy tons of water at a time.

Roughly half of a humpback's diet consists of small fish such as sand lance and capelin, which tend to aggregate where the water is disturbed. Humpbacks take advantage of this by feeding cooperatively. When they sense that fish are near, the whales swim together in a circle to attract and corral their prey. Then they dive and exhale, creating a "bubble net." As this net floats to the surface, it traps fish, and the whales swim upward through it, gulping the food that it contains.

At other times humpback whales eat krill that they obtain by constant feeding. A humpback that recently died in these waters had close to a ton of these small animals inside its stomach. Obviously, it is to the whales' advantage to seek concentrations of their food, and they will swim great distances to seek it in rich northern waters. In order to make some sense of their migrations, we will try to match our sightings of whales to the conditions under which we find them. And to do that, we will constantly be trawling too.

In some ways *Regina* is ideal for ocean research: broad-beamed, close to the water, stable, quiet. But she is hard to maneuver and slow as molasses, lacking adequate power and equipment. Much of the work for which modern research vessels use machines is performed with muscle power. As in the old days, this requires more time, coordination, and a lot of hands.

All through the morning, Peter, Judy, Toni, and Don have been hauling out equipment. During lunch each student signed up for one long-term project. Shortly after, the toilet covers were taped shut; there are certain waterbound samples we would rather not reclaim. Then the first trial runs began.

***

1400 hours. The sea is calm. There are twenty-eight hands on deck. Under Patrick's direction, the members of the mizzen watch move about the ship, striking square sails, trimming the jibs, and sheeting in the main. From the pilothouse, Fran runs the engine at "slow" to maintain a constant trawling speed. On top of the forward deckhouse, Gregg and Clay rig a heavy block and then swing a boom called the topping lift out over our lee rail. As Kathy and Lisa steady the boom with opposing lines, Peter stands on the rail underneath it, hooking on the "bongo nets" with shackles. Conical, fine-meshed, ten feet long, these hang side by side from twin steel collars and taper down into collecting bottles at their narrow ends.

In order to calculate how dense the plankton are, what depth they occur at, and whether the swarms are vertical or horizontal, one must control the trawl's path length and time, ship speed, net depth, and even the slope at which the cable cuts the water. So as Peter watches from above, Toni checks the protractor and calls out cable angles. Lawrence operates the winch. Helene keeps her eye on its drum and sings out every fiftieth turn. As the cable runs, it grows hot with friction: Someone must hunker down beside the gearbox, slapping on a lubricant as thick as lard. This person is called the "greaser." Root is appointed by acclamation.

Meanwhile Francis Noel-Hudson dusts a glass slide dipped in gold. As usual, he looks rumpled, vague. The tongue of his belt flaps in the breeze. His hands are sensitive, a dentist's, as he rigs the bathythermograph. This foot-long brass torpedo contains a needle on pressure-sensitive springs. As the instrument is lowered and raised at a steady rate, the needle will scratch a profile of water temperatures down to six hundred meters on the gold-plated slide inside. Francis will use that graph to locate the thermocline, a layer of constant temperature and density that whales employ to transmit sounds.

Farther north, as the ocean grows colder, it will also grow less salty, diluted by floating ice and glacial runoff. To correlate salinity with density and temperature, Dave Oldach will follow the halocline, or transitional layer, for salt. His Neuston bottle will stay open until it reaches a preset depth and then snap shut under pressure to collect a water sample.

Across the deck, Earle Henderson, from the mizzen watch, stares down into the water intently. He is a dark, rugged young man who in this pose resembles Rodin's *Thinker*. In fact he is just concentrating on a foot-wide circle of wood beneath the surface. The more opaque the water is, the more plankton it contains. By lowering the Secchi disk and noting when its black side and white side disappear from view, Earle can note the water's clarity, and thus gauge its fertility as well.

To correlate clarity with turbidity, Deborah, in the chart room, studies the local currents. And to correlate currents with undersea geography, Brenda runs the sonar, printing out profiles of the ocean floor.

Correlations. Co-relate. It seems like a lot to go through each day for a few stray digits plotted on a graph. I want results, and now.

I find them back amidships, where the bongo nets swing, dripping, as their contents are emptied into color-coded buckets. Each holds a pint of pink stuff, what you might throw up, say, several hours after eating spoiled sushi. "Pretty good," says Peter. "Copepods and arrow worms. Sea squirts. A starfish embryo."

"Look, Pete," says Toni, obviously pleased. "A baby octopus." Helene takes the glop to the lab.

By now the winch cable has been transferred to the otter trawl for our last test in the sequence, and as the net is winched in, a dozen people gather at the stern. This must be the most important test, I think. Ever eager, notepad at the ready, I ask what everyone is looking for. The answer is which evidence to eat for supper.

As we sailed north, the coast grew sterner by the hour; there were forests of dark spruce, bleak headlands, and a bifurcated stone hump called Barse Rock ("I wonder how it got the name," quipped George). During second dog watch, between six and eight P.M., a fog set in. Looking for a lighthouse with an indicated range of fifteen miles, we reckoned ourselves at most six miles off but couldn't find it.

When you stand on the bow of *Regina,* looking forward, anything modern is behind you. Your view is the same as it would have been decades, if not centuries, before: black anchors, foot-square catheads beveled smooth from wear, the steep thrust of a tree-sized bowsprit, with the rope nets spread below. As the fog brushed our hull and purred in the headsail gear, I stared at that view for an hour and thought about those who had done the same before.

I tried to imagine how the first explorers felt along coasts such as this in boats even smaller than *Regina,* without radar, power, or oil lamps. Later, at the peak of the whaling era, profits from one right whale would cover the cost of a two-year voyage. But Ferdinand and Isabella spent less on Columbus's voyages than on a typical court ball. For him, and especially for a crew that was ignorant, ill-equipped, and underfed on a diet of hard-tack and seabirds, with no coats or even hammocks to sleep on, sailing alone with the known world months behind them, what terrors a night like this one must have held.

I was still brooding on that in the aft salon, near midnight, when a different kind of danger loomed. At a quarter to twelve, a fishing boat came out of nowhere, dead ahead, its engine noises muffled by the fog and its running lights not on. But Kathy, alone on lookout, picked it up in time to call out and prevent a crash. Artistic, moody, whimsical, in her sky-blue gear and Christopher Robin rainhat, she could not look less like your standard image of a mariner. So much for images. When it mattered, she was there.

A few minutes later, when the main watch relieved us and we laid below, I looked at her face and the others' in the lamp's red glow. As we pulled off our boots and harnesses, I felt a sudden tenderness and pride. There was no need to account for this. My watchmates' tired faces and the soft, unbroken breathing of the other crew in the bunks that ringed the cabin said it all.

3 July. 45°N/57°W. East of Scaterie Island. Waves Five Feet. Sky Clear.

We've sprung a leak. The bilge keeps filling at a steady rate. The water inside is two feet deep. We are running the pumps and checking the level twice each hour. If this situation worries the crew, they aren't letting on. What George plans to do he hasn't said. In the meantime, life goes on as usual: We eat, sleep, stand watch, handle sail, and learn to steer.

If you drew a line lengthwise down *Regina*'s middle and another athwartships and then backed up six feet to look at where they crossed, you would wind up leaning on the binnacle. The word, originally *bittacle*, comes from *abbitacola*, Italian for "little house." *Regina*'s is a varnished octagon of spruce roughly four feet tall. The compass card floats in liquid in a brass-ringed dome on top, and compensating magnets hang like clock chimes in the hollow space below it. To the left and right of the compass, brackets hold spheres of iron the size of grapefruits, one red and one green. These are also magnetic adjusting devices. Invented for the Royal Navy by the physicist Kelvin, they were referred to by generations of British seamen as "Lord Kelvin's balls." The wheel is oak, four feet across from its bottom to the brass-capped king spoke, and must weigh a good sixty pounds.

What is it like to steer a ship this size? Like those dreams in which you're due on stage but suddenly forget your lines. When you look up at the half-ton mainsail boom or the square sails billowing high above with your watchmates clinging to the yards, it's hard to believe that the whole machine is under your control. Looking forward, you can't see what lies ahead in the water or even the front sixty feet of the vessel itself. So you steer with your eyes glued to the helm.

43

A tall ship does not respond to the helm as surely as a powerboat or as immediately as a sloop. In a strong breeze, with five thousand square feet of canvas set, *Regina* falls way off in a matter of moments. But because of the size and shape of her hull, she is much slower to bring back on course.

The trick, I am told, is to "bracket" the compass swing within a narrow range and begin to correct each movement gently well before you reach the ordered course. My usual mistake thus far is to fail to anticipate in time. As the helm begins to wander and its swings become more drastic, I am forced to play catch-up and overreact to each swing, first one way and then the other.

That is known as "worrying the helm." It results in a back-and-forth motion called fishtailing, which has a nasty effect on the captain's mood and everybody else's stomach. You don't know what *nervous* means until you've felt that swing or listened to the sound of sixteen huge sails luffing and snapping or felt the forty tons of rig that you ostensibly control lean too far over.

Such mistakes invariably happen when the captain is on deck; the joke among us beginners is that George puts magnets in his pockets when he comes to check the helm. This morning I was doing fine, I thought. Then George came forward in a huff. He'd been lying down when he sensed without looking that the helm had wandered. When he checked the compass in the pilothouse, he found that I was seventeen degrees off course.

How could that be? I asked. According to my compass, I was steering the ordered course. Gregg suggested that I might want to set down my metal coffee cup someplace other than the helm.

"The ocean is a different medium from land; it's fluid, and whatever lives in it or on it must adapt accordingly. For larger animals this involves hearing, locomotion, sight, and body structure. More than their counterparts on land, they must be at home in three dimensions and must stay in constant motion. In fact, you could almost say as a rule of thumb that anything that's alive out here cannot stand still." So Judy explained in class today. She was offering hints that would help us distinguish distant whales from drifting objects. As she spoke, it occurred to me that according to that description, *Regina* herself is very much alive, a creature of the sea.

First of all, the ship is in constant motion, both sideways and up and down; it reflects the movement of the wind and waves.

At the same time, it transmits that movement to everyone and everything on board, and like the progress of the ship itself through seas and currents, our own every move becomes, involuntarily, a product of opposing forces. Each moment is a compromise, a negotiation that engages vision, balance, eyes, ears, all ten toes. You learn, without being taught, to stand back on your heels, to "walk with the whole foot," feeling the deck you tread on. Standing still is itself a dynamic process; the so-called sailor's roll serves to lower your center of gravity, and uses sixty percent more calories than walking on firm ground. Whether stepping across raised thresholds or trying to put toothpaste on a brush, you are always gauging, and compensating for, the powers running through you or the air that's flowing past you. Even asleep, you are responding with your inner ear.

Nor do any of the solid things on board stay put. Most objects are in almost constant use. Many play double or triple roles, and to save space or to justify the space that they require, things are forever being moved, improved, repaired, or recombined. In the middle of caulking the deck the other day, I went down to use the head and then got caught up in a conversation. By the time I came back on deck, the seams that had been open twenty minutes earlier had been resealed and trimmed, the black fire ax had turned red, and the toilet whose seat was still warm from my behind lay upside down on a scrap of old sail, with its pump in a dozen pieces.

Not even the hull itself is rigid. The wonderful creaking that surrounds us below decks is caused by individual timbers "working," that is, sliding back and forth against one another. I am told that this happens in all wooden boats and increases as they age. Needless to say, *Regina* works more than most. And the more she works, the more she leaks—from above, through the sides, from below. To lie in one's bunk at night and hear the ocean trickling through and accumulating in the bilge is to realize that even a foot-thick hull is not "solid." Not a moat but a membrane.

At noon it is lunchtime, second seating, for the idlers and the watch just coming off. Under the blackboard, a large rubber pan holds the dirty dishes from first seating, a half hour before, and a bucket full of scrapings. These slop gently as the ship rolls.

Next to the bucket, a body lies spreadeagled on the floor, face down. Craig is peering through a trap door out of which a louder slop rises, along with a smell like that of sewer drains. On *Regina*'s last trip south, a rat who didn't know his place trundled up through this hatch at suppertime. As all eyes watched it cross the room, the third mate leaned back, raised his arm, and before you could say "Jim Bowie," the rat was hanging from the scuttle on the point of a five-inch rigging knife. Now, as Craig gazes into the depths with a flashlight and mutters, "Bilge is high," others make their way to the port-side table, stepping between his legs or a couple of inches from his head as if he weren't there.

Because the ship is rolling, pine slats called fiddles have been inserted around the table's edge. Al sets down a light lunch: vegetable barley soup, ham, macaroni and cheese, fresh corn-bread, and raw carrots. Every four feet along the table there is also a jar of peanut butter and a box of crackers, just in case we get hungry between first and second helpings. First to arrive are the idlers, the members of the crew who do not stand watches; then comes the fore watch, rubbing cold hands. Everyone gets in line at the table's center, fills a plate, and then chooses someplace to sit down. When George moves to the table's head, most of the students attempt to sit near him. The regular crew, for the most part, migrate to the other end.

George launches into Old Salt Tale Number 101. Lo and behold, it has the same hero as the previous hundred. "When we were off Tenerife . . . One day in the Galápagos . . . Well, Eliot Richardson seemed to think . . ." The others try to chip in as if on cue or to ask questions. Judy is keeping up with him, bemused (she seems to have heard it all before), while Dave is a little too attentive, golly-gee-whizzing at George's heels. The truth is, George is so knowledgable and so vital and takes such delight in what he's seen that it's hard to get too annoyed when he carries on. Here he is king and knows everything there is to know. Still, it would be nice, just once, to hear him ask a question that solicited an opinion or idea or judgment, not just information. As if there were something someone else on board might teach and George would want to learn.

Meanwhile, down the table it is *Animal House,* with goofy chatter punctuated at decreasing intervals by Lisa's roly-poly laugh. After one particularly dumb exchange, Root leans across to Fran and whispers. They both smirk. Lisa, about to stop prattling, notices their look, pretends she hasn't, and proceeds defiantly into another gust of laughter.

Gregg arrives. Late, as usual; there was just one more thing he had stayed up on deck past our time on watch to finish. Grinning in response to Lisa's giggles, he parks himself alone at the foot of the table. There is a fresh welt caked with engine grease on his forearm, and—I hadn't noticed this before—he is missing the end of a finger on his right hand. He sets the heaping plate before him with the same spare, stubby gestures he employs when handling tools and begins to eat slowly, steadily. Only after the plate is clean does Gregg look up and join the conversation.

Talk at meals seems to alternate between inane chatter and interminable silences. So far today it has been the former. So when Gregg begins to speak, I tune in expectantly. "Well," he says, "the wind has begun to back now."

"Uh-huh." Long silence.

"How's the reefer doing?"

"50 p.s.i."

"OK."

Two minutes pass.

"Fran."

"Say what?"

"You seen the gaskets for the hydros?"

Nine weeks times seven days, three meals a day . . . I can already feel my brain dissolving. Get me *out* of here!

4 July. 47°N/60°W. Cabot Strait, off Port aux Basques.

During the night the south wind backed as predicted, and when the fore watch came on at four, we were barreling forward, driven by strong westerlies. The mizzen watch had set all headsails and staysails and squares, and the ship heeled hard to starboard. Water broke over the bow, running aft in chilly wavelets. Then it gurgled out through copper-clad holes at the edge of the deck and through oak flaps in the bulwarks. Bunches of mist blew by.

To wake up and step out from the stuffy drowse below into all this, all at once, made my heart leap in spite of the hour. By five we had entered Cabot Strait. As we passed between Newfoundland and Cape Breton Island, the sky began to lighten.

Regina's lines are made of hemp, not synthetic fibers, and her sails are not Dacron but real canvas. Patched and weathered, mottled by age, they change color constantly like theater scrims, depending on the source and slant of light and the time of day. On this tack the main was sheeted in tight and the squares were braced sharp to leeward. When the sun rose over Newfoundland, its first pale rays shone through the fog-stained square sails, from behind, and their lit side steamed.

When I came off the helm at six, I went to the aft salon and found Gregg leaning over the sea charts, reckoning our position. To his right, above an untouched cup of tea, the clock read 1007 (Greenwich Mean Time). To his left the two-foot-thick mizzen-mast came down out of the ceiling and passed through the floor, making sounds like an upset stomach. Lights on the navigation gear winked, green and amber. On the shelf overhead, a row of cedar boxes held the mates' and master's sextants.

The aft salon is "captain's country." Here, in the old days,

George would have been served by the steward and had his officers to dinner. The entire space is carpeted. Its walls are paneled with mahogany. One holds a mirror flanked by African masks. There are portholes with curtains and a brass lamp hung in gimbals from the cabin's roof, with "Home Sweet Home" etched on its chimney. The lamp was swinging gently as I tossed my gloves and watchcap onto the red baize-covered table. In the far corner Kathy sat still, glassy-eyed, unblinking. When the ship rolled, she didn't fall over. So I knew she was alive.

Gregg did not interrupt his work to acknowledge my arrival. But at length he set down the dividers and, moving as if under water, carried his mug to the table and sat down.

"Got a minute?" I asked. There could be no sillier question. Behind the door to the captain's upper cabin, George was snoring softly. In old drawings of tall ships, I said, the square sails are parallel to one another. Why had we just braced ours in a spiral?

"For a couple of reasons," Gregg replied. "First, there's the wind speed. What is it now?" He waited for me to find the right gauge.

"Sixteen knots?"

"OK. With gusts to twenty. That is the 'true wind speed,' measured at the mizzen truck. It's different from the 'apparent wind speed' at the waterline. There the wind is slowed down by friction. Since all parts of the ship are connected and moving at the same speed, you brace the uppers less. This compensates for the difference in wind speeds at different heights and gets maximum drive all along the mast. OK?"

Sure, fine. More than fine for six-fifteen, when I'd been awake since four.

"Then there's the wind direction," Gregg went on. "Again, you've got 'true' and 'apparent.' Say you've got the wind like this." He held out his hand in a way that looked like a karate chop. "That's 'true.' And you're headed like this—no, better still, like this." He held the other hand up to it at an angle, sighting along the finger with a missing tip. "Since the ship isn't standing still, she makes her own wind, based on how she's heading. So the actual wind available to fill her sails is a vector of the two. It's not 'true,' right? It's 'apparent.'"

Gregg couldn't talk without his hands. But as usual, his gestures were not rapid or expressive. He wasn't demonstrating for his listener so much as visualizing for himself. And as he did this, warming to his subject, he became intensely, almost obliviously focused, like a surgeon laboring to explain complex procedures to his patient's relatives, unaware that all they want to know is if the patient will survive.

At this point, I wasn't sure that *I* would. "Have you noticed the shape of the sails?" Gregg asked. (What, more?)

"Rectangular?"

"Well, the course is. But the others have a scooped-out lower edge" (he traced a scoop shape with his hand) "to let air through as well as trap it. A sail is an airfoil, like a wing; it works by creating a differential in air pressure on either side. By changing the shape of the foil, you adjust the vacuum behind it. The higher the halyard, the flatter the sail. Can you think of what happens when we sheet in or take up on the tacks?"

I couldn't.

"Well, what you're doing is changing the curve of the sails and the turbulence around their corners. You're controlling *lift*."

He paused to make sure I got it. This is a man, I thought, who cannot recognize an idle question when he hears one. He was taking me more seriously than I take myself.

"I'm oversimplifying," Gregg said. "But that's basically it. Well, for the square sails, anyway. That's where you get your drive. To steer the boat, you use your fore-and-aft sails to move the center of effort closer or farther away from the center of resistance. Sorry. That's a vector of the lateral resistance (of the hull and water, adjusted for currents, of course) and the apparent wind. Wait, hold on, let's go back a step. Do you know what the 'moment' is, from physics?"

He mistook my nod for affirmation.

"OK. Well the 'angle of attack'—"

The clock began to sound. Five bells. An expression like a battered fighter's when the round ends must have crossed my face, because Gregg broke off, looked over at Kathy, who was out for the count, and stopped talking in midphrase.

"Thanks, Gregg," I said, after a moment had passed.

He smiled wryly. "Well, that's the general idea."

0830. Morning meeting. George: "Well, folks, as you may have noticed, *Regina*'s been a little *thirstier* than usual these last few days. Fran has traced our difficulties to somewhere near the stern, and I suspect that one of the bolts that fastens the engine to the hull has worn through. This is no cause for immediate concern, but it's something we oughtta have a look at.

"Just past one this morning we altered our heading to oh-two-oh magnetic. I've decided to go north inside, and our present course will take us up the western shore of Newfoundland to Corner Brook. Now as Judith can testify, Corner Brook is a perfectly unremarkable town whose great virtue as far as we're concerned is its marine supply stores. What I propose is to put in there, go over the side for a good look at the hull, make repairs, and get going again just as quick as we can. We should be at the dock by suppertime tomorrow.

"Now, more immediate business—uh, Deborah, could you please poke Rob? This being Saturday, it's time for our first field day, a positively marvelous indoor-outdoor sport. Mr. Cowan, would nine o'clock suit you?"

Bill Cowan and the main watch were on duty. "I want to brace first," he said. "Make it nine-fifteen."

By nine thirty-five, when we all got started, the sea had kicked up some more, and *Regina* was ploughing through the whitecaps. Water coursed across her decks. Our flag, which we'd hoisted to honor the Fourth of July, snapped taut at the end of the mizzen gaff in a twenty-five-knot breeze.

Field day boils down to this: All hands assemble at the bow or stern and work their way toward the middle, scouring every inch along the way. During the next two hours, all the cabinets below were emptied. Foot grates and shelves were handed up through the skylight and a fire hose was passed down. On deck, meanwhile, the combination of twenty active bodies, equipment, soapsuds, high seas, and the deck's steep tilt made for treacherous footing. Every forty seconds, you had to pause in the midst of the most domestic duties and hang on as a sea passed over.

For my *faux pas du jour* I had tucked my new waterproof pants inside my boots, instead of vice versa. When the first wave washed across, it left them full, up to my calves. Amused, Helene stuck a lab thermometer down my left boot. The temperature inside it was fifty-three degrees.

Luckily, below decks, the heat had been turned on. This consists of radiators down along the baseboards, run on hot water shunted off the main. I added my wet towel to the socks and gloves already wedged around them and crawled into my berth. Once inside, I stripped and marked the national holiday with a change of underwear.

At supper, everyone was in high spirits. George brought out wine, and Al had baked apple pie. Inspired by the wine, he told us jokes, and assuaged by the pie, we listened. "I had this girl-friend once. A real one-baggah. Man, she was so ug-ly I made her wear a bag over her head when we made love."

Silence.

"Any a' you ever seen a *two*-baggah? *She's* so ugly that you both wear bags. You get it? In case hers falls off."

It's eight P.M. Toni and Don have hooked up a video monitor in the main salon to show a BBC program about humpback whales. We gather around to watch it. In the dark, I listen to the timbers working, deep protracted groans in a cadence punctuated now and then by squeaks, and rubbing sounds and random crackles. Among the odor of damp wool and cries wafting down through the open skylight—"Stand by your t'gallant gear . . . Let go the buntlines and clew lines . . . Hawwwwwl on your starboard sheet"—the electric colors of the screen, with its kelly green graphics, seem too bright. Surreal.

More sounds: the slosh of water in the bilge below, the unbuckling of climbing harnesses, a rattle of pans in the galley.

And then, all at once, there is *Regina* on the monitor, her sails aflutter, bright white against a brilliant Caribbean sky.

Glancing away, I examine the scene around me. With the ship heeled this far over and the bilge so high, the lower bunks on our lee side have been leaking badly and are sodden. Lisa's is the worst. She now sits wrapped in a damp wool blanket next to Clay, who is wearing long johns stained by rusty water. As I study their shadowed, tired faces, I feel the presence of those who huddled in this space on similar nights sixty years ago and listened to the same beams groaning.

Turning back to the monitor, I see the ship as strangers see her—glamorous, carefree, sexy. As *I* saw her, from a distance, nine short days ago.

5 July. 48°N/59°W. Gulf of St. Lawrence

Five foot six, 160 pounds; maybe twenty-nine years old or maybe forty; full-faced, heavy-featured, with thick lips and the gait of small black bear—that's Fran. Everything about her broadcasts *lumpy, crude*—except her eyes. The expression in these is so bright, so shrewd, and so delighting in its shrewdness that it makes the rest of Fran resemble a disguise, a costume she's been forced to wear.

Fran is the only person on board besides George to hold Coast Guard and commercial licenses. She has told Helene that she knows five languages. She told Scott that early in the Vietnam War she "spent time" on U.S. submarines off North Korea. She told Dave that she once rebuilt a German U-boat "for the hell of it." Fran's current job is teaching shop in a boys' industrial high school. Her home is the fifty-year-old steam tug *Luna*, moored in Boston Harbor. Having purchased and restored the boat herself, she now takes on "apprentices," rough kids from the Boston area. "It's good for both of us," she says. "I treat 'em like shit.

They get to live on board a boat—and learn to tow the line."

When mates join a ship, each usually comes with his own sextant; engineers often bring a set of tools. Fran came aboard *Regina Maris* carrying only two: a broken-off broom handle and a coffee can. Her first time in the engine room, she rolled up her sleeves and knelt alongside the idling main. Then, holding the broomstick between the engine block and the tin can, cupped to her left ear, she listened for a while, stood up, and proclaimed the condition of each cylinder's pistons, rings, and valves.

The other night, in the Cabot Strait, Fran joined me up on bow. She wore black combat boots, a polyester hula shirt, a baseball cap, and a knee-length coat of black fake fur. I couldn't see or hear a thing through the pea soup fog. But Fran kept a veritable stream of information flowing aft: "Triangle," "tide rip," "red nun," "green light, double flash, two miles, two points off." In between, we had our first conversation. She talked; I listened.

"Whaddya do on shaw? No foolin'! I wrote some books, too. One was called *You Got to Pay*. A day in the life of a bill collectah. It's about this guy from Commonwealth Gas. You see, he looks real bored with what he does, but in fact he's a *lot* like Goebbels. Sez you, 'Overdue? I got children here.' Sez he, 'You got to pay.' 'But my mothah is dyin', we need the scratch for dope!' No dice. 'You got to pay.' It was pretty good. A small press published it."

From back aft, a voice called out. "On bow!"

"Hello!" I shouted back.

"Hey, Harvey, you seen Fran?"

I glanced at her. She acted as if she hadn't heard.

"She's here with me."

"Tell her the ONAN's down, OK?"

Fran shifted the chewed-up pencil stub behind her ear but showed no sign of going aft. "The *Globe*," she said, "took another piece. 'The Great Catnip Caper.' Back in '72 I found a lot, I mean tons of catnip growin' in this small town in Vermont. Those days every junior bureaucrat was longin' for a bust. The local drunk, well one of 'em, he used ta hang out at my place. He got in trouble with the cops, so he decided to slip them some hot information, right? I knew what he was up to. I cleaned out the house—I mean of *everything,* right, even aspirin. Then I loaded the cupboard up with fuckin' catnip. So the cops arrive with a warrant, right? And book me."

"Hey, Fran!" They were calling again from back aft.

"I nevah said a word. Just let 'em take me in. Wake up the DA at two in the mawnin'. Pull 'em out of his old lady's bedroom. Man, you should of seen their faces when the lab report came in. I could of split a gut. But I didn't tempt 'em aftah that. No way. I beat it ovah the county line.

"A few years later the Angels owed me fawteen hundred dollahs. What? Hell's Angels, yeah, I'd done 'em a favah. But their assets weren't liquid. What I did, instead of cash I accepted this old Panzer tank. Treads, turret, the works. But no gun. I got it in workin' ordah, stuck on a length of pipe ta make it look like the barrel.

"Well, this used car dealah, his name was Monty—no shit, Monty!—he was a Legionnaire. Like in Legionnaire's disease. Believe me if anyone looked like he had it. This Monty, he had an old Sherman tank parked in his lot. Big hero, right. Everybody's gotta have a gimmick. So one night me and the Angels get into this Panzer tank an' start drivin' around the guy's parkin' lot. He calls the cops. So we point the, you know, turret at 'em. That guy—man, you shoulda' seen 'em freak!"

Joan had arrived for the story's end. Officially cross. "Fran," she said pointedly, "I believe that the ONAN's—"

"Hold ya hawses. I'm comin'. Catchya later, man."

The Gulf of St. Lawrence is a triangular inland sea the size of Kansas with sides four hundred miles long and an opening at each corner. At the western point the St. Lawrence River flows in. At the south lies Cabot Strait, through which we entered; to the northeast is the Strait of Belle Isle, through which we will depart for Greenland.

As we sailed further into the gulf early this morning, the water grew gradually calmer, and yesterday's fair wind died. At 0345 our speed fell below four knots, so we struck some sails and started up the engine. The main watch arrived on deck and, still warm from their beds, were sent up along with our watch to gasket sails. This would have been my first time aloft while underway, had I not been on lookout at the time. Close call! Feeling sheepish but secretly relieved, I leaned my head back and watched the others climbing. With their legs splayed out on the quivering footropes, the nine black silhouettes resembled spider people out of science fiction, bouncing along their web against a dim rose sky.

At lunch we moved our clocks ahead. Years ago, when Newfoundland was still an autonomous dominion of the British crown, it unilaterally declared its own time zone, which no one else shares. To this day the island remains a half hour apart from the rest of the world. So for us noon became twelve-thirty. We had sailed into Newfie Time.

From then on the day was a slow-motion dream of mist and water, of conifer forests and 2000-foot-high headlands the color of crumbled chocolate. Cape Ray, the Anguille Mountains, Cape St. George. The droning of unseen breakers. Fog. More fog. The bluffs poked through like worlds condensing out of chaos. Shearwaters, petrels, and terns appeared and vanished. Cormorants hurtled by. An osprey watched us from the top of a blasted fir tree, screaming.

Finally, sticking up like a bobbin through its spool of clouds, a lighthouse on a granite outcrop signaled our destination. This was South Head, fifteen hundred feet above the sea, at the entrance to the Bay of Islands.

Tacking east, we headed in. Pretty soon, all sounds except *Regina*'s disappeared. This large bay is actually a sunken meadow flooded by the ocean. We motored up it slowly, past small islands that resembled tufts of green wool stuck in molten silver. Farther on, the water grew tea-brown; split logs and dead fish clogged the surface. Ten minutes more, and the source of this change came into view: three smokestacks, an enormous mill, and a low town spreading out behind it.

***

Corner Brook, five P.M. We are tied up to a pier that rises seven feet above our rail, designed for ships like the huge red freighter at its other end, which is loading wood pulp for Shanghai. All we can see of Newfoundland is the pier's cracked side and the nostrils and chins of some people peering down. Viewed from below, their faces call to mind old horror movies. When I climb up a shroud to get a better look, they still do.

Several dozen locals line the pier's edge, families mostly, out for a Sunday stroll. The women, in curlers and cotton frocks washed too many times, talk about us as if we're not there. Two box-headed little girls observe our every move through wide pale eyes. Their fathers, with bulbous noses and bangs cut square, wear shirts buttoned up to the collar and ironed jeans. As the family dogs, all chows and Pekingese, rub up against their work-boots, the men study our rig intently with serious, hatchetlike faces. Questions drizzle down:

"Where from, bize? Where bound?"

"Why de fixed gaffs? Was she ever schooner-rigged?"

"Bass-ton. Sout' of 'Alleyfax. Wait. Dat's New Brunswick. Bass-ton. Down roun' Nova Scotia way?"

It's as if the "rude mechanicals" stepped out of a Shakespeare comedy, dressed up in clothes from K Mart, and affected the speech of nineteenth-century Ireland.

Even so, *their* speech is nothing compared to my shipmates'. Half of them have found things that need doing aloft, all, curiously, on the side that faces shore. From spar to spar, they are calling out, with exaggerated cool, "Haul," "slack," "belay." Then Jack emerges from the aft companionway with a kerchief wrapped around his head and a lit pipe in his fist. ("Clutched in his fist," you can almost hear him thinking. "Gnarled. Clutched in his gnarled fist.") Meanwhile, Clay is calling his Levis "britches." Just last night, he tells a man on shore, while he and the mate were "jawin' on the quarterdeck . . ."

Quarterdeck me arse.

If I didn't feel so much like an imposter myself, I might have more distance and be less embarrassed. What is this foolishness? What impression is it making? In the middle of one student's peroration on the rigors of life at sea, an old man in briny hip-boots interrupts, "Does your captain really mean to cross de Davis Strait in *dat?*"

On the dock before supper, I chat with a sign painter and a loader from the mill. They tell me this plant is one of the largest pulp and paper operations in the world; in one continuous process it turns timber into newsprint bound for Boston, Miami, and a dozen other major cities. It is owned by an English-based con-glomerate called Bowater. Since they located here in 1925 until just a few years back, Corner Brook was a company town. Both men were born in the Bowater hospital, lived in Bowater hous-ing, and shopped in the Bowater stores. The plant still employs most of the population and runs twenty-four hours a day.

"Why here?" I asked. "Well, dere's de timber, first of all. Tree firms bought up de rights to all of Newfoundland." (*Tree firms?* What a funny phrase, I thought.) "Dat's right. Bowater here owns de timber rights from Sout' Brook clean true to Bayvurt."

"Bayvurt?"

"On de coost. It's French for 'Green Bay.' And apeart from de timber, dere's de Humber here, to float it down. And dere's dis harbor. You won't find one more protected closer to da sea."

"What happens in the winter?"

"Oh, well. It freezes solid. In '78 an ice bar formed way out across de mout' of Bay of Islands. Even de icebreakers couldn't get true. For tree months. We were cut off, surely."

We are joined by a fisherman holding two large salmon who asks whether I would like to buy them. I call Al, who praises the fish but says they are too expensive. The man gives a quizzical, half-hostile look and turns toward me. I ask if the fish came from the Humber River.

"Hardly," he says, scowling. "From shore-tied nets. It's hard work," he adds bitterly. "I used to be a sealer." Pause. "So was my father. T'irty years." He watches my face as he says this. I have no idea what he is driving at.

"You like de seals? You here to save de whales? You're Green-peace, aren't you?" I assure him that all we do is *study* whales to discover where they are and how they feed.

He relaxes for a moment but then thinks better of it. "Well, den, just don't discover too much. After submarines discovered de salmon grounds, de big bize, Russians mostly, followed after. Dey're all gone now, why not? All de fish are gone too."

After supper, a walk into town, which was drab and weary, like a county seat in West Virginia, circa 1954. There was a Woolworth's, naturally. A mail-order store, a discount hardware, discount clothes. The half dozen people I passed on the street looked as if they'd been discounted too. Worn out, poker-faced, and incurious, not one of them returned my smile.

At the drugstore I bought a Coke and the local papers and sat down outside. Across the square, kids were lined up for a movie, hooting to friends in an old black Ford that shone like patent leather. As it circled by for the third time, two rows of yellow light bulbs on the theater marquee came on. Hot night, small town. I had almost forgotten it is summer. This was not what I'd expected, but it wasn't bad, not bad at all, to be on my own for a change, to smell cut grass and feel nothing move.

"Can you *believe* this?" said the unmistakable carborundum voice as Fran plunked down beside me.

"Believe what?" She looked frazzled.

"I sure wouldn't want to walk alone here after dark."

"Why not?"

"Ya see the way these people look at you? 'You're strangers, man. Don't jaywalk *here.*' No foolin'. It's like Deutschland über Alles, nineteen thirty-four."

"You been to Germany?" I asked.

"All ovah. Military brat."

"Army?"

"Nope. Navy. Jewish Navy. My fathah was one of Rickovah's boys."

"Is Grost a Jewish name?"

"No, but Gadowsky was. He was commandah of the sub base at New London. Man, you should of seen 'em. The whole fuckin' place was crawlin' with 'em. One guy, this commandah, he ran the Navy's only kosha' submarine.'"

"I hear that you did some work on subs yourself."

"Well, not exactly," Fran said with a tight-lipped smile. It curved upward like a dolphin's. "Naval intelligence, off Nawth Korea."

"What was your job?"

"All kindsa shit. Sometimes we'd listen ta the Chinese listenin' to us." She cocked her head. "Or mess around with codes." She was grinning broadly now, all snaggle-toothed. "Or *wire to fire!*"

On anchor watch, I sat down with Gregg Swanzey, and we talked for the first time about our lives back home. Gregg and I are the same age. He entered Cornell as an engineering major, but studied a lot of biology and anthropology while there. After graduating, he went west to work as a commercial fisherman and wound up "interested in boats." That interest led him to whale-watch operations off of Baja California and finally brought him east again, to the third mate's position on the ocean research vessel *Westward*.

As we talked about how a career takes shape, getting older, and what settling down would mean, I realized how starved I had been for personal conversation. I know so much less about my shipmates than about the people with whom I work at home. And yet, I am already entrusting them—as they are entrusting me—with so much more.

By eleven o'clock the others had started drifting in; you could hear them telling one another to be quiet two blocks away. The tide had risen, closing the gap between our rail and the dock. From the lab I listened to the thumps as people jumped on board. Then I curled up for the final hour of anchor watch with my *Corner Brook Daily News.*

First, sports: The Bay of Islands Men's Darts League held its annual dance and presentation of awards last night at All Hallows Hall on Fudge Road. Randy MacDonald of Labatt's had tied for a triple, *plus* he had the most tuns and finishes and was thus named series MVP. In a photo, Randy and the lads stood grinning ear to ear. Which was no small distance.

On the facing page ("More news from the World of Darts"), my eye was captured by a small box with a bulletin inside. This stated that a steel-hulled sailing vessel, the 990-ton *Arctic Explorer*, had been reported missing five hundred miles off Cape Bauld. A search was started after the ship failed to make regular radio contact. There were icebergs in the area of the sinking. The water temperature was forty-three degrees. There were thirty hands on board.

6 July. Docked, Corner Brook.

In the next day's paper the inch-square box had become a banner headline. *Arctic Explorer* had indeed gone down. Eighteen hands were rescued from a single raft after forty-six hours at sea; eight others are known dead, and four are still missing. The ship's representative in St. John's won't speculate as to what caused the sinking, but survivors report being awakened by "a loud thud." One man who watched from the life raft as his fellow workers leapt into the water said, "You are watching as you drift away and there is no way you can get back to them. It's terrifying."

Is what we are about to try responsible? *Their* ship was seven years old. Leased out for seismic exploration, it was specially reinforced, with an expert on ice aboard. They went down exactly where we are bound. There are forty-four icebergs reported in the Strait of Belle Isle alone.

John Ruskin once wrote that the goal of education should not be just to make people do the right thing but to make them enjoy it. It is hard to imagine that I will ever enjoy laying aloft. But somehow that strikes me as the key to this whole experience, so I've been forcing myself to go up whenever possible at quiet times. Moving about in the rigging after supper, I experimented with different places to clip on, different ways to balance on the footropes and cross from side to side. I went way out on the yardarm. Slowly, very slowly. Then I tried going higher.

At the foretop (where the lower mast overlaps the upper) is a platform called the top. This juts out from the mast a few feet, like an overhanging eave. How does one climb upward over it to the topmast? For someone whose usual main exercise is turning pages and whose wrists could be mistaken on a dark night for the legbones of a cornish hen, this was no easy question.

Time to let the body answer. Leaning back, I reached up, grasped two iron bars (the futtock shrouds), and held on to them while my feet kept climbing up the shroud below. Each step higher forced my upper body further outward until it was nearly perpendicular to the mast, like the body of a climber rappelling on a rock face. When my feet were right underneath the top, I half pulled myself, half crawled, up and over the platform's edge, then pivoted, stood upright on it, facing out, and then looked down.

Viewed from this height, the deck became a rabbit hutch, a hundred-foot-long village in which every ten feet was a separate neighborhood. People passed between them, going about their business, disappearing into one hole and popping up through another. Kathy snoozed in the bowsprit netting. Amidships, Gregg and Scott cut thread in some brass pipe. On the port side, next to the after deckhouse, Fran was welding. Over to starboard, Bill worked five-inch needles through the corner of a sail. Deborah, from the mizzen watch, was washing clothes in a bucket; on the fantail, Rob and Jack sat gossiping. So little space, I thought. But how much it accommodated. How much living it contained!

7 July. 50°N/59°W. Esquimaux Channel.

Last night I dreamt I was caught in a web or netting. Ropes stretched everywhere. Each time I grabbed one, it gave way. The more I struggled to break free, the more I became entangled.

I woke in a panic to find that the fishnet above my bed had fallen down, the plastic I'd taped up had sweated off the wall, and my life preserver had wound itself around my ankles. Time to rearrange the bunk. Again. I tore down the fishnet altogether and consolidated bags of "clean" and "dirty" clothes; who's kidding whom?

There was time for all this because we were still dockside, stuck in port waiting for the sheets of lead required to patch the hull leak. Some workmen finally brought them and went over the side at once. But they came back up a minute later; the harbor was so polluted that they couldn't see their outstretched hands. We had had enough of Corner Brook. George decided to cast off at once and to make the repairs ourselves in clearer water.

Noon. *Regina* tiptoes through McIvers Cove. Third mate Patrick, raised on the Mississippi, stands on the cathead with a sounding lead, heaving and hauling, calling out, "By the mark, five. Five! By the mark, four. . . ." Eight of us have just hoisted the half-ton anchor outboard on its davit. Gregg stands on one of its swaying flukes, barefoot, not holding on, with a sledgehammer on his shoulder. Motionless, clad head to foot in black, he could pass for Vulcan.

On deck Lawrence waits, also in black, gripping the long iron lever of the chain brake, looking like an old-time railwayman about to throw a track switch. His eyes are fixed on Gregg, who listens to Pat, who keeps calling back to George, on the roof of the aft deckhouse. George watches a point on the shore for twenty seconds, rechecks the wind, and asks, "OK on the bow?" Gregg waves. "Let fall!"

Gregg steps off from the hanging anchor onto the cathead, raises the sledgehammer over his head, and slams it down on the chock. The anchor crashes. Chain roars out after it through the hawsehole. The whole ship shudders and complains. But as soon as the hook is fast, she rounds up slowly and comes to rest. Then points like a happy old hound to the fresh sea breeze.

Brenda, from the mizzen watch, steps up to the taffrail, wearing nothing but skintight rubber and looking mighty fine. Five foot two from her toes to pigtails, she needs help with the diving tanks, which the mizzen watch deckhand, Alan Abend, eagerly provides. As he helps her into them and up onto the rail, he holds on to her hips a moment more than is required, and his gaze is definitely not on the horizon. But Brenda doesn't notice. All business now, she checks her wrist gauge, pushes off backwards, and becomes a splash.

On *Regina*'s opposite rail there is more splashing as the residents of McIvers come to call. They approach in a dozen dorries with broad gunwales close to the waterline and swooping orange bows. Each boat holds up to fourteen people—grandmothers, four-year-olds dressed in miniature boots and slickers. Before we can say hello, they are being handed across the rail. Before you can add, "Sure I'm crazy with delight," the entire village is aboard. The only exceptions are some teenage boys who continue circling, lobbing what seem to be squid guts at their girlfriends in another dory. Courtship, Newfie style. But the girls are up to it. They giggle, lure the lads in close with squeals—and retaliate with a volley of dead cod.

The only problem with this jolly scene is that we're still slowly sinking. Because the water is so cold, our best divers, Brenda and Fran, have had to take turns going down. They have found the leak and fashioned a patch but can't hold on down there well enough to nail it on. Then Gregg has an idea. He borrows Fran's wet suit and jumps overboard with a rasp and a toilet plunger. Once below, he uses the rasp to clean off a spot on the hull and affixes the plunger to it. Holding on to the plunger with one hand, he hammers in long copper nails with the other.

Done. Our guests depart. We raise the anchor and stow the chain. Set staysails. Set the main. Fall off. Shake out the squares. Al starts supper. Toni goes off to the darkroom. Corner Brook disappears astern. The fog is clammy and the breeze is cold. Feels great to be underway.

8 July. 50°N/58°W. Gulf of St. Lawrence.

As the weather has gotten harsher and people spend more time below, the tension over small things has been rising. *Regina* runs like a timepiece, a perpetual-motion machine. Her three watches are like gears engaged in sequence, and the members of each watch are the teeth on those gears. So when any one person fails to engage, it throws off everybody's timing. One day it's the galley slave; she forgets to wake someone for supper. He goes on watch twenty minutes later, hungry and pissed off. Another time, the watch coming on is late. "You lay in bed after we woke you," charge the members of the watch going off. They've been out in the rain four hours.

"Bullshit," say the others, still logy. "You forgot."

"Forgot, my ass. You asked about the weather."

"Yeah?"

"Yeah."

"Well, you should've come by a second time."

Last night brought the affair of the coffee. Usually, when Joan goes down to wake the main watch half an hour before they are due to relieve us, she checks to see that we've left four pots of hot coffee waiting for them. But because we were busy tacking, Kathy did the waking, and we each assumed that someone else had checked the stove. Nobody had. The pots never perked. So when he stepped on deck at four in the morning, Bill threw a tantrum—how he wants his coffee, when he wants his coffee, what his watch requires of ours, is that so much to ask. . . . I could hear him letting Gregg have it as I hit the sack, and today at morning meeting Bill was still carrying on.

Who is this guy, anyway? It's amazing how little I know about him, or any of these people, given that every day I place my life in their hands, as they increasingly place theirs in mine. What are the personal qualities that matter here? Are they the same ones that I've valued back on shore? Whom can I share my fears with? Who will come through in the clutch? Will I?

On helm today at 0320 hours it was peaceful, calm but cold. My hands had grown stiff on the wheel, and I was tired when Root showed up to offer cake and company. Root Liebman is a twenty-one-year-old Floridian with an amiable freckled face and an over-sized head on a powerful but prematurely pudgy body. His speech is backwoods Florida. He chews tobacco constantly, and his teeth and lips are coated with its slime. Ask Root why he wants to be an engineer and he says, "Why not? You make good money, man. You get ta stay in an air-conditioned trailer while the other poor bastards work all day."

Still, Root, like Fran, has an underside that I can't quite fathom. He sleeps with his old guitar, and as he plays the same songs over and over with great sensitivity—they are mostly groaners by Tom Waits—you get the sense that he's known hard times. Sardonic, gentler-spirited than he lets on, he seems older than the others, certainly less gung ho.

Had he noticed, I asked as we stood in the dark, that when people are feeling least sure of themselves, the first thing they do is start instructing others? By way of reply, he launched into a fine imitation of Joan when she is nagging. We both laughed. "She needs to loosen up," I said.

"What she *needs* is to get her brains fucked out. 'Do this. Do that. George says.' Some people don't never get crazy. But you got to break out. Smile at your mama and walk on."

1300 hours. On helm again. A stiff northwest breeze has turned the weather brilliant. Everyone's spirits are improved, and we've readjusted to our sea routine.

This morning's plankton tow went fine. Standing by now for the afternoon's tow, Peter, Lawrence, and Helene have gathered around, and we are singing in four-part harmonies. Bill passes, pausing to appreciate Helene in her brand-new orange Gore-Tex jumpsuit. Calvin Klein. We catch each other's eye, and he winks at me, as if this morning's squabble never happened.

We have seen a fin whale today, along with petrels, jaegers, and murres, all distinctly northern birds. My favorites are the humble fulmars, pigeonlike creatures with snow-white bodies and elegant black eyes who would look at home in medieval tapestries. They hover about the rigging day and night but never perch there. When a flock takes off from the water with short, arthritic strokes, the sound is like that of wet flags snapping in the breeze.

We also saw ice for the first time, cubelike chunks up to twenty feet across and twice as high. They were just as I'd imagined—white in the center and translucent toward the edges, with a dull glint coming from within. Everyone dashed below for cameras. Everyone, that is, except Judy, Don, and George. Hadn't they seen the icebergs? Deborah asked. George glanced at the chunks that were drifting past. "Not yet," he replied.

2320 hours. In areas where there is ice, *Regina* will not sail after dark if it's foggy. At the foot of the Strait of Belle Isle, we therefore crossed to the Labrador side to seek a sheltered anchorage. It was a wild night, pitch black, with gusts of twenty-eight knots or more. Up on a bluff, the lights of Blanc-Sablon were like windblown sparks. After we anchored, Clay and I were sent up, for the first time, to "gasket the main," that is, to secure the furled mainsail by cinching it to the mainmast with long ropes called gaskets.

Regina's mainsails and mizzen sails are fore-and-aft sails, just like those on a sloop or schooner. When not in use, they are hauled in along long fixed gaffs and bundled and tied to their respective masts. To get to these masts (on the centerline) from the shrouds (above the rails), you must cross a lot of open space on sagging ratlines, standing on one line while gripping the parallel one five feet above it with your armpits. On a night like this, both lines sway back and forth like jumpropes. Stretched between them, you are jerked this way and that like wash hung out to dry.

Tonight we began at the top of the mast, where the distance to cross over from the shrouds is shortest. With Clay on one side of the mast and me on the other, we started gathering the sail in toward us and worked our way down along the mast by dropping from ratline to ratline, passing the rope back and forth around the mast and canvas in a downward spiral as we went. It took forever. Just when we were done, down on deck, Joan said, "Hold on, you've caught the outhaul *inside* the gaskets. It has to stay outside so it can be hauled to set the sail. Go up to the top, undo it, and start over."

Fine. The clear night was spectacular, and there was now no rush except for the one that we were getting from the sight of stars exploding into view as a high wind shredded clouds.

When we reached the bottom ratline a second time, I jumped the last six feet down to the deck. And realized as I landed, that for the last ten minutes, working hard aloft, I had forgotten to hold on.

9 July. 51°N/56°W. Red Bay, Labrador.

On maps of the north, a line is sometimes drawn from the north coast of Alaska east to Hudson Bay, then southeast across Quebec to Labrador and the Strait of Belle Isle. This represents the tree line, separating forestland from tundra. We have now reached that ecological edge, as well as the geological edge of the vast

Canadian shield. When we came on deck this morning, the wind had entirely disappeared. The water and sky were both flat gray, and the shoreline, some of the oldest rock in the world, was desolate. Cartier, observing this same sight in 1534, called it *"la terre que Dieu donna à Cayn"*—the land God gave to Cain.

Before we cast off again, the crew received a special talk about ice. From now on, lookouts must be more specific in their reports (we reviewed the terms *broad, fine,* and *points off the bow*), and the person on helm must refrain from conversation. If something is sighted suddenly, the lookout should shout back a course change, which the helm must immediately obey. Square riggers head up into the wind very slowly and only with great effort, so the order would normally be to fall off.

Underway, we motored slowly, not even bothering to shake out sails. Except for the spout of a fin whale and occasional chunks of ice called growlers, there was little change in scenery to indicate we'd moved. Indented by rivers, unforested, sea-torn, the cliffs stretched on, their grim line broken only by occasional outposts. L'Anse au Loup, Pointe Amour, Capstan Island, Cap Diable . . . We ticked them off on the charts as the engine droned and the hours slid by, while keeping our eyes peeled for a tiny two-humped island. At 1430 hours it poked through the mist. With Mad Moll to port and The Louse to starboard, we sneaked in behind the island, anchoring in the small, still, perfect harbor it concealed.

Along the water, tiny wooden houses stood on stilts. Each had its firewood stacked outside in tepee style; the stacks were larger than the cottages themselves. The houses farther back were bright-colored cubes with gables—cheerful, rugged, prim. In the Scottish Hebrides, each might have had a spot of pasture. But these houses backed up only on a ring of cliffs that walled off the surrounding wilderness and were perched on solid stone. The whole village, named Red Bay, resembled a folk art diorama. Imagining winters there, I hoped it was well glued down.

We had stopped off to visit the site of a large European colony said to predate Massachusetts Bay by eighty years. Across the harbor, Saddle Island sat like a cork in the mouth of a bottle. On its lee side, a few dozen figures scratched away at scattered excavations. A makeshift dock led out to a barge. Pipes and contraptions ran from the barge's deckhouse to the waterline. As soon as our wheel was lashed and the sails were furled, a couple of men came over from the island in a launch and invited us ashore.

We were met at the dock by a tall man in muddy Wellington boots, a red sweatshirt, and faded jeans. He introduced himself as James Tuck, professor of archaeology at Memorial University and director of the dig. With his graying sideburns, chestnut hair, square jaw, and crow's-feet at the corners of blue eyes, he looked like he'd just arrived from central casting. He did not look particularly thrilled to see us, however, and didn't want to interrupt the work in progress. But if we would break into three groups, he would be happy to have us shown around. We did as he asked; I wound up with Tuck's group. As we strolled toward the first site away from the water, he told the following tale.

In 1976 an archival historian named Selma Barkham was sifting through sixteenth-century Spanish documents for references to Canada. Ten years before, she had become intrigued by recurrent stories that Basques once lived in the Maritimes. Some of these stories were recorded; for example, on his so-called Voyage of Discovery in 1534, the first thing that Jacques Cartier discovered was European fishermen in a place called *Hable de la Ballaine,* or Harbor of the Whale. Many of the stories were hearsay or oral history. Though widely believed, they had not been verified. So Barkham set out to discover if they were true. Having taught herself Spanish, then Basque, and then Renaissance legal idioms and script, she set up shop at the Basque national archives at the university in Orñate, Spain.

Basques began hunting whales in the Bay of Biscay some sixteen thousand years ago. In the Middle Ages, the Basques were a major maritime power, and by the sixteenth century their commercial interests stretched from the Mediterranean to Iceland. The syndicates that their business spawned in turn created an incredibly complex legal and bureaucratic tangle. In fact, Basques were considered so quarrelsome (litigious, if you prefer) that in

Europe at the time the word *Basque* was used as an unflattering epithet for *lawyer*. So Barkham found plenty to go on and was soon up to her elbows in regulations, lawsuits, and mortgages.

Many of these concerned shipping. Poring over them, she began to find sailing directions and recurring place names for up to a dozen sites, such as Schooner Cove in a letter of 1540. The most frequent was Grand Bay or Buteris, perhaps a corruption of the French word *buttes,* for cliffs around a harbor. A line in a lawsuit read, "He was standing in the cabin beside which they boil down whales when he overheard them say . . ."

Still more intriguing was the case of a ship, the *San Juan,* which went down in 1565 "due to loss of a cable." Like Yankee whalemen in 1840 (and Gloucester fishermen today), Basque crews received pay as "lays," or shares of the catch. Since the *San Juan* went down in the harbor, fully loaded at the season's close, her crew received no pay for the previous six months' labor. When they arrived back home, they brought suit against the owners. From details that emerged in the testimony, Barkham narrowed down probable sites for the mishap and the whaling operation. In 1977 she persuaded Tuck and his assistant, Tip Evans, to search for the actual location, beginning here at Red Bay.

As Tuck said, standing in a hip-deep square pit of marbled clay, "It wasn't hard to find. The gardens across the harbor contained as many fragments of red Spanish roofing tile as turnips. That put us on the track. Our breakthrough came here" (a low stone wall with a grainy black crust) "and here" (a similar vein of black in the pit's clay floor). "From my work on prehistoric Inuit sites I recognized this at once: charred blubber." The dig was on.

In addition to the roof tiles that lay everywhere (one ship alone had brought in six thousand), wine glasses, shop tools, rosaries, and coins were also soon revealed. This was domestic refuse, not the leavings of shipbound transients. As the work progressed, it became increasingly apparent that large numbers of Europeans had actually lived and worked here over a period that spanned decades and that this tranquil bay was the New World's first major industrial site. Now, thanks to four years of Barkham's and Tuck's parallel endeavors, a fairly clear picture of how it operated has emerged.

Basque fishermen first came to Newfoundland in the 1530s. Lured by the inexhaustible stocks of cod, they returned to hunt the more lucrative *sarda,* or black right whale. By 1540 a large-scale commercial whale trade was thriving along this coast. Crews sailed from Spain in the spring, arriving to catch the whales' migration up the coast to the Gulf of St. Lawrence. They stayed for a second season when the animals, fattened up on late summer plankton, swam out through this strait, then processed the catch and set sail in time to avoid the ice and reach Europe by Christmas.

During the six-month season here, the workers lived on the island while their mother ships lay at anchor, much as *Regina* is now. When whales were sighted from watchtowers along the coast, the men rowed out to catch them in twenty-six-foot shallops called *chalupas.* Less sturdy than future Nantucket whaleboats, these couldn't stay fast to a harpooned whale. Instead, they would attach a drogue and then follow the animal for hours or days. When it finally died, they would manually tow it back into port, the whale kept afloat by its own internal gas and blubber.

At the central cookery, the whales were flensed and tried out. Tuck showed us the gray clay imported from Spain, soaked by carbonized fat, and the spot where the forty-five-gallon copper cauldrons stood. These were wood-fired. Once the oil inside had boiled (and if the tank had not exploded, as they sometimes did), it was poured into barrels split lengthwise, half-filled with water. Once its impurities had settled, the oil could be graded, skimmed, and stored. For that, each oven was provided with a cooperage; Tuck pointed to where adzes, draw knives, and barrel staves have been found. Under terms set by the Spanish throne, all the barrels, called *baricas,* had to be made in Spain. When finished, they were broken down into marked sections, stacked aboard ship to save space, and reassembled on arrival here.

How big was the operation? At its peak in the 1560s and 1570s, nearly one thousand men were quartered in Red Bay, producing a half million gallons of oil in an average season.

How lucrative was it? Back in Europe, whale oil was vital for lubricants, lighting, medicine, soap, and pitch. By today's standards, the 55,000 gallons in the *San Juan*'s hold were worth six or seven million dollars. In fact, if you think of that ship as a tanker and then think of the state regulations, overseas refinery, prefab construction techniques, multinational syndicates, and takeover bids, the whole thing comes to look a lot like petroleum in our time. For example, during the oil shortage of '74 (whale oil, 1574), the price of a barrel soared (in today's terms) from four thousand to ten thousand dollars. Windfall profits rivaled those from the Caribbean treasure trade.

What became of it all? A dozen years later, the pride of the fleet was conscripted into royal Spanish service. England-bound. Before Francis Drake put an end to them, they had put an end to forty thousand whales.

After our tour, I climb up the northern hump of Saddle Island, joined by a couple of graduate students from the dig. We have now reached the latitude of permafrost. The seal it forms three feet below the surface traps cold water, making the "saddle" between these hills a variegated sponge of liverwort and bog.

We stand on a point, looking out to sea. On this same spot the lookouts must once have stood, drinking red Catalonian wine, tending fires to guide the chalupas home. A rain squall walks over us, as it would have walked over them. Accustomed to weather by now, we pull on our oilskins and continue talking.

I am struck, I remark, by the gap between what they have discovered and how they go about it. "Yeah, well," shrugs a dark-haired girl, "that's archaeology."

"Did you ever get the urge to drop your brush and tweezers and just bash on through?"

"Not once," she laughs.

"Not *once?*"

"Eight hours a day!"

The dig on shore began in 1977. The following summer, Tuck's group was joined by an underwater team led by Robert Grenier, head of marine archaeology for Parks Canada. Their first dive turned up an oak plank. Oak doesn't grow in Labrador. They went down again. On the second dive, they discovered a Spanish galleon. The pure frigid water of Red Bay had preserved its pieces perfectly. Less than thirty feet below the surface, they found the *San Juan.*

"What is it like down there?" I ask Michel Audy and Denis Paget. They and four others from the diving barge have dropped by to see *Regina.* These are not small men. Dressed in tangerine jumpsuits with sky-blue logos on the breast and sleeves, they occupy the aft salon the way sausage fills its casing. "Down there," says Michel, "it is *cold.*" How cold? Today, on June 9, it is thirty-five degrees. Too cold for lobsters, and even for French Canadians in wet suits. The solution, Denis explains, is "hot suits" through which water at body temperature recirculates from a boiler unit on the barge. After being down for hours at a time, the men surface feeling sleepy, with skin as pink and as wrinkled as a baby's. If a hose burst while they were down, they would be in major trouble. But the method works and has tripled available diving time. As for the sensation, says a 230-pounder with biceps like Michelins, "Eeets . . . oo-là-là."

The *San Juan,* ninety feet at the keel, went down fully loaded; perhaps if she hadn't stayed so late in the season to pick up those last few barrels, she wouldn't have caught such an autumn storm. When it hit, the ship dragged, then grounded on the rocks of Saddle Island. Her keel split. But no one was injured, and the vessel stayed half afloat long enough for valuables to be salvaged. When she finally went under, she went gently, almost whole. Since then, the weight of winter ice from above split her down the middle like an orange, fanning out ribs and frames symmetrically from both sides of the keel.

Right now the parts of the ship that have been raised are submerged in tanks of harbor water in a shed on shore. This water has preserved them for 416 years, and no better way could be desired. At some point a number of the pieces will be taken off to Ottawa for study. After that, they will be reburied in the harbor of Red Bay.

Stepping down into their launch from *Regina,* Michel and Denis invite us to a party. Their place. Tonight. How will we know where it is? I ask. "You'll know."

Red Bay is a village of three hundred people. When we get there, it's plenty bright out for nine P.M., but no one is visible. Where they are hiding I can't say. Up the hill past three small churches (Baptist, Pentecostal, Catholic) and the village's only store stands a dairylike prefab building. Over the door, a sign says "Stagger Inn." We do.

Bright lights! Liquor! Action! Song! Everyone from the dig is there. We humble sailors stand in the doorway, blinking like a pack of moles. Beer? Dancing? Sure I remember how.

In the wee hours, I am led off by my clog dance partner to see the *San Juan*'s remains. She unlocks a hangarlike shed by the water's edge. Inside it is dark and deathly still; we stroll from tank to tank in silence. Reaching down blind into icy water, she hands me a piece of beech, then an oak stave with its grain still perfect. Bilge board and part of a block. Because of the time spent on *Regina Maris,* I can recognize them, naming each one as I hold it like a hand. And smiling, in the darkness, as an actual hand takes mine.

Later, as the Avon comes toward shore, a final beer and parting. Three hours from now this fog will lift. We will raise the hook, sail out around the underwater wreck of 1565, past a steel hulk gone aground 301 years later. An iceberg will split and roll like a whale as we sail beyond Twin Island, past Scab Rock on the *San Juan*'s wake in our own frail home, *Regina.*

FORETOP

10 July. 52°N/56°W. Labrador Sea.

As the sun rose this morning, we sailed through the Strait of Belle Isle, snaking our way out past dozens of growlers, and at last reached open ocean; next stop, Greenland, 250 nautical miles east, 800 north.

I'd had the dawn watch and was just snoozing off after breakfast when George Nichols called down through the skylight, "Uh, Deborah? Are you available? I believe I do see an iceberg now."

From on deck it looked more like a castle. Half the length of a football field, 170 feet high, it had split down the middle into three great pinnacles or turrets. Seas flowed in and out of a central canyon; breakers crashed against the outer sides. Though the bottom ten feet or so had been polished smooth, the flanks higher up were like crumbling battlements. They didn't sparkle, didn't even reflect the light; they were full of debris scraped off another continent and pitted, gunmetal gray.

Having grounded itself in water ninety fathoms deep, this old iceberg stood still, like an island, as we floated past, and the feeling it produced was desolate, as of something ancient and possessed of great experience now dying.

Soon there were others, less broken up, drifting very slowly. Some were angular, some craggy, some as sinuous as a nude by Henry Moore. One iceberg twice the size of *Regina* had a perfect sphinx head; hundreds of small dark seabirds nested on its peak like hair.

The gray sky was oppressive, somber, but intensely bright against water the color of graphite at high noon. Jutting up from one into the other, the smoother icebergs didn't just reflect the light; they swallowed it, digested it, and glowed. Emerald, lilac, aquamarine, they seemed to distill and concentrate the colors that we couldn't see from underneath the water and above the clouds. Nothing could have been more full of beauty—or devoid of life. The combination mooted every thought inside my head. As we stood at the rail and stared, the initial whoops gave way to a baffled quiet.

Just past past Belle Isle itself, however, that quiet was shattered by a sound like giant vacuum cleaners sucking on a throw rug. We had met up with a veritable farewell party of harp seals and minke, fin, and humpback whales.

By observing and responding to the humpbacks' dives, George synchronized our movements with their own. Undisturbed, they breached repeatedly. Peter, Don, and Toni stood on the forward deckhouse, their electric shutters whirring, shooting high-speed photos through lenses the size of coffee cans. Judy scribbled in her census books, alluding to "apical notches" and "odd scars in the seventh quadrant" and "the cow with two juveniles." All of this I found frustrating, though exciting. When I did catch a glimpse of the animals at all, they looked all pretty much the same to me—big, black, and wet—and I seemed to have a real talent for locating the spot where a whale *had been* before it dived.

Once clear of the coast, George ordered our largest square sail taken down so that a new one could be "bent on." The course, as it's called, weighs 250 pounds, and the yard to which it attaches with a bolt rope the width of my arm is a full-grown spruce. By the time enough of us had gathered to attempt the job, the wind had risen sharply, and *Regina* was meeting seven-foot seas head on.

I was one of the first aloft, and by the time nine others had joined me, I found myself forced all the way out on the yardarm. With so much weight on the footrope's center, its ends rose right up to the level of the yard itself. With the yard on a level with my thighs, there was not all that much to hold on to as each new plunge lifted us up and forward, roller-coaster style. As we pitched, we were also rolling, and the new course, hauled up by the sheets in one great bundle, swung back and forth like a wrecker's ball. It had started raining. I was wearing rubber boots, which began to slip and slide along the footrope.

Once we had fastened the sail to the center of the yard, it was unfolded outward and secured along its whole length. The next job was to lean over the yardarm and roll the sail up onto it for gasketing. Fat chance! Stiff as could be and soaked with rain, the canvas weighed too much for even nine of us to handle. Each time the others kicked back on the footrope to gather a "byte," my legs swung backwards, out from under me. Fright made me worse than useless, too scared to let go with either hand and help furl. As my fingers cramped around the cold iron jackstay, I could feel blood draining from my face. I wondered whether I was about to black out. I thought, "That's ridiculous." Then tried to laugh. Then panicked.

What to do? With four other people between me and the mast, there was no way to get off the yard. "It's only your fear," I kept telling myself, which was like telling someone on a bad acid trip that it's "only the drug." Then the brunt of the squall arrived. The sail grew heavier still. The others gave up gasketing and filed in toward the shrouds. By now I was practically paralyzed. Left out on the yardarm, I clung to the stunsail ring, looking down, and saw only water.

And then I saw Dave Oldach, waiting in the mist like a fireman on the Golden Gate Bridge, as if to talk me down. In fact he said nothing, just slithered on out and stood beside me for a while. That was all it took: just being there.

On deck I felt grateful to Dave but angry with myself. Humiliated. After my good experience off Blanc Sablon, this was not supposed to happen. I thought I was over it. Now I dread it, worse than before. I'm not sure that I can go up again at all.

2000 hours, in the galley. During Don's talk on vertebrate morphology, the sea rose higher. People began to be sick. Experienced Al Stearns had the right idea—to keep our stomachs full—but he might have made a wiser dinner choice than lamb. Dinner now over, I'm standing in front of the galley sink, shifting from foot to foot on the slippery floor, inhaling a mixture of diesel vapor, fat, and steam. The hatches are all closed for weather; it's muggy; the oven has raised the temperature to eighty degrees. I have just carried two ten-gallon pots of water from the stove. The portion of their contents that did not land on the floor now sloshes against the walls of the stoppered sink. As the water tilts one way, I shift weight in the other direction. With each roll, a reef of dishes pokes through the rippling grease and then disappears again with a sucking sound.

My partner for this tag team event is Joan. She rinses; I wash. Under the circumstances, I am trying to watch what I'm doing as little as possible, and I am ready to admit that a few of the dishes I send her way might not be jiffy clean. But after a while I have the distinct impression that the flow of rejects in my direction has grown greater than the number of dones I send in hers. I don't want to argue, but I think that I'm changing the water often *enough,* thank you, given the weather, and if she bugs me one more time I'm gonna—

No need. Just as she's lecturing me on why rinse water should be boiled, her face turns the color of lamb; she clutches her stomach and disappears through the hatch in an updraft like the wicked witch of the West.

Ten minutes later I'm done. I squeegee the floor, then slide the dishes back into their cupboard (and believe me, they do slide). In the main salon, it's time for a class on plankton. Peter is writing on the chalkboard. Each line of print sags slightly in the middle and is higher at either end.

11 July. 52°N/53°W.

Fifty-five miles northeast of Belle Isle, it's three in the morning. Nothing is visible on deck or from it. Rain falls steadily. The temperature is forty-two degrees, the wind northeasterly at thirty knots. Rather than fight it, we heave to. *Regina* wallows on the long swells, slipping sideways, drifting.

We have lashed the wheel, and I am the only one on deck, on lookout. We are crossing the Labrador Current now, a frigid river that flows south straight from the Pole and brings the icebergs. Not far from here, a big one met the *Titanic.* Since then, most ships steer south of this route, by law.

It's hard to stand here, see nothing, and yet *not* project the dangers you are looking for. That blur—is it my imagination? What about the light I thought I saw five minutes ago but can't find now? That brightness two points off to starboard, that's for real. But is it a ship's light miles away (we haven't seen anyone for days) or bioluminescent plankton quite close by? A week ago I spotted an ominous light and called Gregg forward. He told me I was not required to report the rising moon.

The rain is very fine, though steady. It clings to my stubble, which tastes of salt. Fulmars cluck and coo among the headsails; when the birds swoop past our starboard running light, it freezes their motion like a strobe and colors their outstretched wings bright green. Over and over the bowsprit rises—six, eight, ten feet off the water—then presses heavily down, like the heel of a giant hand on dough. Water surges across the deck, aglow with the krill it carries. I am knee-deep in sparkle. My seaboots are coated with glitter. Over and over they light up from ankle to calf, and then go dark.

Over and over . . . To break the spell, I look at the foremast, letting my gaze rise spar by spar. The yards are always larger than you expect, especially at night. There is such audacity in the design! Who could conceive of such a thing, not to mention actually build and sail it? If you let your mind climb *that* one all the way, it might never come down.

Lucky for you, it has to. Settle down now. Concentrate. You shift weight, stare once again at the darkness up ahead, and try to see only what is there. Settle down, for others' sake. And let your mind recede into its task.

1510. Underway again in fifteen-foot seas, the thermometer at forty-two. When I was on helm last hour, the wave tops were even with my eyes. We are heaving about like a Marx Brothers movie of ships at sea; half the crew is ill, and almost everyone not on watch is in bed below. Instead of lunch, I ate crackers, a dozen or two. I don't seem to get seasick, in the sense of throwing up; instead, I become irresistibly sleepy, almost faint.

One way to stave off getting sick is to keep busy. So in the drylab between watch rotations, I try to get caught up on my journal. I love this deckhouse, from the green brass of its portholes to the stout Douglas fir (the foremast) passing through its roof and floor. There's a faint smell of fish and formalin. Water thermometers swing on their hooks. Cameras and field glasses click against the bulkhead. Over my shoulder the skull of a goose-beaked whale is mounted on the wall. Plates of baleen hang overhead, swinging forward and aft, forward and aft, with a whooshing sound, like fans.

12 July. 54°N/52°W.

Much calmer now, and colder too. The last traces of coastal fog have disappeared, giving way to a sky that is all bleached glare and a strangely colorless ocean. Air temperature is forty-four degrees. The water temperature has plunged to forty. When you draw seawater in the canvas bucket, it numbs your hands. The wet lines leave your fingers raw, and when you come below after standing watch, the pads of your hands grow puffy.

Because of headwinds, we are forced to motor; the engine's constant mutter lends a sameness to the hours. This morning there was an unspectacular plankton trawl. Apart from what came up in the nets we have seen no other life—or sun or vessels. Nobody feels too frisky. There is not much to report on. A dreary, uneventful day.

13 July. 57°N/52°W. Labrador Sea.

The same.

14 July. 58°N/51°W.

"Hey, Scott," Fran asks, "what's the difference between creosote and this coffee?"

It's breakfast, second seating, half the places empty, Fran in the middle, as usual, close to the food and speaking, as usual, too loudly. We are 350 miles northeast of Belle Isle, almost halfway across the Davis Strait to Greenland. With the engine on, the main salon has acquired the stench of diesel fumes. With the hatches closed (it's thirty-nine degrees outside), the air below is stifling.

After Fran has spoken, nobody looks at her, but every head inclines in her direction.

"I don't know," says Scott. He wants no part of it.

"The difference between creosote and this coffee is *the cup.*"

At one end of the table (where the scientists and George are seated), conversation stops. At the other end (the fore watch, mostly), there's an intake of breath and a couple of stifled laughs. Coffee is big in the news again. Since we entered open ocean, it's been a rule to have four pots ready at all times. This means that they sometimes stand on the stove for hours. To make matters worse, George insists that the corrosive swill be perked much too long, and the result is that we can enjoy a coffee lift without all that coffee flavor.

So last night Dave (the veteran of many an encounter group on shore) set out to work with the situation creatively, convincing Clay to doctor the contents of one pot with cinnamon and cloves. Unfortunately, the doctored pot, which they forgot to mark, was the one from which George poured his wake-up cup at six-fifteen this morning. He was not amused.

Nor is he now. Perhaps the only thing that our captain likes less than being crossed is expressing anger when he has been. At such times his lips grow thin and stubborn and his cheeks go slack. That's how he looks as we wait, and he says nothing.

Adopting the fools-rush-in approach, somebody asks, "Why not brew two strengths of coffee, one quart for the captain, the way he likes it, and three quarts for the twenty-nine others on board?" At this point, a hundred years ago, the operative word would have been *keelhaul.* George smiles tightly. Mumbles, "Coffee is ready only when it can hold up the spoon." Forces out a watchful laugh. When nobody else joins in, he adds, "Our coffee is *superb* and will remain so." End of discussion. Spite in the guise of charm.

Before conversation can resume, the curtains of a bunk behind the table part and rise beneath an emerging wave of flesh: Rob Trainor. Rob is our youngest student, a member of the mizzen watch who doesn't say much but goes about his business affably. Because his frame is, shall we say, well insulated, it's hard to tell how far down the blubber ends and the muscle begins. He is certainly someone you want to have hauling with you on a line, yet even when doing more than his share, he *looks* like he's slacking off. Now due on watch, having slept through breakfast, Rob could not have chosen a worse time to breach. As he shambles past the table, he grabs a few pancakes to take on deck, oblivious to the silence in the cabin and all eyes on his hand.

"Drop it!" George barks. "You're too late."

The hand opens. The pancakes fall. Everyone else looks up, then down.

As it turned out, breakfast was the high point of the morning, during which my mood grew worse and worse. Maybe I'm just too old to spend time listening to dormitory-style conversation, Outward bounders everywhere I turn. And as usual, the people with least to say seem most compelled to say it constantly.

Maybe it's because they're so out of their element that they feel the need to talk as if they weren't, trying to carve out a personal space and role. The problem is that if that's their way of dealing with the anxiety we all feel, if what they are really saying, hour after tedious hour, is, "This is me," then you can't very well reply, "Shut up" or "Go away." And of course, you yourself can't go away, as you certainly would on shore.

People have begun to linger before choosing a place at the table, waiting to see who sits down where. But this is frowned upon. When I tried it at lunch today, not only was it noticed, but it also failed, and I wound up in a crossfire between wild-and-crazy-times-at-Smith and how-many-minutes-my-mom-cooks-eggs. I sat on the bench and glowered like one of those anvil-shaped black clouds that foretell approaching squalls. For the whole meal I said nothing, and nobody sought to draw me out. I guess they preferred not to get rained on.

Skipping dessert, I went out to the fantail and sat up on the steering box. Sheltered from the wind, with my back against the pilothouse, I stared at our wake.

Bang. Pause. Bang. Pause. Bang. . . . Alongside the pilot-house port-side door is a closet called the Doo's Bait Locker, used to store light gear such as heaving lines, to which we need easy access, and as a space for drying clothes because it's right above the engine. Apparently someone retrieving wet gloves or socks hadn't hooked shut the door, which was now repeatedly swinging open and banging closed. Fuck that. It could tear itself off its hinges for all I cared. I stretched out on my back and closed my eyes, feeling too annoyed to address what was annoying me, like an angry man alone in his kitchen, letting the faucet drip.

A minute later the swinging stopped. I heard someone come around the corner and sit down on the steering box, no doubt watching me and waiting for a chance to socialize. Maybe if I feigned sleep, he would go away.

"This is really hell," said a voice—Bill Cowan's. I opened my eyes. He was letting his own travel lazily, caressingly across the mizzen sail above us, out along the gaff vang to the bright calm sea. "Anotha' lousy day in Paradise," he drawled, and suddenly looked me straight in the eye. Was he mocking me? Trying to make me laugh? Confused, I didn't answer. He took another tack.

"Haahvey, listen, boats are a very intense environment. They make *everybody* moody. You are constantly at the mercy of factors beyond your control—the work, the weather, people. There's always a couple of cone eaters on every trip. People you didn't choose to be with and you don't wanna be with. I once had these two Hispanic kids in my watch. On the *Mary Day.* The three of us would be up on deck together and they'd refuse to talk English. Drove me crazy. But you can't let bad feelings hang around. A boat's too small. You gotta speak up right away. Haul 'em out, get 'em up on deck, then send 'em overboard."

That burst the bubble of my anger. After some talk about the ship and the way things have been going, I asked Bill more about himself. He has lived his whole life, he replied, around Camden and Rockport, Maine, where he worked in shipyards from the age of seventeen. His father and brothers all earn their living from the sea, and his uncle is a tanker captain. Bill himself holds a seaman's card and has spent time in the merchant marine. The pay is great and the work isn't hard, but it's boring as hell, he said, "like living in a motel." So after many such trips, having also been a sail-maker's apprentice, Bill left the merchant service for work he truly loves, on sailing vessels along the coast. On the last of these, two years ago, he was first mate.

"A windjammer?" I asked.

"Cargo schooner."

"Cargo?"

"Yup. She is—she was—a beauty."

"Sold?"

"Sank. In a hurricane." He seemed uncomfortable.

"Were you aboard?"

He nodded. Now it was Bill who looked away.

Amidships, Gregg and Lawrence were busy caulking. When I asked if I could join in, they both looked surprised. It was proba-bly the first time I had sought out extra work when not on duty.

"Oh, for a life of sensations, not of thoughts!" The sticki-ness of hemp, the sound of the hammer—iron on oak, the pop-ping torch, and the bubbling pitch. A gentle rolling. Bursts of spray. Sharp whiffs of piny tar smoke blowing aft on the salt sea air . . . We worked side by side for two hours and in the whole time spoke maybe a dozen words.

Then a plankton trawl, a long nap, and supper; an hour of writing, followed by quiet chats on deck, as the sky dimmed, with Helene and Craig. Turned in, feeling good, at nine.

Midwatch. Arriving on deck, I found Kathy and Lisa conducting a speed check, *Regina* style, by tossing trash off the forward rail and timing its progress aft in the crossed beams of their flashlights. Kathy's stopwatch measured 6.2 seconds from shroud to shroud, which translated into seven knots.

That's about as exciting as things would get. With no staysails and only a couple of square sails set, there was plenty of time for the warmth of the aft salon, and boning up on navigation. George has been offering classes in the subject, and despite my extreme deficiencies in math (which trace back to a high school teacher who was misnamed Mr. Witty), I find the material fascinating.

In open seas, George explained last night, it takes two fixes to approximate, and three to confirm, one's exact location with a sextant. These can be moon lines or sun lines or star lines, so long as they intersect, but before you can calculate where they meet, you need a starting point. And since everything looks the same, what you do, in a word, is invent one. For longitude, you agree on a zero point at Greenwich and measure local time as distance east or west from that zero point. For latitude, you posit a plausible position north or south and then calculate what the altitude of a given star would be *if you were there.* Then you do the actual star sight and calculate the difference. Depending on which altitude is larger and what the difference is, you can now establish that you are somewhere on a "circle of equal altitudes," or CEA. Successive star lines then transect that circle and determine your exact position on its arc.

We are taught to think of science as quantitative and precise, and in one sense navigation is—the trigonometry alone requires six sets of tables. Yet what fascinates me here is the imaginative leap that must precede these calculations, how we must first invent a fiction against which to measure truth. The navigational technique is called *assumed positions*.

Our present latitude is a few hundred miles north of Moscow's. At this time of year, the darkest it ever gets here is "nautical twilight." The horizon is always visible, so one can take star sights nearly all night long. And so, toward the end of our watch, at 0300 hours, I find Gregg on the quarterdeck, looking east, with a sextant in his hand.

To see him standing there, against the vacant sky, is to be reminded just how small and how impermanent we are. And to admire all the more the way his feet are planted, the dignity in his upturned face, his hands controlled and quiet, his mind the same. He is not posturing, not even thinking of himself. Yet as he aims and reads the instruments, he is aligning himself, literally, with stars.

Unaware that he is being watched, he figures a moment. Rubs his eyes. "Fifty-eight. Twelve. Fourteen," he says to no one. "Sunrise at four-oh-nine."

15 July. 61°N/50°W.

At ten A.M., with the sea a dull smudge and the pearl sky glowing like a surgeon's lamp, our lookouts spot icepack, a solid white line in the distance dead ahead. Unlike icebergs, which form on land, drift ice develops from the freezing of the sea itself. Though easier to anticipate, it is also more treacherous and can surround a ship in no time. In 1915 another 144-foot barkentine, Sir Edward Shackleton's *Endurance,* was caught in the Antarctic pack. It crushed like a walnut beneath him.

On hearing of ice, George himself climbs all the way up the mainmast and orders a ninety-degree course change. Because the pack has crept around the southern tip of Greenland and on up the western shore, we must abandon our destination, Julianehab, and instead sail northward, seeking an open port. With no adequate leads in the ice, we veer out to sea and continue north all day with the pack on our starboard side. When the light dims, we heave to in open water. Air temperature is down to thirty-seven degrees; ocean temperature, to thirty-one.

16 July. 62°N/51°W.

Having bypassed Julianehab, we had hoped to put in at Frederikshab, a hundred miles farther up the coast. But nearly a full day later we have still not reached this icepack's northern edge and must therefore bypass Frederikshab as well, continuing north instead of east, staying parallel to the shore.

It is 0430 hours; a pale polar sun electrifies the fog. Overnight the drift ice has aligned with the direction of the wind; every now and then it makes a sound like grinding molars. On bow lookout I am told by Gregg, and then by Joan, and then reminded, it seems, by everyone else on deck, that if I even *suspect* we're approaching ice, I should shout my own commands directly to the helm. Visibility is less than eighty yards.

At 0600 George raises Godthab on the radio: "Come in, Greenland, this is *Regina Maris,* Whiskey Yankee Foxtrot five four one three. Over." A contented, drowsy voice responds in English. I imagine some slightly flaccid, good-natured Scandinavian face at the other end, slow hands and yellow hair, a beer paunch in a navy-blue sweater, the sun through Venetian blinds creating stripes in dust on the radio controls. "So you'ff found ice," the voice says. "How far does it extent? Ofer."

"Uh. That's what I was hoping you'd tell me. Over."

"Sorry, sir. Can't help you there."

"I didn't catch that, Godthab. Say again?"

"It's the weather serfice, captain. All of them they are out on strike."

I offer to bring George coffee. He says no, it makes him jumpy. Catches my look of amazement. Smiles.

By 0700 all we can do is evade the floating flak by changing course almost continually; for "bearing," the logs read simply VMO, for "various maneuvers ordered." It's strange to think of the others sleeping peacefully below. Approaching a dense group of ice pans, George quips, "Hit these and we'll wake up even the bosun." In my anxious state, I think he has said, "Wake up the bosun." I rush below to the fo'c'sle and rouse Lawrence, who rushes back up behind me. On deck, bleary, responsible, pulling up his pants, he gasps, "I'm ready, George."

"For what?"

Confusion. Explanations. Laughter.

For the next twelve hours we proceed dead slow, heading north, west, southwest, any which way to remain in open water. If the wind turns westerly, it will force us back into the ice, which will consolidate around us. Floes are everywhere, ranging in size from six to sixty feet across. Yesterday the solid pack shone white; today it has veins of startling green, like emerald ink. Fog, fatigue, and tension breed hallucination. At one point it feels like a sea of milk filled with oversized animal crackers.

All afternoon there are two lookouts on the catheads, two on the forward deckhouse, one aloft, and a mate on the foremast shroud. Patrick, the mate, communicates with Fran in the pilot-house by walkie-talkie. Fran's radar screen looks like a windshield splattered with raindrops. "Pat," she radios forward, "you've got one dead ahead, two hundred yards."

"Roger, Fran. What size?"

Silence. Maybe she hasn't heard him.

"Fran?"

More silence.

"Fran, what size?"

"Oh-my-sweet-Jesus size!"

We swing hard to port and manage to avoid it. But over the next few hours, we are not so lucky. Whenever pans lie ahead on both sides, we are forced to choose the smaller one and run it down.

Curiously, through all this I feel tense but never really frightened; our collective caution is equal to the danger. As so often on *Regina Maris,* you are asked not to exert extraordinary skill but to place extraordinary trust in the skill you already possess.

Meanwhile, the research continues. The ice edge teems with life. Today alone we have observed a harbor porpoise, gannets and a greater scua, countless murres, pilot whales riding our bow wave like surfers, three sperm whales, and four humpbacks. Two of these were yearlings, frisky little seven-tonners who kept checking us out momentarily and then hurrying back to the grown-ups' sides. As usual, all were observed at length and photographed. That's what we're here to do.

17 July. 63°N/54°W.

I awoke for midwatch overwhelmed with an all-consuming sadness and the strange sense that I'd just dreamt an entire eighth-century Anglo-Saxon poem. In "The Wanderer," a man describes his life of exile on the sea. At one point he dreams that he is back with his "beloved lord" receiving gifts of treasure, hearing comrades' voices in the bright hall. Then "the joyless man/wakes up and sees instead the yellow waves/the seabirds bathing, stretching out their wings/while snow and hail and frost fall all together." Care is renewed for him "who must continually send his spirit over icy waves." A litany concludes that all is hardship in this world beneath the heavens: "Possessions are fleeting; friendship is fleeting;/kinship is fleeting; man is fleeting;/all this earthly framework is growing empty, and will come to naught."

Up on deck, the cold and damp were numbing, and the ocean, black with whitecaps, had the look of a photographic negative. My first rotation was on bow. As I faced what the

Anglo-Saxons would have called a *hrimcalde* ("rime-cold") sea, the residue of feeling from my dream persisted and grew stronger.

What in the world was I doing here? Why was I standing in sleet in the middle of nowhere at one in the morning? What was I trying to find out or prove? The speaker in that poem was in exile, but I *chose* to do this, almost as if I could not stop myself from moving on. It had always been this way; maybe that was why I had no "bright hall" to dream of coming back to. I had made a botch of it; I had failed to find, or at any rate to keep, my hearth back home. Indeed, it was from this emptiness, this absence, that I was fleeing. Yet nothing could feel emptier than the prospect at which I now stared.

But maybe I was getting too particular; maybe this was something anyone would feel, faced with the blank screen of the darkened fog night after night, alone. If not this sorrow, it would be another, I thought, and asked myself how there could be such sadness, wondering where it comes from.

All I could think to answer was no answer, the Buddhists' "noble truth," that life is suffering. You feel it as our prow divides the wet black world in half: Time's fabric splits, then mends astern.

18 July. Docked, Godthab.

All through the night and morning we continued northwest, dodging drift ice; the noon fix put us farther out from port than twenty-four hours before. But this afternoon, having cleared the pack at last, we ran east, entering Godthabsfjord in early evening. Sailing in, we could see no hint of the town that we knew was there. A blue-black fog bank hundreds of feet high rolled over us between the fjord's steep sides, and as the ship crawled farther into it, you could almost hear the choruses of Wagner echoing.

At the fjord's narrow head, a sharp U-turn to port brought

the town and harbor into view. A jet-black, flat-topped mountain looming overhead made the place look like a Steven Spielberg set. The first ship we encountered was a wreck with its foredeck buckled by ice and the paint scoured from its bow. Farther on, past a dozen shrimpers, small boats were moored five rows deep. We docked beside three blue fishing boats with harpoon cannons mounted on their bows.

I was all set to go on shore at eight when I realized my watch was on—for the third straight time on a night when our ship reached port. I did some figuring: We'd be on duty from eight to twelve tonight and from eight A.M. to noon tomorrow, which was Saturday. So with early closings, I'd miss all the shops and markets.

Not acceptable. To be mopping the wetlab floor, with Greenland seven feet away, after sailing fifteen hundred miles? No way. I asked Gregg to let me go ashore. He said to ask George. I cornered George. He looked annoyed and said it was up to Gregg. It was almost eleven by the time some others returned, and Gregg, seeming disappointed in me, said that I could go.

It was still light out. As I stepped ashore, a bleary blond man in his thirties also stepped off from a shrimp boat moored astern. I asked for the time. He held up his watch. It read 11:20. He answered, "Haff pest tvelf," and wobbled toward a waiting car. "Are you driving?" I inquired.

"No, I am drunk. My wife, though, she iss drifing, yes? We'll give you a little look round." The Toyota, which had ads on its roof, turned out to be Greenland's only driver education car. We lurched off with the man, his wife, and small daughter up front and me in the rear. As Gerhard pointed out the sights, he grew increasingly convivial and loud. Every now and then his wife Christina spoke sharply in Danish, after which he piped down.

Godthab is Greenland's capital, a town of ten thousand people. But at first sight it looked less like a capital city than a mining camp. There were no streets or squares or parks, just a series of structures thrown up along a roadside. The dominant and most depressing ones were five-story, blocklong housing projects with water-stained concrete sides. They had never been painted. Most of the windows that weren't boarded up were broken. There were graffiti in Greenlandic on the walls. Looking in vain for some shrubbery or lawns, I thought at first that their absence might be due to the climate. But there weren't open spaces, yards, or playgrounds, either. There was no sense of relationship of one building to another or to the space between. What I was looking at were warehouses, pure and simple, built cheap to store Eskimos.

Farther on, the same proved true of the town as a whole. An apartment complex for Danish engineers, the sports arena, and government offices did look a little fancier, in the spare style of a ski resort. But they too were prefab, planar, and awkwardly set down, and even the fancy Hotel Grønland was flanked by Quonset huts. The whole place felt like an outpost dropped onto the land, not sprung up in relation to it. The human population seemed an afterthought.

Gerhard moved here from the Faroe Islands when he was five years old. His father worked on ships, and he is now cook and part owner of the boat I saw him leaving. He has been to Denmark once but has no wish to return. I asked about the Greenland winters. In his childhood, Gerhard said, a single storm dropped seven meters of snow, and the thermometer once hit minus thirty-five degrees Celsius. In December the sun does not come up until almost ten A.M. and goes down again by four. It was midnight when Gerhard told me this; I could see a half mile and said so. "Yes, well," he said apologetically. "Tonight is so very dark only because of the rain."

We drove on over to the "old town." Settled in 1721 by the Danish missionary Hans Egede, this resembles an eighteenth-century Danish village, with a yellow wood-frame church and surrounding homes on stone foundations three feet high. Farther up the hill stood smaller bungalows, where Inuits live. These were practically windowless, clustered together and painted in primary colors like the houses in a Monopoly game. All stood on solid stone. In fact, there is no such thing in Godthab as "below ground level"; even toilet waste must be stored and collected weekly.

We stepped out of the car to examine one cottage. It was cornflower blue with maize-colored trim. Its picket fence, pump house, and steep roof made it look quite Danish, out of a story by Hans Christian Andersen. But the whole thing was igloo-sized. "How many people live in there?" I asked Gerhard. "Oh," he said, "probably eight or nine."

Back in the modern part of town, we drove past Greenland's first civilian airstrip, which was built two years before, and the studios of Radio Greenland. There is also television here. It transmits week-old news reports and second-run films by cable. Passing police headquarters and the new one-story jail, I asked how many prisoners it contained. "Maybe a dozen," said Gerhard. "Trunkards. In the morning when they wake up, they can go home."

On the main street again we encountered packs of Inuit teenagers. Some were sitting on the curbstone. Others leaned against the wall of a dance hall built of corrugated steel. Many staggered; two were fighting; all were extremely drunk. As we rounded a curve, I saw five kids talking with some people from *Regina*. The teenagers shook their long, black hair and gesticulated crazily. Backlit by the midnight sky, they looked theatrical and frightening. Christina did not so much drive past them as aim for them, with her high beams turned on. They stopped in midgesture, staring, trapped as in a frozen frame from a silent film, projected by carbon arc light.

In Greenland, as in Alaska and the Canadian North, displacement of native ways has created serious social problems. Gathered in towns, deprived of nomadic life and a hunting culture, many of the people now have literally nothing to do. Squeezed by the loss of traditional work on the one hand and an influx of skilled Danish immigrants on the other, they can't find jobs and are thus reduced to wards of a state that is three thousand miles away. They sit in their concrete tenements, draw welfare, and drink. The suicide rate in Greenland is four times that in Denmark.

Those are statistics. Just now, however, I didn't need what I'd heard or read to realize that the town was not quaint or happy, that something here was frighteningly wrong. With the image of those wasted kids still dancing in my mind, I was delivered back aboard *Regina*, feeling both excited and disturbed by what I'd witnessed and eager to learn more.

The first thing that this required was to get on shore again, and with that aim in mind, I asked George if we could talk right after breakfast. He said to meet him in the pilothouse, where we wouldn't be disturbed. But in fact I was already quite disturbed. It seemed pretty stupid to take me along as a writer and then not allow me to get off whenever we reach port. I assume that the others did not spend weeks in the library reading up on Greenland; nor did they buy Danish kroner back in Boston to save time for talking with local people when they got here. If I'm going to be stuck below decks making baggywrinkle, how am I supposed to accomplish my own work, for which I came?

"Your *own* work?" George asked. "Aren't you on watch?"

Of course I was; why else would I ask to be excused?

"Maybe you can get someone from another watch to swap with you."

"Why would anyone want to stay on board?"

"Then you've answered your own question."

"George, this isn't play for me."

No answer. Then, "If I'd known you were going to be this way, I would not have taken you along." Eye contact down from ten percent to zero. Silence. Finally, speaking ve-ry slow-ly and de-lib-er-ate-ly: "As I believe I've explained to you before, special status on a boat is not a good idea."

"I haven't noticed any scientists standing watch or doing dishes."

"Ideally they would. And to be frank with you, Harvey, I may have made a mistake in that regard. I have seen a lot of crews in my time, and oddly enough, folks seem happiest when they share the dirty work; I can think of one scientist, and I'm sure you know who I mean, who would be feeling better right now if he pitched in a little more.

"The point is not whether a privilege is big or small or even justified; either way, it makes the person who receives it *different*.

It disturbs how people feel about the others in their watch and how they pull together."

"But my status *is* different: I'm older, you took me on different terms, and I have a specialized task to perform. I'm a professional. We signed a contract. I've got to produce. It's to your benefit as well as mine that you let me pursue it the way I know is best—"

"You are not on board this ship to write about Greenland."

Take a deep breath, H.O. Calm down. How can I make him understand how much of a writer's discipline is aleatory, necessarily random, purposefully unfocused, following his nose? No, I'm not here to write "about" Greenland, but if someone respects the work I do, he should respect my way of doing it, and not deny me my equivalent of the plankton trawl. Why should I have to justify so fucking much? Can he really not appreciate what this involves?

"I appreciate your dilemma," George said. "And I think this is too important for a snap decision. I will take it under advisement and give you an answer in twenty-four hours." I stepped outside.

"Oh, and Harvey . . ."

"Yes?"

"As long as you're so dreadfully stuck on board, there's something you might find useful. Three Inuit whaling captains are coming to have a chat with me. Why don't you join us? In the aft salon, at ten."

At ten o'clock, Ujunquaq, Teresee, and Nicolaj Heinrich seated themselves around the table, and the rest of us pulled up chairs. How quiet it seemed! No people coming in and out; no ocean sounds; the lamp at rest on its brass gimbals.

Hardy Larsen, administrator of the local marine biology lab, served as translator. Peter and Judy showed the guests our humpback catalog, explained what we're after, and asked them to tell us about the current state of Greenland whaling. Nikolaj then explained how belugas and narwhals are still hunted farther up the coast, in the traditional way, from kayaks. Because these animals remain plentiful, there are no legal limits on the catch. A few times he has seen them two hundred miles to the north, where we are bound, in the company of bowhead whales. The latter have, he hopes, escaped extinction.

Kayak hunters also remain on the south and east coasts but have been displaced in many spots by commercial operations. Our guests themselves use fifty-millimeter harpoon guns and sell most of what they catch. Their whale hunt is thus not, strictly speaking, for subsistence. But the kill *is* based solely on local demand for meat, and whatever is caught is promptly used.

The number of humpbacks sighted is increasing. In 1979 over 220 were seen, some in pods of twenty animals. Those that are captured all have full stomachs and look healthy. The annual quota of ten, set by the International Whaling Commission, has already been reached this year. However, the main prey of Greenland's whalers are not humpbacks but minke whales. These, Ujunquaq said, are still abundant. The annual quota of 420 (120 for Norway, 300 for Greenland) has never been filled, and Godthab takes only 25 per year.

Though minkes are erratic in the open sea, said Teresee, they move more predictably on their shallow feeding grounds. Therefore, the whalers simply stay at home and watch for them from the windows of top-floor apartments. When whales come into the fjords, the men launch the boats, pursue them, make the kill, and tow the captured animals to shore for flensing. Up until five years ago this was performed on the town beach here in Godthab. It is now banned under new pollution laws and must be carried out in nearby bays. Every part of the whale except its intestines and skeleton is brought into town and sold. Most of the flesh is cooked, but the blubber is eaten raw or pickled into *muktuk,* a great delicacy.

According to Nikolaj, the minke whales have grown more restless in the last few years. "They need their peace and quiet," he explained, but the increased underwater noise from more and larger boats makes whales "unhappy." He and the other men then spoke with concern about a greater threat now being planned. The Canadian government wants to exploit the natural gas reserves that have been found northwest of Baffin Island. They hope to bring liquid natural gas through the Davis Strait in supertankers and insist that their methods will be foolproof. But our guests said that the underwater noise—let alone an accident—could destroy the fish and mammal stocks on which Greenland's livelihood depends. When we expressed a desire to learn more, they said that the man to talk with is Finn Lynge. He is away, but they will arrange a meeting for when we return to Godthab a few weeks from now.

After lunch, I walked into town with Gregg and David for a few beers at the Hotel Grønland. Drinking Tuborg at a linen-covered table set with silver, looking out through plate glass windows, I found the stillness almost disconcerting. So was the total absence of Inuits; except for the view outside, we might have been in Copenhagen. When I said so to the young receptionist, she grew uncomfortable. Once encouraged to talk, however, she told me that she was Danish and that she had landed her job for the summer even though a trilingual Greenlandic friend had been turned down for the same position weeks before. I would have liked to ask more, but the girl's boss suddenly appeared and summoned her away.

Gregg and Dave were waiting in the lobby. The instant that we stepped outside, a procession drew near. It was a funeral. Behind two coffins walked two men, each bearing a large wooden cross. They were the fathers of a teenage couple who had committed double suicide. Stolid with grief and poverty, the mourners took no note of us as they passed by. I felt like an intruder on their grief, their lives, their culture. I turned away, and my glance fell on the American Express plaque mounted on the hotel's wall. I hated it. I wished it didn't glitter so.

In Godthab no one owns residential property outright. Though those who can afford to build may do so, the land on which they build still belongs to the city and reverts to it when they leave. Perhaps the rule is meant to reinforce existing patterns of ownership or to control growth; there is certainly scant evidence of planning. Even the small, bright, handsome homes and church in Old Town, to which we now strolled, had no layout such as one might find near an English commons, an Italian piazza, or a New Hampshire village green. The buildings seemed to have been wedged in wherever the rocky slopes allowed.

We came upon a fish stall. It was an open-air, sturdy structure, very Scandinavian in its butcher block design—and this in a place where any wood, even matchsticks, has to be imported. Inside, a half dozen wizened Inuits were selling skins with the blubber still on, spread out terribly red and bloody on the ground. Above them, on even bloodier tables, were the hearts and heads of seals. Checking for quality, an old woman dressed in furs lifted up one head and peeled back the skin, turning the seal's face inside out like a glove. Satisfied with the flesh underneath, she dropped the whole head, still inside out, into her plastic shopping bag.

Alongside the original boat-landing site, which is now no longer used, we passed a beached whale carcass—a humpback, probably flensed elsewhere and then washed ashore—and walked on up to Hans Egede's yellow frame Lutheran church. I opened the double doors. It was packed with worshipers. "The funeral," I thought, and withdrew at once to an outcrop twenty feet away. As Dave and I sat down in a clump of scrub grass, ptarmigan rose out of it and scattered. Seconds later the doors of the church flew open and a flood of people in traditional dress poured forth.

Every one of them was grinning ear to ear. First came some very old women, their eyes reduced to sunken dots by joyful squinting, their whole faces wreathed in wrinkles, and their throats encircled by bright beads. Even before they were down the steps, they were passing out fistfuls of cigarettes and lighting up, emitting clouds of smoke and gales of laughter. More and more people emerged from the doors behind them, in high sealskin boots edged with arctic fox and polar bear fur and parkas encrusted with beads and embroidery, black, yellow, red, and blue.

Last out were a dazzling young couple with their daughter between them; it was apparently her confirmation. Cameras appeared from under sealskin parkas. When all of the guests began snapping photos, so did I. The extended family grouped and posed. The father beamed. The little girl stared out from underneath her straight black bangs. But I couldn't take my eyes off her mother.

She was dressed in a quilted print jacket and tan sealskin pantaloons with broad stripes of deep brown fur. Over these she wore a tunic trimmed in lace and bands of embroidered flowers and draped in triangular nets of maroon and yellow beads. Her purse was scarlet leather, and her boots were white sealskin, thigh-high, with a cuff of red ribbon appliqué. But this outfit was nothing compared to the woman who wore it. Twenty-five or so, she had a willowy, tall European figure and a classical Inuit face, with brilliant teeth, almost blue-black hair, pure skin, and uncannily clear eyes. When those eyes met mine, she realized I was staring at her. She stared back and then began to laugh.

That got me laughing too. My presence *was* a bit preposterous. But not unwelcome; they had joy to spare. Soon everyone picked up on the joke and joined in. They laughed at me looking; I laughed at their laughing while watching me laugh. I laughed. They laughed. *We* laughed together until the reasons for the laughing were forgotten and the only thing that mattered was the pure free pleasure of it all.

Each month on his or her numerical birthdate, each Greenlander over the age of eighteen receives a sheet of seventy-two "points." These are coupons that must be presented with each liquor purchase, one for a beer, four for a whiskey. The system was ostensibly designed to ration the sale of alcohol and thereby prevent, or at least limit, the kind of social harm that liquor has caused among Inuit people elsewhere. Yet some believe that the government's goal was less benign, that whites have ways to get around the system, whose real purpose is to keep the native population under control.

Whatever the true intention, in practice things have backfired. "Points" made liquor contraband. And for unemployed, uneducated youths, that contraband has become a source of status they cannot earn in other ways, and drinking in public is the way to flaunt the status. A black market has sprung up, with one sheet of seventy-two points bringing up to one hundred U.S. dollars. This is no small temptation for tourists with points to sell; it made me wonder what my shipmates were discussing with the locals so excitedly last night when I happened by.

Thinking of the night that lay ahead, a guest from the tourist board had advised me not to walk alone. There is "an edge" to things here, he said, and the situation is more tense than it may appear.

But there are times when you want to sense the spirit of a place, when even the protective presence of your friends gets in the way. So I took my boat knife with me, left my wallet and watch on board, and set off alone toward the town.

As on the night before, gangs of teenagers staggered out of the mist and then receded. Several times one or more approached and circled me. But not one spoke or even returned my cautious nod. Godthab is the only place I've ever visited where young people haven't sought contact. I did not feel frightened by this fact. I felt sad. Their collective idleness hung heavy as the smell of processed fishmeal in the cold dank air. Their past had been completely severed from their future. What was missing here was hope. No welfare state could compensate for what they'd lost.

At half past eleven I bumped into Al, who was also wandering. As his tousled head came through the mist, I thought of Hamlet's father's ghost; from the look in Al's eyes, I wondered whether he was stoned. He was unusually quiet. "This," he said, with a slow swing of his head, "is like a dream."

I nodded. We leaned on a gate and looked at the sky, then looked at the sky some more. At midnight he walked off alone. I watched him disappear, slowly absorbed into the undark night.

19 July. Godthabsfjord.

We will be coming back to Godthab, ice permitting, in a week or two, but for now the plan is to get out and find some whales. This morning, while we were making preparations for departure, George gave me his decision from the day before: I will not be excused from any watch at any time.

I had expected as much. What I had not expected was to feel, in some strange way, relieved. That feeling resulted from the way that way George presented his conclusion. I still did not agree with it, but after three years of conditional and duplicitous maybes back on shore, there was something cleaner, even more compassionate, in a direct no that was stated unapologetically.

George's decision grew out of a premise that was different from mine, an ethic that was simpler, less individualistic, and more absolute: "Right" is whatever is good for the ship, and "wrong" is whatever impairs its operation.

When I said this out loud, I surprised myself at least as much as George. "There's no doubt about it," he replied, as his shoulders dropped an inch or two, and the life came back into his voice.

But is this a paradigm of how to live, or an escape from real life? I asked.

"That's the big question, isn't it?" George answered. For some, he suggested, ships are a flight from the moral and intellectual complexities of home. Out here one's options and responsibilities are really very limited, one's choices simplified. He added that even for a captain, it's that way: only a finite number of situations can arise, and the appropriate response to each is predefined. As soon as a situation has been diagnosed, one knows what must be done and follows through in the appropriate way.

Of course, he went on, such thinking has its virtues. For one thing, the challenges are all objective, indisputable. Faced with a storm, a change of wind, fog, or ice, you simply *react,* and there is never any looking back to ask, "Could I have prevented it by acting differently?" Second, you learn that just as such things arise, they always pass; the squall blows itself out, and you go on.

I thought back to a squall we encountered last week. It had come at the end of dawn watch, with what seemed like a full gale approaching. Everybody was rushing about, excited, busily downhauling, reefing, and gasketing every sail. The main watch was straggling up on deck, and we were all gathered amidships, waiting to be relieved, when Joan asked whether I had taken the ocean salinity readings for eight A.M. Typical, I thought; at a time like that, the science logs were not my main concern.

But she had been right, and I was wrong. My willingness to jettison my own routines had been a form of panic. She understood that it's precisely in a crisis that routines are most important. Just continuing our normal business under stress helps make extraordinary danger ordinary; we cannot control the storm, so we control ourselves by not renouncing what is ours and will be, still, when the squall has passed. That night the anticipated storm veered off before it reached us; later, it was good to have done the logs.

Just now, George had referred to "diagnosis." I asked him how a captain's responsibilities compare with those of a doctor. Well, in terms of ethics, he said, you could simply substitute *patient* for *ship* in defining what is right. And both, he added with slight distaste, have their paternalistic aspects. But as a captain, you yourself are always vulnerable, at equal risk. And the difficulties you confront aren't self-inflicted. They are not, as with so much disease and environmental harm, man-made.

20 July. 65°N/54°W. Little Hellefiske Bank.

According to Ujunquaq yesterday, humpbacks may be seen all along the coast from Cap Farvel at the southern tip to Umanak in the north. From April through August they keep moving northward, so that is where we are bound, passing Eqalunguit Nunat, Kangarssuk, Pisugfik, Angmagssiuik—all uninhabited landmarks, merely points on a chart.

We will be reaching major iceberg waters in a few days. But for now we are getting a free ride on the Greenland Current. Because it is relatively warm at roughly thirty-eight degrees, the current supports abundant marine life. It also produces constant, unbelievably dense fog. For the past two days we have been sailing survey "transects" plotted along lines of depth and temperature. So far there is no sight of whales and no break in the dismal weather. Today I am galley slave.

There could not be a cozier duty. If the aft salon is *Regina*'s brain, the galley is her heart and womb and belly; with its odors of roasting meat and fresh-baked bread, it's like a country kitchen on a winter's day. People on watch pass through with reddened faces, trailing cold air behind them, snatching some tea or bouillon. People off watch come to gossip as you set the table; to insist that their watchmate's bunk is roomier, cleaner, drier; to debate what would taste better—strawberries or peaches—as they chew on crackers and mend sails.

In this climate the name of the game is calories, and all afternoon I've been listening to Al deliver homilies in passing to the gang on watch. "It takes *ena-gee* to keep wawm up they-ah. Faw-get that tea. Drink chicken soup." I'm reminded of the joke about an Israeli battleship named the *Ess Ess, Mein Kind*.

For tonight Al has planned a special supper. Along with the fifteen pounds of potatoes, he's cooking two roasts, butternut squash and onions, a three-bean salad, and whole-wheat rolls. Watching him work with a half hour to go and the diesel burners roaring at full throttle is like watching a pilot prepare to land.

The stove is a classic Shipmate model without heat controls or gauges. "How do you regulate this thing?" I ask.

"Feel. Touch. Smell." He opens the oven door, prods the roasts, and holds his right palm above each in turn. "This heah is hot." He moves his hand to the other side. "Heah, coolah. Coolah over heah"—as he points with his right hand he squeezes a roll with his left—"heah, scorchah." Sliding the two trays of rolls so that they swap positions, he looks up and catches me staring. "Haavy, did you fill all the shugah bowls?"

In a minute I'm back with the sugar. He's now got the oven closed and three mixing bowls filled with butter and flour and eggs. "How much shugah?" he asks, with a gesture toward the recipe beside me. I hand him the slip of paper and step out to the main salon.

Back again, I can see that he's made no progress. Facing the sink, Al asks once more what the recipe says about sugar. He is holding the slip of paper in his hand; what's going on?

He points to the paper. "What is this word?" he asks me.

"Scoops," I say. He studies it.

"Scoops. Right. You know, I'm not what you'd call a educated man."

"God damn shit fuck piss." This is what I hear as I come down from pumping the day tank. The brownies are now in the oven. Al stands in front of it, slicing into a twelve-pound roast beef that is slightly more brown than pink. *"Damn it,"* he says, and shakes his head. "George likes it rare."

Ten minutes later, the food's on the table. I've brought out the side dishes, but nobody starts to serve before Al arrives. This is his moment. He comes from the galley, bearing the roast beef surrounded by vegetables swimming in natural juices. Ignoring the chorus of "wows," he says to Craig, "I really ovahcooked the roast." George goes to help himself. He sets aside an outer slice, another, and then another, working his way toward the center. Watching him, Al tells Sid, a little louder now, "I'm so pissed off; I ruined the meat." He stands with his big head bobbing, waiting to be contradicted.

Oblivious, or elaborately not hearing, George says nothing. Al waits a few more seconds and then walks off.

WHAT MELVILLE WOULD HAVE LIKED TO KNOW (OR HOW TO BUILD A WHALE)

Suppose it's a couple of million years ago, the Cretaceous period, and you are God. Reptiles have had a good run but have started, understandably, to bore you. So you bring on the mammals. Warm-blooded, bearing live young, with their legs underneath them instead of splayed out to the sides, they can run and cover distance; they are smart; they lend new zest and personality, a certain *je ne sais quoi* to the Creation. Seeing that it is good, you next devise "adaptive radiation," starting with primitive insectivores, then partitioning out the land environment among rodents, bats and primates, ungulates and carnivores. By the Eocene era, all the modern mammal orders are in place.

Time passes. Then one night, you sit up in bed astounded, thinking, "What about the seas? I forgot to put any mammals in the water!" Rather than start from scratch, with a whole new class, you decide to take some existing land mammals and just modify their form, from a plantigrade (flat-footed) to a semi-aquatic pattern. By shortening a neck here, flattening a tail there, making the fur more dense and oily, you come up with otters. Beavers. Shrews. And snow-white animals whose huge webbed paws and pointy, streamlined heads suggest their half-land, half-sea status: polar bears.

Another success! From that it's a small leap to true aquatic mammals—sea lions, walruses, seals. Charmed (and who wouldn't be?) by Hoover's forebears, you ask yourself (it's your nature), "Why not go all the way?" You imagine an animal larger than the dinosaurs but almost as smart (and at least as kind) as the ultimate ape (still waiting in the wings). It would inhabit all oceans, traveling thousands of miles at will, and "refuel" while underway. Be equally at home in arctic seas or tropical lagoons. Dive to a depth where the pressure is one hundred atmospheres, then surface and literally leap through air. It could locate others of its kind through a hundred miles of water. It could navigate. And sing.

What special problems would such an animal face? And how, from the standpoint of design, would they be solved?

The first problem for any whale is size. Little things are light; big things are heavy; gravity presents no problem for a fly, and indeed, if a man were the fly's size, he too would be able to walk along the ceiling. But body weight (the pull of gravity) increases geometrically with volume. As one scientist has noted:

> You can drop a mouse down a thousand-yard mine shaft; and, on arriving at the bottom, it gets a slight shock and walks away. A rat would probably be killed, though it can fall safely from the eleventh story of a building; a man is killed, a horse splashes.

Whales, by comparison, can't even support themselves. If stranded in shallow water, they will suffocate beneath the weight of their own bodies. Only the buoyancy of displaced water lets them achieve such enormous mass, and even then it requires structural adaptations.

In order to *float,* they have porous bones filled with lighter-than-water oil, and relatively few of them; neither flukes nor dorsal fins have skeletal support. In order to *travel through water,* the bodies those bones support are subtly streamlined. Rear legs are gone, of course, and front legs are reduced to paddles for sculling and steering. Body parts that protrude in other mammals, such as ears, are set beneath the skin to cut resistance. The air passage and digestive tract are separate, with nostrils moved up to the *top* of the head; whales can thus feed without breathing and breathe without lifting their heads out of the water. The head itself is a rigid ram or nosecone, with all seven vertebrae behind it fused. Only the shoulder moves. All other parts of a whale's long torso are immobile and undifferentiated, like a hull or a fuselage.

That impression is reinforced, of course, by bulwarks of blubber up to eighteen inches thick. Yet we now know that even they are designed to cut effort and boost speed. Sandwiched between skin and muscle, the blubber is not attached (the way ours is) to either. As the animal moves through water, its fat undulates beneath the skin like a continuous ball bearing, cutting drag. Unlike the rigid surface of a ship, whales' rippling sides decrease resistance by *responding* to the flow.

Blubber also helps to solve a second problem, temperature control. The amount of heat a creature generates depends on the mass, or volume, of its tissues; the amount of heat it dissipates depends on the area of its skin. As body size increases, area and volume increase at dramatically different rates, so very large animals have great mass in proportion to their surfaces. What this means can be seen most vividly when a great whale dies. Deep down, the heat produced by decomposition is retained by its well-insulated body. Temperature begins to *rise,* not fall; in a few days, the flesh inside is actually cooking. This accounts for the fact that these corpses fill with gas and float, and sometimes explode with enormous force.

Though such power to hold heat is a virtue down in the frigid depths, it becomes a problem when whales are active near the surface. Contrary to what was thought for centuries, the main challenge these blubber-clad giants face is not staying warm but cooling off. Whales have no sweat glands and can't pant with their tongues. What they use instead is a vast capillary network functioning as a heat exchanger and a system of vasodilation in which intertwined veins and arteries distribute the heat of outbound blood or send it on back toward the heart. And the whale voluntarily controls this process, deciding the amount, extent, and direction of the flow.

The third major challenge whales face is diving. To understand how they can go down so deep and stay so long requires a few quick words about respiration. Breathing in mammals is controlled by two linked mechanisms. One is oxygen tension, which depends on hemoglobin. It is not particularly sensitive—there is no response until blood levels fall by half—and can be resisted, within limits, as we hold our breath. Carbon dioxide tension is, by contrast, very sensitive and is linked to myoglobin. Our response is involuntary and extreme; at CO_2 levels approaching ten percent, we black out within sixty seconds. Thus for any animal underwater, the trick is to "fix" or neutralize free CO_2 and limit the metabolic processes that form it.

When humans dive, our hearts automatically slow down, and peripheral blood vessels narrow, concentrating blood supplies and oxygen near the brain and heart. This reflex helps, of course, but compared to what whales possess, it's downright primitive.

What happens when great whales dive? One can follow it step by step:

1. The animal hyperventilates; thanks to powerful muscles in its bronchial tubes, it can empty its lungs completely and refill them with fresh ("tidal") air.

2. As the whale dives, a larynxlike structure called the goosebeak closes the internal nostril like the ball in a snorkel tube. Cartilaginous stiffening rings around the short, thick windpipe keep it from collapsing. Myoglobin starts to saturate with CO_2; since a whale has ten times as much as humans, this fixes metabolic wastes, holds off the CO_2 response, and keeps unattached oxygen free for other uses. Oxygenated blood collects in vascular reservoirs at the base of the brain.

3. As air in the lungs compresses, the flexible ribs contract. All air is forced up and out the lungs, away from the exchanging surfaces, into sinuses and a muscular sponge of air sacs called the melon. The lungs collapse completely. Powerful sphincters seal the windpipe closed.

4. The animal stays down and goes about its business, using the energy stored in its muscles anaerobically, thereby creating an oxygen debt. It is seven hundred feet below the surface. Fifteen or twenty minutes pass.

5. Time to come up now. So long as the air remains in nonabsorbing chambers, there will be no exchange of gases. Trapped by the mixture of oil and mucus that these sinuses contain, nitrogen won't bubble out into the blood and cause the bends.

6. The whale breaches and blows. Out comes the oil and nitrogen emulsion. Out comes the pent-up air. Time for some badly needed oxygen. If our model is a sperm whale, it has been down a mile or more. In ten minutes on the surface, it will breathe fully fifty times.

There is one final point to be made, just in case you are not impressed by all this hardware. Though much of what I have described is involuntary (as with more primitive systems found in man), evidence is growing that cetaceans consciously control some of these functions. In the same way that it can cut off blood flow to its tail in order to save body heat, a diving whale can apparently shut down entire systems such as the digestive tract to save oxygen for more essential functions. At the Scripps Institute, dolphins have been seen to blunt their own CO_2 responses voluntarily. Some scientists believe that in humpbacks this is learned behavior, passed on from mothers to humpback calves. If these animals can in fact adapt their CO_2 response, that makes breathing based on the oxygen response more voluntary. It gives them the opportunity to judge a potential threat and decide just how long to stay down.

Hearing Don Patten lecture about these things, you get a different perspective on humpback whales, an image less like the lovable, whimsical beasts adorning coffee cups and Christmas cards and more like an update of Leviathan—too much of everything to justify a sentiment, more systems than a 747: engine, tugboat, pressurized reactor in its own containment vessel, power station, submarine. Being aboard *Regina* also increases the sense of how different these animals are from us in terms of how they must perceive the world. Today, when our first two Greenland humpbacks rose up through the slush ice, the contrast between how they and we have gotten here was stark. They didn't plan it for six months, spend three months in the yards, buy rope, solicit grants, onload 263 cartons of supplies, study charts and plot their progress, or stop along the way. They simply started. There was nothing besides themselves to take along and nothing to leave behind.

So let's play God again for a minute more, not way back then but now. If you were the glow in this fog bank, watching the whales and humans pass in this cold ocean, would they please you equally? Would you say that one had been more deserving of your bounty? Lived as you'd intended? Could you tell which loves you more?

21 July. 66°N/56°W.

We are now twelve hundred miles north of Maine, running north-northwest toward Baffin Bay. A following breeze has freshened; the mizzen and main are set "wing and wing"; the fog has transformed itself into sleet and rain. We have entered true polar regions now. Though gray, benign conditions veil the change, you still feel it all around you and inside you. Weather? Magnetism? Vibes? Something is different but hard to name.

"Everything that rises must converge." I remember reading once that at either pole, the first business every day would be to decide what time it was; since time is a function of longitude, where all the meridians connect it's whatever you want it to be. At this latitude those lines begin to angle steeply inward, and we cross degrees of longitude in hours. The variation between true and magnetic north is now twenty-six degrees. The loran signal grid does not reach up this far, and even the omega radio waves that do are so warped by curvature that the "reliability of the system cannot be determined," as the chart's droll prose proclaims. So we're left with traditional navigation now: the sextant and the compass.

It's hard to take astronomical observations in a constantly cloudy sky. With dead reckoning therefore so important, all of us have been trying hard to hold course when on helm. But even when *Regina* handles easily, the compass hardly moves.

The phenomenon we're seeing is called compass dip. Above sixty degrees north latitude, the earth's electromagnetic waves converge not only horizontally (along the surface) but also vertically, curving down like the ends of gigantic rainbows into the magnetic pole. Caught between this celestial force from overhead and the pull, from below, of gravity, our compass needle slows its spin and attempts to point straight upward; if it could, it would stand on end. But the glycerine in which it floats, grown viscous from the cold, prevents this. As a result, the compass lags. There's a gap between what the instruments confirm and what you feel.

The quality of light has also changed. Horizons are smaller. The sky seems lower. Still overcast, it grows thinner, paler, brighter every day. Though the sun never sets, there are times you'd be hard pressed to point directly at it. In this weather it isn't a ball, a disk, not even a glob of light—just a glow, diffuse and luminous, like the inside of a fog lamp on a London bridge, a radio tube, the belly of a firefly. From hour to hour, the sky does not change color, just intensity. It fades toward midnight, brightens at noon, its dull glint half absorbed and half rejected by the furrowed sea, like acid on wax or ink on a porous stone.

0830 hours. Main salon. After a grueling watch from midnight until four, Sid, Helene, and Craig slept through breakfast, only to be rousted out the minute it is done for morning meeting. "Meals are optional," they're told; "this isn't." They roll down out of bed with their blankets wrapped around them and huddle along the port-side bench, glowering like Cheyennes at a memorial for Custer.

Item: whales—or the lack thereof. Based on bottom scans and environmental logs from the past few days, the scientists think we may be too close to shore for this time of year. We will give these grounds twenty-four hours more and then move out to deeper and colder water. Meanwhile, there will be two trawls today, at 1000 and 1400 hours.

Item: logs. You are getting careless, folks. Last night two consecutive entries were inaccurate; no one was informed, the batteries did not get charged, and the freezer thawed. "Do that again," Al warns, "and we'll all be eatin' crackas."

Last item: socks. Guess who. "Now, people," George says, "personal effects are not to be left in the main salon. If your hats and gloves and other gear get wet," (if?) "they will dry off nicely in the Doo's Bait Locker or, if you get Fran's permission, in the engine room. The main salon is public space. I want these radiators cleared. Anything still here at oh-nine-thirty will be used for rags."

0840 hours. Meeting over. Without having spoken or changed expression, Sid, Helene, and Craig rise up in their gray wool blankets, drift back to their bunks, and are gone, like three puffs of smoke.

1000 hours. Just off the helm; next duty station, logs. I open the door to the engine room and step over the threshold backwards, clipboard in one hand, wet socks in the other, not holding on. A bad idea: As my boot hits the companionway's top step (a round steel pipe), it rolls off the greasy surface. On the way down, I land on my ankle, kneecap, hipbone, ass—and grab hold just in time to prevent my skull from hitting too. When I come to a rest three rungs from the bottom, I am upside down, looking back through the stairs at Fran.

Her back is toward me. She is bent over, turning a large iron valve wheel, shunting a pump from the bilge to the fire hose. She doesn't even look up to see whether I'm OK.

I gather myself together and start working my way around

the cabin, taking readings: water temp, pressure, volts, and amps—AC, DC, full, half full. I squeeze past twelve car batteries strung together. Dozens. Past cracked, thirty-year old gauges. Jury-rigged machines with their paint worn off, two-thirds of them built for a purpose other than the one they serve, every one "torn down" and reconstructed too many times to keep track of. *Regina,* of course, was not designed to hold an engine, and this "engine room" is no more than a hold in the stern with a slippery floor laid down and very few places to hold on. It is too low to stand up in, too cramped to work in, too dark to see in, and too close for anyone but Fran to remain in for very long. Yet this is where Fran hangs out for days on end, her bunker and her lair.

I check the ONAN, move along to the saltwater feed line, generator, boiler, and then back around the main. "Hi, Fran," I say. She is still bent over and does not respond. Weird. It isn't noisy, with the main shut down.

She is wedged between two punky frames, in the shadows, sweating, her full face gleaming, her thick neck dark beneath the brim of a baseball cap worn backwards over matted hair. Her hula shirt has lost half its buttons. A vise grip dangles from an empty belt loop by its jaw. In this posture, Fran's body appears to have lost all shape; she resembles an otter, a troglodyte under an ancient bridge, a troll.

I touch her arm. She jumps sky high. I have startled and embarrassed her somehow and stand there feeling dumb, I don't know why. "Hi, Fran. Can I dry these anywhere?"

She points to the sloping transom.

"But it's filthy there."

"No foolin'. Jesus Christ. How long you been on this buggy? You still thinkin' *clean?* We're talking' *dry.*"

At 1500 hours the deck was deserted, except for the helm, and deathly still, which was unusual for this time of day. The mercury stood at thirty-six, and the breeze was raw. If you sat down on deck and stared at the forward hatch, you would have seen a green sou'wester hat appear, like a prairie dog's head from a burrow.

This was not strange; it happens all the time.

But the next sight to cross that line was naked shoulders, followed by round breasts prodding a tight bright tank top, nipples hardening in the cold, a naked midriff, taut bikini bottoms, full thighs gathering goosebumps as they spread and rose, and Lisa set her naked foot on deck, borne forth from below on a column of hot air and a gush of laughter.

Kathy followed, poker-faced, in a one-piece Speedo. Then Brenda, Little Red Riding Hood in her scarlet long johns only, followed by Joan in a painter's cap and sundress, then Canan and Helene.

Eat your heart out, Amundsen. Tough luck, Peary. Cook never had it so good.

Where *Regina* women lead, their men soon follow: Pat in a union suit with a baggywrinkle tutu; Al in a jockstrap and a fishing hat, with basketball; Root, wearing black shoes, black socks, black bikini underwear, and a Sony Walkman; Francis in a life preserver; Sid sporting aviator shades and snorkel gear.

As the officer of the deck stood by (in boxer shorts), George watched the chronometer back aft. "This is it!" he called. The brass bell rang. We grouped and posed for posterity, with Kathy holding up a portrait of the sun that she had painted on a pie plate and, crouched in the foreground, Scott, whose placard read:

REGINA MARIS
21 JULY
66.36
THE ARCTIC CIRCLE

2300 hours. Like well over half the crew, I could not seem to turn in tonight. Maybe it was the afternoon's excitement or the light that was, bizarrely, growing brighter through the barred glass hatches. After a pleasant supper and a good class on navigation, I chatted with Patrick up on deck and then came below to the sounds of Renaissance music through the fo'c'sle door. One knock with its old brass minianchor brought a "Come in, Harve" from Lawrence (nicknames have made their appearance recently).

Inside, Helene and he had propped up sheet music on cylinders full of Freon and were playing a recorder duet by Josquin des Pres. It sounded sweet and reached back to the aft salon, where others sat reading, bullshitting, and thinking up desperate measures to attract the whales, such as paint the hull pink, tie-dye the sails, or position a wooden jockey on our bowsprit, lamp in hand. If our search out on Hellefiske Bank is as unsuccessful as the past few days have been, we will head farther north to krill-rich Disko Bay.

For Craig, that name rang a bell tonight. Pulling down a worn copy of *Captains Courageous,* he confirmed that the master of the ship in Kipling's book is Captain Disko. Also that the name of the spoiled city boy who falls off an ocean liner, is rescued by the fishermen, and becomes a man in their rough company, is Harvey! This brought a good laugh all around. But I was in no mood to be amused; in an hour I'd turn thirty.

That was hardly a calamity. Why, then, was I so moody? I think it had something to do with my dream the other night and the lingering sense of having built no hearth, of having reached a turning point and yet achieved no turning. Even this scene, which should have been an escape from all that, was becoming a reminder. I looked at the kids who sat good-naturedly beside me. On shore I would be their teacher. On the ship, if age were the criterion, I belonged with the scientists or mates. But in terms of what I knew that mattered here, I was a student—one of the most frightened and least qualified. In this world of Anglo-Saxon verbs, what place—what *use*—was there for my adjectival life, with its judgments, its distinctions, its damned Latin?

I was really getting going.

"Hey, you, old guy in the corner!" Lisa called.

"Just don't start losing your grip aloft," teased Sid.

Toni asked if I could still recall the words to Motown songs. I left the cabin.

Alone with my thoughts on deck, I stood near the starboard bow staring into the midnight sun, a pale orange ball fifteen degrees above the north horizon. Above and in front of it, the entire sky was overcast. But below, for the first time since the ship had left Corner Brook, there was a gap in the clouds like a lead in ice, and through that gap the sky was a nacreous violet-gray.

All at once there was someone knocking on the door of the wetlab. From the inside. Strange. I turned around and opened it. There was no one there. But over the sink, on the test tube rack, I found an envelope. And in that envelope I found a joint.

Now there are at least a half dozen reasons why drugs on a ship are a bad idea. We'd received an extremely stern talk about this before the ship cast off. But tonight being what it was, and where it was, and me off watch, with the brooding quiet and unsettling light, and the gift—for that's what it surely was—right there . . .

Wide-eyed, along *Regina*'s rail once more, I watched the overcast split open like a seam. As blue fog boiled off its edge and floes of cloud broke free, I felt deeply shaken—I could not say why—and then something in me broke off as well, and drifted, this whatever-it-was that I couldn't name, as a voice inside that I hadn't known was mine said, "Let it go."

Helene passed by and bumped me playfully. Brenda showed up with some cookies she had baked. And then came Al. "Hey, buddy," he said, with a wink and a few slow nods. We put our four elbows on the rail and leaned outboard together. "What a amazing sight!" Al said. The sun had emerged and was cutting its way like a blowtorch. Like a laser beam through the seam of clouds. In the jaws of the sea and sky, a tongue of flame.

22 July. 68°N/54°W.

Imagine the sound of a wood chair breaking. Now make it a two-by-four. Now think of a ten-ton tree three feet in diameter, straining as if to split, nine inches from your nose. That sound now comes from the mainmast, stepped behind my pillow. It's 3:25 in the morning. The ship is rolling fifteen degrees to each side, and I am lying face up with my head at the fulcrum of a hundred-foot-high lever, bearing its freight of spar and sail against a furious wind and sea.

Sounds like screams, and like gunfire: rat-a-tat from the small planks, sharp unpredictable squawks from the masts and beams. Because this "working" of plank against plank increases as a ship grows old, *Regina* now leaks badly in rough weather. At the extremity of each roll, the bilge water she has taken on creeps up her "ceilings," or inner walls. It stays there a moment, silently soaking the bunks on one side. Then, as the vessel steadies, water roars back toward the centerline, gathers speed, and breaks like a wave against the other side. Though I'm not due on deck until four, it's hard to hold myself in bed. I swing down to get dressed.

My feet land in icy water. Five feet forward a door has torn off its latch. Again and again it swings open, blocking the passage-way, then whips back hard against the wall. With each swing it seems like a camera shutter opening to reveal the main salon. Three people are shivering in wet blankets in the glow of one red bulb. Kathy tries to secure a pot that has fled the galley and is cannonballing around the deck. She advances on it in a way that looks like pantomime—slow motion, uphill. Just as she reaches it, the ship rolls the other way; she skids backwards, arms akimbo, as if the film has been reversed and speeded up.

My own arms ache from bracing, half-awake, against the

sides of my berth. It resembles the inside of a clothes dryer. Sweaters and socks and tools lie tangled in the blankets. I need twenty minutes to dress, what with keeping my balance, losing it, being thrown down, and having seaboots yanked out of my hand as if on invisible ropes. On its usual hook, the climbing harness has tied itself in knots.

At a quarter to four, the mizzen watch deckhand half walks and half slides down the aft companionway, his face windburned and flushed. "Fore watch!" he bellows. "On deck *now!*" He careens past, repeating the message, his oilskins streaming. Glad, as only a green hand could be, to witness a full gale, I follow.

Water. A black wall. Twenty-five feet high, fifty yards away, rushing toward us broadside. I freeze in the doorway, thinking, "Perran." Once, in another gale, a scientist was standing helm one night when a wave like this one struck. He heard it first, a sound like an oncoming train, and turned just in time to see it coming at him over the roof of the after deckhouse. He was torn off the wheel, held flailing underwater with his hood twisted around his face, swept overboard—or so he thought, until his head smacked into a scupper.

The wave was forty yards away. My watchmates, coming up behind me, pushed me out on deck. Steel safety cables had been rigged on both sides, fore and aft. Scott yelled, "Clip in." My harness buckle snagged.

The wave was twenty-five yards off. Still tangled. Fifteen yards: I worked it free, clipped in, took a deep breath, and braced. When the wave was five yards off our starboard rail, *Regina*—all 500 tons of her—heeled violently to leeward, sidled up and up and over the water, paused atop it for three seconds, slid across, rolled sharply back to windward, shuddered, and then settled with a sigh in the following trough. As the water she'd shipped rushed out through the scuppers, coils of line that had been dragged off their pins rose and fell in the ebb like kelp.

A voice above me shouted, "All hands aloft to gasket the squares!" It was Patrick, halfway up the foremast shrouds. The members of his watch had been kept on with ours and were climbing up behind him. Sheets of rain cascaded down along the shrouds like water in a log flume, splashing off one person's boots onto the shoulders just below. Clouds blocked out most, but not all, of the midnight sun. As the four tense silhouettes clung to the bouncing web of rope, they were jerked back and forth—spun suddenly clockwise, then just as suddenly the other way. Francis (I knew it was him from the duct tape holding up his pants) had taken off his gloves to get a better grip, and his pink hands shone through the storm. He was beckoning me aloft.

With the canvas soaking wet and heavy, the mizzen watch needed help to handle sail. Two of my watch were already on the manual pumps, another on lookout. "Come on," said Dave, "Let's go."

I unclipped, ran to the rail, and, terrified, stepped up, swung outboard over it, took two steps up. On deck, Joan must have seen my expression as I pivoted and faced inboard to climb. Reaching out through the shroud, she poked me on the calf; I kicked as if taking a reflex test. "Would you rather not go up?" she asked.

The waves were twenty-five feet high, the wind at fifty knots, with puffs to sixty-five. I had planned to go. I was willing. Would I *rather* not? I hesitated. "Come back down," she said. "Take Root's place on the bow. Send him."

The bowsprit was buried in water. Root perched high on the forward deckhouse, clipped in to the radar cage, holding on with both hands. Approaching from behind him to avoid the foredeck, which was underwater, I called out. Root didn't hear. I thumped his arm. He turned; for once all the cool was leached out of him. He stared.

"Joan says to lay aloft. I will relieve you here."

He lifted a hat flap and cupped his ear. "Say what?"

"Joan wants you up aloft."

"What about *you?*"

"I'm just not comfortable up there. It's just—"

"You think *I* am?" He seemed about to spit. "Goddamn. I mean, what the fuck? I hate it there. Hate it like hell. But when

someone says 'go,' I *go.*" He unclipped and staggered away in a
fury, pitching violently sideways twice before he slipped from
view.

Moments later I saw him climb onto a shroud with the
others. The order in which they got aloft put Root farthest out
on the upper topsail yardarm, near the earring. When you are
relaxed up there, you drape your belly forward over the yard,
taking weight off your legs, which kick out behind against the
footrope, at an angle. When you are nervous, you tend to stand
upright on the line. This tenses your back and throws great strain
on your legs. They cramp up rapidly; you grip too tight and sweat
and start to wonder if you'll fall. So looking at Root's splayed
ankles, ashen face, and white knuckles clutching the jackstay, I
knew that he, and Lisa and Rob as well, were having a very hard
time.

After what seemed forever, they came down. Root reap-
peared beside me. I explained that I had only acknowledged my
own limits; the last time I went aloft in rough weather, I had not
been helpful; I had spoken based on knowledge of myself, not
him, and blah, blah, blah. All true. Based on my knowledge of
my *current* self. But also true that if I don't go, somebody else
must. "Honesty," "good judgment"—the words curdled in my
mouth as I spoke them. What I really felt was shame.

Joan arrived and yelled, "Let's get the main and mizzen."
The wind was still rising, approaching a force nine gale. All hands
were now up on deck to keep the pumps at work full time. Root
turned to go. "Hey, Root?" He wouldn't look at me.

I spun him around. Our eyes met. "Root," I said, "stay
where you are."

In the hour that followed, I helped furl and gasket every sail
on the two aft masts while stretched out between catlines like
wash on a windy day. When Clay and I were doing the main
topgallant staysail, its gasket slipped out of our hands. The rope
did not fall down but hovered to leeward in the wind like a
pennant twenty-five feet long. When finished there, we moved
forward to the headsails. It took seven hands to downhaul the
flying jib.

With the sails clewed up and double-gasketed, we were able, at last, to ease her. Hove to, with her yards braced sharp and a handy-billy shackled on the steering gear, she rode much better, drifting sideways, sliding across the heavy swells. By eight A.M. the wash on deck was moderate, and the breeze was down to thirty knots. At nine, one watch could lay below.

Gales at sea comprise a set piece of many books, and the crew's responses have been analyzed in much detail. I remember mostly this: it was exhilarating; we worked hard, and time went very fast. Once I was actually working, I became intent and serious, no longer panicky. It was as if the whole storm were shut out by a series of tasks that were immediately, and literally, at hand.

In *Moby Dick,* Melville writes that for the first mate, Starbuck, courage was not a state of mind but a practical tool. Observing George, Gregg, Joan, and Root, I saw courage: not defiance, but acceptance, of whatever challenges the sea imposed. Not a statement, not a gesture, but a tool like other tools—intelligence, strength, poise—consistently and patiently applied.

The night's real hero is *Regina.* Guided by hands that knew her and respected her limits, she seemed alive in her element, like a conscious being. She had been through this, and much more, a hundred times and knew exactly what to do. Her every spar, block, bolt is an optimal solution, an age-old answer to the single question it is asked, perfected over time. Together, these parts embody the experience of thousands over centuries. Today I feel bound to them, and in their debt, for the courage and craft that even in death give service.

Coming down from the maintop this morning with my hat blown off and my hair soaked back, I saw George, who had been on deck for the past ten hours, standing at the foot of the mast. His hands were in his pockets. His wet white beard thrust upward. He was watching me, and he looked like Father Time.

I swung down and stood beside him. No question, he'd been waiting for me. Beaming: "Happy birthday, man!"

RIG

23 July. Moored, Godhavn, Disko Bay.

On deck today for midwatch, the world which had been so violent the previous dawn, was now flat calm, rinsed with pale light and a dewy clarity like that which follows fever. From amidships you could hear the smooth sea lapping at our bow. The gale had set us thirty miles off and forty north of last night's destination. Rather than double back, George chose to save Great Hellefiske Bank for later, on our way down south. The immediate plan had become to run north past sixty-nine degrees and put in at Disko Island.

At three A.M. the island's black volcanic profile loomed two points off our starboard bow, while the rising sun revealed a line of icebergs in the violet mist to port. Newly calved from the Jakobshavn Glacier, riding north on the Greenland Current, these were larger and less ragged than any we'd seen before. Oblong, pyramidal, domed, white tinted lavender or marbled by the pastel sky, they seemed a procession of ice gods, sorcerers convening silently on their way to the top of the world.

Awestruck, in answering silence, we clustered along the rail. At 0400 the mizzen watch arrived and joined us. The hour came and went. No one could break the spell and lay below.

But at last, one by one, we did. When we woke up three hours later, *Regina* was at anchor in a tiny harbor. We lowered away, putt-putted in to the town's sole dock, and stepped ashore through an arch made of humpback jawbones seventeen feet tall.

It rises slowly, like the sun behind a thousand-foot-high headland, like the sound of gulls overtaking your boat from astern. However, it's not gulls, not birds at all, but the yelp of huskies draped across rocks all over town as they greet the arctic day.

Lying alongside sledges or chained up to Mercurys and Evin-rudes, they stretch in the lazy sunlight, preening; summertime is a sledge dog's paid vacation. Out of reach above them, drying racks dangle split fish and strips of seal, its odor alternately sweet and rotten. Unpaved streets seem to dead-end in icebergs—glittering Gibraltars just offshore, aground. On the other side of town, the west face of volcanic rises still wears morning's shadow, balanced like a basalt bonnet on the gneiss head of the land.

For a long time nothing moves. At length, a grandmother clad in sealskin passes with two smiling four-year-olds in tow. Then a young man driving a forklift, wearing a black leather jacket, "YAMAHA" in bright yellow letters running down one sleeve. Now we smell sweet bread baking and hear someone start to hammer on a plywood roof: tap, tap, then rat-a-tap as the muscles of arms and fingers warm. Close by, three puppies nurse. Their mother keeps an eye on me and yawns. I yawn back, happy in the unexpectedly blue sky, the foreign yet familiar peace of village life, in Godhavn, aka Qeqertarsuaq, on Disko Island.

Though the bay that separates us from the "mainland" is two hundred miles north of the Arctic Circle, it is fed by an offshoot of the warm Irminger Stream and supports rich stocks of halibut, shrimp, and cod. Godhavn is the only town on this 2000-square-mile island. Founded in 1773, it was for many years a port of call for Dutch and Danish whalers and up through the nineteenth century the center of North Greenland. Today the main catch is shrimp, and the eight hundred residents live in small bright houses clustered at unlikely angles around a red-walled octagonal church nicknamed the "Lord's ink pot."

To sit down beside it now, on ground that stands still, with my head bare and the scent of wildflowers rising, feels like a fantasy so soon after yesterday's gale. Aboard ship you are sometimes off duty but always on call, and you know the source of every sound and odor. So it's a double pleasure to just let my mind wander as I look around.

There are no institutional buildings to be seen. No housing projects, traffic, shops, or bars. Few people, either. Those I have passed have been friendly. David and Clay confirm this, back from a stroll: What a nice change from Godthab, they remark.

A large blond bearded man in coveralls approaches; if the hammer he holds were heavier, he could pass for Thor. "How do you do?" he says with his hand out, formal, firm. "I am Finn Steffans. Welcome." He is on his way home for a coffee break. Would we like to come?

Coffee? Danish coffee? In an instant the Cinnamon Twins have climbed into the pickup's cab, leaving me, Mr. Nimble Aloft, to vault its tailgate. I land in a heap, on a heap of harnesses and reindeer skins.

Finn's house is one year old, China blue and square, with a very steep roof and a chest-high stone foundation. It is the last on its unpaved street, one of a dozen or so that loop around a barren bluff to dead-end at the ocean. Working together, we unload the harnesses, skins, and rolls of fiberglass insulation into a workshop as clean as an operating room that occupies the whole first floor. Then we follow Finn up a set of stairs with huge pelts—no, they are coats—hung on either side.

It's my first time inside a home in four weeks. With its woven rugs and brightly colored houseplants glowing on the varnished windowsills, it could be my family place in the Berkshire Mountains. Well, not quite: There's also a stuffed puffin on the mantel, glaring at an even more stuffed razorbill, and outside, sealskins drying on the line. "Make yourselfs at home," says Finn, heading off to the bedroom to check on his napping child.

I go to the bathroom. In the mirror, framed by the window behind me, something bright and massive seems to perch atop my shoulder. I turn and look out the window. It's an iceberg. Though we're easily two hundred feet above the water, its white crown is inching past, on a level with the house's second story.

Back in the living room, Finn has laid out bread and jam and coffee (the kind the humans drink), and as we eat he speaks, in halting English, about his life here.

Finn has lived in Greenland for a decade. He first came when stationed here with the Danish army, found that he liked to hunt, and decided to stay when his tour of duty ended. He didn't like Godthab, though—with ten thousand people, it was growing too developed and too crowded—so after two years there, he headed north to Godhavn. In the eight years since, this town has also seen "a lot of growth," but Finn likes it here, for now. He has married and settled down. In the summers he works as a carpenter, and in winter he hunts narwhals.

Narwhals are the ocean's unicorns, small snow-white whales with a six-foot spiral horn. They live exclusively in arctic waters, coming down to Disko with the ice in autumn and retreating toward the pole by early April. We had noticed side trawlers equipped with harpoon guns in the harbor. "Is that how it's done?" Clay asks.

No, Finn replies, those boats are for minke whales. They are too small for catching humpbacks—all ten in the annual quota go to fast South Greenland boats—and narwhals are hunted in a more traditional way, which requires that large groups of people work together. Some go out in small boats through leads in the ice pack, find a whale, and strike it with hand-held harpoons. Then other people, who have been waiting on the ice itself, follow the struck whale toward shore on foot. When it tires, they haul it up onto the ice for butchering.

Twenty narwhals are taken in this way each season; last year Finn caught five in a single day. This hunt is not commercial fishing. After shares have gone to all who participate, what remains is given away, first to relatives and friends and then to anyone else who wants it. Like beluga whales, to whom they are related, the narwhals are prized for their outer blubber, which is pickled into muktuk. The lucky few folks who own electric freezers pack them full in December and can still enjoy their muktuk come July.

"What else is hunted?" David asks. Foxes, says Finn, and reindeer. Arctic hare. In winter, walruses. "Last veenter," he continues, "some people they were catching ptarmigan. They found a large hole in the snow. Then they heard a loud noise. It was polar bear. They followed it, yes, and shot it dead." He pauses, touches his forehead gently with his palm. "To *shoot* a polar bear. I do not like it. Many of these people here, they still are feeling not so good."

Where does Finn do his own hunting? Southward, mostly, he replies, near Søndre Strømfjord. To the east are hundreds of thousands of square miles of ice, an area that would cover North America from Maine to the Mississippi. I ask if he ever goes inland from this coast. He doesn't seem to understand the question. I repeat it. "Inland?" he says this time. "No. There is nothing there."

Dave is still thinking about narwhals. Does Finn believe that the males' long single tooth is used to establish dominance? Has he ever seen them fighting? "Narwhals fight?" asks Finn. He looks almost offended. "Nooo. I think not. They are very—*sweet* whales." A look that could only be described as love comes across his soft blue eyes.

The sign, on our way back to the ship, reads "KBH," the acronym, in Danish, of the Royal Danish Trading Corporation. This is a latter-day Hudson Bay Company. For decades the state-run monopoly, KBH still constitutes the main or only retail outlet in most of Greenland's towns.

Having made our request in the office, we are led by two highly amused, half-sober Inuits to an outer warehouse. Inside, it is musty, piled ten feet high with reindeer hides. Leaning twenty against the wall (where they stand up on their own like cardboard), we select a few that are least clotted up with fat, dried blood, and tissue. We assure one another that they'd be a steal at any price and make our purchase.

Back on board there are lunch guests. One of them, from the Institute of Geophysics at Copenhagen University, is an expert on shooting stars. The icecap, he explains, is like a vast collecting pan. Any meteorites that land on it are instantly doused and preserved, uncontaminated by terrestrial life, dust, or pollen. Then they are carried coastward by the glacier and eventually "spat out" at its mouth. These meteorites are condensed debris, small bits of exploded stars. Some contain carbon, that is to say, they are organic. Their estimated age is four and a half billion years.

The other guest is an elderly man name Persild. Hearing

about our reindeer skins, he says, "Oh, my." It seems that those untanned hides are meant strictly for outdoor use, for throwing over sledges. If we take them south, they will rot and shed, and we'll never get rid of the hairs. How did we know where to purchase them? asks Persild. "Ah," he replies when told, "so you've met Finn Steffans, have you? He is one of the greatest hunters in all Greenland."

After lunch I set off out of town, down a coarse sand beach that stretched for miles, with a long surf rolling in. Pieces of ice the size of kitchen tables bobbed on the gentle breakers and piled up on the sand.

I followed the shoreline out to a headland and around its other side; then inland, upward. With the views becoming more spectacular at every turn, I began to feel light-headed, dizzy. Soon my stride grew longer, and I found my footsteps quickening beyond my own intention or control. In the full arctic sunshine, with no mist, no dust, and little pollen, the air was so pure and the light so sharp that it was almost painful, as if someone had turned up the contrast too high. The whiteness of the ice, the blueness of the water, and the breadth of the sky had a different kind of beauty from any I'd ever seen. It was absolute. Devoid of shadings, it reduced things to geometries. It dazzled.

I turned toward the interior and began to climb the igneous rises. From a distance these striated flat-topped bluffs several thousand feet high had reminded me of the American Southwest. But close up they were very different, made of jet-black knobby stone so sharp it could cut your hands. In sheltered spots this was upholstered, as it were, with wildflowers—similar species to those at home, only in miniature form. In other places there were scabs of lichen, pink and pale green.

Up and up and up I climbed, with a swirl of snow buntings overhead for company. At the top of a steep ravine, I heard a chattering scream and was overtaken by a giant shadow. It came on so suddenly that I ducked behind a boulder. Looking up as the attack resumed—for that's what it seemed to be—I saw a white hawklike bird with wings five feet across: an Arctic gyrfalcon.

I recognized it from the scientists' talk at breakfast. Hoping they'd get to see one, they had said it's a very rare and solitary creature, that it lays red eggs, that both males and females feed the chicks, and feed themselves on eiders, ptarmigan, and seagulls. Seagulls? This became easier to believe as I stared from behind a rock at the huge spread talons flexing in the air above me.

To see what would happen, I stood up. The falcon hovered for a moment, screaming twelve feet overhead, and fixed me in its gaze. There was red flesh stuck to its hooked beak. I could see the fierce eyes moving in their sockets. Then it beat its wings, once, twice, rose straight up to the height of the overhanging ridge, and disappeared.

Before my watch began at eight that evening, I went ashore to buy some beer. All that they had in the general store was "Greenland beer," its alcohol reduced to 3.2 percent for special export. I bought a six-pack. Back outside, I heard raised voices. Down at the dock, Al, Bill, and Fran were pooling their resources to stock up on beer and waving sheets of points worth hundreds of kroner in full view of the local kids, oblivious to the agitation that this caused. It pissed me off. I was glad that I couldn't stick around.

At eleven, after an anchor watch spent on the foredeck playing Root's guitar, a few of us made the last run in to shore to pick up stragglers. Several of those we came to get were not at the dock, so Gregg set off to find them. While he was gone, a small angry crowd of kids surrounded the rest of us, haggling for points and jeering. In less than a day, some of our crew had created their own black market.

Things got uglier. Somebody spat at me. Someone else snatched Clay's pipe out of his mouth and started tossing it around. Clay asked to have it back; the kid just raised the pipe above his head and waved it. Clay is a wiry man, not large. Lawrence is. When he went for the kid's throat with both hands, the boy threw Clay's pipe on the ground and ran. Just then, Fran and Al came lurching down the hillside. "Somebody call the cops!" shrieked Fran. As if there were cops to call.

Gregg returned, with young Jack, who was drunk, in tow. With the whole shore party now accounted for, we herded them into the Avon and cast off.

The ones who were drunkest found it all quite funny. I didn't, though, and on deck for the final hour on watch, I tried to figure out my feelings. True, those people were harassing us. But if you come into a socially tense scene in a place like this and try to cash in on the frustration, of course things will get nasty. Back in Godthab, I had heard that some of the crew were profiteering; Gregg had raised the issue in a meeting and asked people to think a little harder about the effect that such behavior had on the local kids involved. Naturally, those who were not at fault spoke up to support Gregg's view, while the ones who were guilty said nothing. I found the dispute disturbing for two other reasons. First, it made me acknowledge divisions within the crew that I've been trying to ignore but are developing nevertheless between the rednecks and the hippies. Second, it made me ask again whether the ship is not a special situation, where the way we act is unrelated to the way we live on shore. I was feeling not just angry but also *disappointed,* as if Al and Bill and Fran had let me down. As if by being so insensitive they had undercut the "moral of the story" I am always so intent to draw, the frame of mind toward which my temperament and education point me. Once again, the prose seemed to deny the poetry; reality escaped my need for themes.

A laugh rang out back on the fantail. This was odd; there had been no voices for an an hour. Coming around the deckhouse to investigate, I found Fran standing in a circle with three teenage Inuits, "signing" back and forth with them in the language of the deaf.

Another of Fran's languages? When I asked her later why she knows it, she replied, "I'm gonna have to."

"Have to? When?"

"Sometime. A couple or three years." I recalled when she hadn't answered me in the engine room and the volume of her voice at meals. I didn't know what to say.

"It's all right, man. You know what?"

"What?"

She smiled. "It was really a gas to find someone I could *talk* with for a change."

24 July. 69°N/53°W.

This morning we sailed past a lineup of great white icebergs fresh from the glaciers, broken off clean and beveled smooth. From the crosstrees I counted seventeen, like planes on a runway, with the same aspect of waiting to embark on long journeys. Passing one off our port side, I wondered where it would be three years from now.

In the evening, Don gave his introductory lecture on marine mammal reproduction—hot stuff for a celibate time at sea! Very little is yet known about how whales actually reproduce, so much of his talk was confined to their anatomy. He told us, for instance, that right whales' testes weigh nineteen hundred pounds; that the females have up to twelve conical vaginal folds with which they grip and squeeze the male, whose penis, in turn, has a prehensile end. And then we saw pictures of dolphins.

Much of their mating behavior, Don said, may be more social than purely sexual in nature. In any case, their play is longer, in relation to actual mating, than that of almost any other species. It includes all kinds of lovely affectionate gestures: nuzzling with bottlenoses, hugging with flippers, stroking each other's slippery backs. One pair dived down separate, broke through the water's surface mated, and leapt out still mated, spinning through midair belly to belly, end over end over end.

25 July. 69°N/52°W. Off Jakobshavn.

I'm on the wheel at 0600 hours, steering toward the eastern shore of Disko Bay. Having circled the sky at a height of six degrees off the horizon all night long, the sun now oozes upward like a squashed fruit, spreading its pulpy light across a wreckage of ice and stone. The Jakobshavn Glacier, so-called Mother of Icebergs, sprawls dead ahead, grinding seaward at the rate of sixty feet per day, dropping aircraft carrier–sized icebergs into the blue-black sea.

Seven miles offshore we meet our first ice. Closer in it is everywhere; there is often one floe ten yards to starboard and another just as close to port. These chunks are not pack ice formed from the frozen sea. They are splinters, dumptruck-sized, of larger icebergs. It's impossible to guess just how much farther they extend beneath the surface.

Under normal conditions the person on helm may let the compass wander up to five degrees, holding course over time by balancing the swings to either side. But when maneuvering here, straying even one degree could cause real trouble. Square-riggers don't respond like sports cars; steering is hard work, you have to know what you're doing, and at such times in the past it's been routine for a deckhand to take over. So I am surprised, to put it mildly, when George does not replace me at the helm.

My arms are tired, and my back is tense. I keep my eyes glued to the compass and my fingers tight around the wheel. George stands on the roof of the after deckhouse, above and behind me. Amidships, everyone maintains silence so that the helmsman can hear and repeat the captain's orders.

—What's your bearing, Harvey?
—One seven eight.

—Come to one seven nine.

—One seven nine. (Twenty seconds pass.) One seven
   nine, *on.*

—Steady. (A half minute passes.) What's your bearing?

—One seven nine.

—Come two spokes to port.

—Two spokes to port.

—Come four spokes to port.

—Four spokes to port, aye.

—What is your bearing?

—One seven eight.

—Steady on. . . .

There are all kinds of intimacy in the world. This one proceeds, uninterrupted and unadorned, until I lose track of time.
I almost lose myself in the hypnotic counterpoint of order and
reply, the sense of being one not just with George but with the
whole crew and with *Regina,* moving forward in my hands.

At last we reach the narrow mouth of Jakobshavn harbor. I
am still not replaced but take her straight in to the wharf—this
too is a first for me. George is preparing to dock into the wind
and has Al Abend standing by with a heaving line when a man
on the wharf lets us know that we can't put in; another ship is
expected. So it's out again through that narrow harbor mouth to
hunt for an anchorage among the growlers.

More pressure. Later I will notice how George and I lapsed
into "sirs" and "ayes," the traditional language of command.
Later I will be proud to have come through in circumstances that
allowed no latitude for blunder. I will realize that I never looked
up, never got to see the sights I steered us through—and will feel
honored by the trust that let me steer. At the moment, though,
we are casting the lead line constantly, finding sudden changes in
depth from twelve fathoms to as little as four, along with tricky
currents. After a half hour of unsatisfactory soundings, George
takes the ship out to deeper water and turns her over to Bill
Cowan. His orders are to drift with the engine on.

"Is the main watch all assembled?" George asks. "OK, fore
watch, breakfast. I don't know about you folks, but I am *stahv-*

ing." Passing the binnacle, he notices me still there and turns back. "Harvey, my friend," he says, "I guess we can let these people have the helm."

One quarter of Greenland's population lives in four towns that ring Disko Bay. This one, Jakobshavn, sits on the east or "mainland" side. After breakfast, George took the Avon into town alone and returned with permission to dock until six that evening.

Most of the crew immediately went ashore. We purchased some canned Danish gourmet food and then walked east to the edge of town, where seal meat hung from driftwood racks and the land began to rise. Just past the meat racks, we met a boy of eight who was playing with his husky puppies, balls of white fuzz with razorlike teeth, bad breath, and bright pink tongues. Their beauty was no accident; in North Greenland it is legal to shoot any other kind of dog on sight in order to keep the breed pure. Even in captivity, the Eskimo dog remains a scavenger and can extract the nutrients it needs from excrement. That explained why the puppies who scampered over had been lying in a human midden. They kept up with us, yip-yipping playfully, for as long as the land was relatively level but turned back when we headed higher.

Once again there was the same volcanic, self-enfolded stone we had seen on Disko Island, only this time it stretched on without a break for miles and miles. The highest shrub in the landscape was several inches tall, and even where scrub grass had taken hold, the rock poked through, as on a billiard table with its felt worn sheer. After a half-mile rise, the slope turned into cliff face—nothing but stone—and we began to climb.

After an hour, we came upon three glassy tarns, jet black but pure. One by one we overcame our shyness (and good judgment), stripped, and took the nearly suicidal plunge into the freezing water. *Splash* went each warm, frail, beautiful young body, *splash*—and beyond them, nothing but stone and ice as far as the eye could see. Atop the next rise we warmed up with a picnic, washing down fish and bread and cheese with Carlsberg beer and Gammel-Dansk liqueur. Then we gathered our things together, climbed a half mile farther, and sat down.

We had reached the expedition's destination. This was as far as we could come, the "margin" I'd set out to find five weeks before.

Looking out, one saw the Greenland icecap—700,000 square miles in area; two miles deep in parts; so heavy that the underlying earth has sagged beneath its weight; so cold that it creates its own weather system; a place where no one on earth has any cause to go.

Looking down, one saw the icecap's edge and the broad mouth of a frozen river. Ninety-five percent of its surface was ice—slabs and crags and pressure ridges, raftered abutments fifty feet high, beginning to fracture and explode where the outermost approached the sea. A few leads of water were emerald-colored. Every now and then an iceberg somewhere calved with a roar like thunder. But you never saw anything move.

We spread out along the bare ridge, black as pitch and sharp to the touch. As if it had been agreed to in advance, each person walked off from the others and stood alone.

It was then that I felt the words fail. To stare at a continent of snow that has fallen centuries before, has been compressed to an enormous density, and may not melt or alter for another thousand years was to come face to face with Time. Even terms of deepest awe seemed suddenly a pretense or false comfort—self-deception, straining to forge relation where there was none, where there never could be. Maybe it was because we're used to seeing the earth clothed in trees and lakes and fields—in nature's garments, things that die—that, as with those naked bodies earlier, no matter how beautiful they are in the cold clean light, there's a sense of shyness in looking on them.

Later, back on board, we skirted the Jakobshavn Ice Fjord, sailing right up to the mouth of the river that we had gazed down at when on shore. We were now at the very spot where a continent-sized slab of ice breaks off into the sea.

The glacial edge was columnar, with vertical fluting that resembled basalt at the mouth of a sea cave. The top of the ice cliff (at the height of our upper topsail) echoed the mountains' pointed forms. Snow-colored at a distance, close up it was streaked and pitted with debris. We lowered the small boats and moved in. In the lee of the ice, the air was dead, wet, cold—like opening a freezer door. I was unprepared for the sudden chill, or the warmth as we passed back out of it. I was even more surprised, as we turned around, by the sight of *Regina Maris,* framed by tabular icebergs twice the length of football fields and seven stories high. It was like seeing her for the first time, once again: How beautiful and brave she looked, how full of life, there, shining in the sunlight! I felt myself blessed to be aboard.

26 July. 68°N/53°W.

Thoroughly rotten weather: thirteen-knot winds in the wrong direction, temperature thirty, wet snow mixed with rain. We are back at sea, and it feels like we never left it. Worse. It's depressing to return from a good time on shore to the tedium of sailing transects. Everyone is tired and moody, and the fellowship of yesterday has given way to quarrels.

No one's about to shake hands, either. In this weather, waterproof gloves are not warm enough, wool gloves turn into rigid sponge, and if you try to wear both, you can't handle lines. So you wind up using none at all. Your calluses grow stiff and crack. When you go below, your fingers swell and your palms get red and puffy.

If you've walked along a lakeshore in a blizzard, you know something of how midwatch feels. It's bad enough trying to move around aloft in even a few layers of bulky clothes, but today I am wearing sixteen garments. At least that keeps me warm. The part I find worse is standing on the bow. There one receives the full force of the frozen rain, increased by the forward motion of the vessel. As lookout, you have to stare straight into it; you can't turn away. So the sleet strikes you full in the face like buckshot,

and the wind keeps your hood ballooning open like a sail. Hail-
stones rattle off your oilskins, turning the hood into a snare drum
with your head inside. You can hear ice crystals scouring the
deckhouse wall and the slush and brash ice rubbing along the
bow. This noise is abrasive, frictive, rasping; when you close your
eyes for relief from the sleet, it sounds like a forest fire.

Midwatch last night was bitterly cold; the sleet kept up for
four hours straight, and we had deck work almost constantly.
When we came off at four, my cheeks were so numb that I could
not form words. This morning at eight-fifteen (we had all skipped
breakfast), George came striding through the passageway, boom-
ing, "Field day, field day, field day!" with exaggerated and in-
furiating cheer. None of us budged, of course.

He was followed three minutes later by members of the jolly
main watch, swinging mops and dustpans as they gamboled down
the passageway. I don't know what it is with these kids. Hor-
mones? A little too much scouting? Canan's idea of a joke was to
reach in and tickle me awake with her ice-cold hands. I swore; she
disappeared. When I swung my feet over the berth, with the socks
still on, Al Abend mopped them. Hardy har har. I took a swing
at him. Patrick and Scott stepped in between.

I don't need this crap, and I don't understand how people
you can feel so in touch with one day can be so insensitive the
next. Maybe it has to do with people in groups, their ugly side.
In the past few weeks I have heard some students talk about
mountaineering and Outward Bound. In every story there's always one member who was scared and threatened to "hold back
the group." So the group drew together and "helped" that person
through—that is, got what it wanted. Then everyone "felt great":
the party line.

There's a quality of bullying oneself as well as others under
all this hearty cheer, exerted in the jaunty, square, desexualized
style of the youth group. You can see where it leads if left un-
checked. What tolerance does it have for individual differences,
for those who are less capable? What room does it leave for
expression of honest fear?

Afternoon watch brought another four hours of raw cheeks,

numb toes, knotted shoulders, rain. But still no whales. The scientific goal seems to have switched from finding them to accounting for their absence.

Off watch at four; a nap until five. At night, a video in the main salon: an episode of *Cosmos* filmed aboard *Regina*. Sunshine lights the aqua sea off Puerto Plata; barefoot nymphs ascend the rig in pink and green bikinis; George (in Bermuda shorts) is interviewed. As a half dozen humpbacks leap about the rail, Carl Sagan furrows his wizard brow and asks, "Could it *be* they are trying to *tell* us something, in a language every *bit* as cawm-plex as our *own?*"

Five minutes later I'm on deck again for nightwatch, intermittent showers, temperature thirty-four, wind westerly, approaching twenty. All sail is set except the main and mizzen topsail. Almost at once the wind picks up, and Clay sights a squall line off the starboard quarter. Everyone is sent aloft to furl and gasket. Outboard, a Manila line has frozen stiff and knocks, like a piece of wood, against the channels. At the mizzen top, it is blowing twenty-seven knots. Pellets of cold rain whistle through the shrouds. There is ice around the footropes.

At 2200 hours I move to the standby slot in our rotation, chilled to the bone. I lay below for a minute and am staring into a cup of cocoa that's still full when some squishy footsteps approach me and a nasal voice declares, "We *eat* below. We *stand by* in the aft salon." It is Joan, all pumpkin-faced and huffy in her streaming weather gear.

I do not answer.

She repeats, "We *eat* below. When we're on watch, we do not leave the deck without permission. We *stand by* in the aft salon." Having entered from up forward, she stomps through the main salon to make a dramatic exit aft. But just then a voice in one of the bunks begins to mimic her, and the silence of those who have been listening turns into laughter. Joan's steps speed up rapidly. She disappears.

Ten minutes later I reach the aft salon. I'm feeling a little better, warmed, and proud of the work I've done in the rig all day under dangerous conditions. George is still up, and angry.

He points at the upholstery, to a wet spot ringed with salt. "Someone" informs him that I've been sitting there with my oilskins on.

Not true. But I'm damned if I'll deny it.

Chicken shit. Summer camp.

27 July. 68°N/54°W. Great Hellefiske Bank.

SHIP'S LOG

0430	68.00°N/54.18°W. Underway. Set main and flying jib.
0515	67.58°N/54.28°W. Set headsails, main staysail, upper and lower topsails.
0630	67.50°N/54.12°W. Struck same. No wind.
0900	67.40°N/53.56°W. Set all sail only to have wind die out.
1015	67.34°N/53.40°W. Struck inner and outer jib, main topgallant staysail, mizzen, and all squares.
1300	67.48°N/54.02°W. Set course, upper and lower topsails. Sheeted in the main.
1450	67.56°N/54.14°W. No wind. Douse all sails.

Another iron-cold, interminable day, with the water khaki-colored and the sky like slate. We're doing a hell of a lot of work for nothing. All anyone wants to do is sleep. Erratic winds. More trawls. Not a single humpback whale.

A lot of the stress and fatigue we now feel is compounded by confinement in close quarters. When the usual ways of expressing or releasing stress are tightly circumscribed, people tend to pass it on. Feeling put upon, they demand to know how much others are doing; feeling out of control, they assert it by "supervising," uninvited, someone else's efforts. Or by *offering* to help instead of just helping. Or pronouncing territorial rights.

To an outsider, the issues that we fight about would seem almost laughably petty. But precisely because the territory is constricted, they express, in heightened form, the whole range of needs and weaknesses that we normally act out in our private and public lives on shore. The scale is different; the emotions are the same.

28 July. 66°N/54°W. Off Holsteinsborg.

Lunchtime. George: "So as soon as my father has finished, Dulles turns to Stimson and says—"

"*Shove it up your ass!*" From the galley, followed by "Fuck you, asshole," and a collision of two big bodies.

"I don't care if you spent a *week* on shore collecting. I don't need no moldy little mushrooms in my reefah."

"Moldy little—they were morels, you asshole. A real cook would have recognized—"

"Big fuckin' deal. Just— get— you— *nobody* goes in the reefah without askin'. Get the fuck outta my galley."

"Who's gonna make me?"

"Who's gonna— *I* am."

"You and who else?"

Thud. A pot falls. Crash. Some cups fly down the passageway.

"*Al. Lawrence.*" It is George, still sitting at the table. In the galley the noises stop. Both men appear. George examines them, looking quizzical, more pained than angry. Seeing that the fight is over, he decides not to intervene. Al bends down to pick up the cookware. Lawrence steps over him, stalks off to the fo'c'sle, and shuts his door.

* * *

The lack of whales has sapped everybody's sense of purpose. It has frustrated the scientists most of all and driven a wedge between them and the rest of us.

Unlike members of the working watches, scientists are designated "idlers"; they knock off after supper and get to sleep through the night. So long as they had their hands full, they were no different from the other idlers (bosun, cook, and engineer), and no one on board complained. But it now seems like the less of their own work they have to do, the less they pitch in to help others or even seem aware of what our work entails.

It's a drag, for example, to be sent aloft on "science watch" at six A.M. after back-to-back hours on helm and bow so that no daylight observations will be lost while the scientists, who went to bed at ten, can sleep until breakfast. ("Wake us if you sight whales").

It's a pain to come off watch and find the four of them complaining to each other over second helpings by the time you sit down. It's embarrassing, when you're bracing the yards, to have to ask the scientist who is looking on to lend a hand. And unlike the mates, who are excused from washing dishes but all do them anyway, not one of the scientists has yet to set a plate or wash a spoon.

I'm beginning to understand, begrudgingly, the point George made to me a week ago about special status. As is, I am pretty antsy. I'd go nuts if I didn't have work to do; somehow by taking care of *Regina,* physically, I take care of my own emotions. By not sharing in this caretaking, by hanging back, the scientists have made themselves unhappier than they need be. It's the dirty work the rest of us can't dodge that binds us to the ship and to one another, even—no, especially—on days like these.

Dull as it is, I am grateful for that coherence. There's a Tibetan Buddhist concept that has been called, in English, "crazy wisdom." As explained by the teacher Chogyam Trungpa, this is the power that will always bring you what you are least expecting and most need to learn. Sometimes it seems that this whole damned vessel *oozes* crazy wisdom and that no matter how much

I think I have learned, she will always surprise me. I'd been feeling so high the last week or so, in the thrall of the personal moral scheme I was so eagerly imposing on experience. I had been confused and then scared; then I had faced my fear, so I was ready (I thought) for Significant Understanding. But no sooner did I have a glimpse, a flash, the slightest glint of any insight while on shore than it was straight back to the same old shit—to life as usual, yes, even on a 144-foot barkentine.

29 July. 66°N/55°W. At Anchor, Itivdleq Fjord.

Yesterday afternoon the weather broke at last. Fresh winds brought whitecaps and blue skies. Changing tactics, we abandoned the outer fishing banks, sailing east and then south along the coast to explore for whales in coves and inland waters.

Along the way Gregg had each of us take a turn as mate and direct the clewing up or setting of one sail. Bear in mind that the course has two sheets, two tacks, two leechlines, four buntlines, and two braces; multiply that by five for the other squares; also throw in the halyards, and don't forget that each sail must be "loosed" in advance and "overhauled" once set—then you'll get an idea of how many steps this routine task involves. For a month I'd been hauling on various lines as ordered but hadn't seen or understood the process as a whole.

Now giving the orders, I was forced to consider the sails as a unit and to think logically about the sequence of my commands as I watched their effects take hold. There was a lot to think about, such as why you raise one yard before you sheet in the sail below it or why you don't make fast the clews until the buntlines have been hauled. As usual, I would no sooner get the basic method right than Gregg would reveal some subtle change:

"When you have them cast off the buntlines, allow a six-second pause between the windward and leeward sides." It was challenging but great fun. Standing amidships, gazing upward, barking out, "Slack! Hold! Belay!" I couldn't have imagined this five weeks ago; even now it seemed a bit unreal.

Twenty miles south we turned east at Cape Burnil, entering this fjord at 1600 hours. Instantly, the wind died. Striking all sail, we motored inland slowly through the absolute and dreamlike silence, through frigid water several hundred meters deep and mirror smooth. The fjord was narrow. On either side, spectacular glacial valleys rolled to the water's edge, devoid of vegetation: rivers of gravel, deltas of crushed stone.

"Hold tight!" says Gregg. "Here comes the biggest fish I've ever caught!" It's 10 P.M., and four of us are in the jolly boat in Eqalugarssuit Cove. We've been jigging for cod and hauling them up on unbaited hooks on sixty-pound, hand-held line. The last school passed by over fifteen minutes ago, and from Gregg's smile you just *know* he's bluffing.

A moment later, however, his line snaps taut, and the whole boat dips two feet to starboard. Scrambling toward the center-line, Gregg braces himself for something big all right, and dangerous: "I'm gonna need help!" he cries. He lets out some line, hauls hand over hand, then loses the ground he's gained and lets out more. Adds, "Harvey, get out your knife."

"My *knife?*"

"Be ready to cut the line."

Now the whole boat is rocking. Brenda has unsheathed her marlinspike. Patrick stands up, brandishing an oar above his head like a lance, an ax, a spear—and starts to laugh.

Not Gregg. "Keep an eye out," he tells Clay and me. "Let me know if you see a fin."

A fin. I know what *that* means. Then it bumps us, and the boat tips hard the other way, and water comes across the port-side gunwales. As we scramble and it steadies up, the long black back appears. I pull out my knife.

"Don't cut!" yells Gregg, leaning back on his line like a man on water skis. He attempts to haul in, hand over hand, gains a couple of inches, loses more. Then exchanges a look with Patrick, plants his feet against the boat's steep side, and lets his body weight fall backward. For one long moment man and fish hang balanced, frozen in action—Gregg in the boat, his catch at the waterline.

He starts to haul in barehanded. I lean out to help him grab it, look into a mouthful of inch-long teeth, and pull back fast. It seems to follow me. A heave, a heavy thump, and it's on board, a monster almost five feet long. We wrestle it to the bilges and tie it down with a double bowline around its tail like a lassoed bronco. "Halibut!" says Gregg.

He keeps on grinning all the way back to *Regina*. Meanwhile Patrick, in the bow, seems moved by a less identifiable emotion. He picks up our smallest cod, a beauty, and examines it over and over, running his hands across fins and scales and peering inside its jaws and gills. He holds it the whole way home.

On the ship's deck, after the whoops and hollers, the photos and the measurements (it's four feet nine and weighs eighty-three pounds), the butchering begins. No sleek trout, this. A horrible old fish—its skin coarse, scarred, and missing scales, its teeth grotesque, its eyes on ugly stalks, one ruined by the hook. Lawrence kneels beside it. He unsheathes his knife and starts to gut. Gregg opens up the stomach, filled with half-digested one-pound fish. They look embalmed, or fetal. Judy takes the rest of the stomach's contents to the lab to probe for fragments of inner ear that will identify digested prey.

Next they cut out the halibut's tongue. Then its heart. Two inches long, it lies in a canvas bucket—beating. Not occasional flickers; a strong, steady pump. And as they go on cutting off fins and tail, and the bright anemones of clotting blood slide out the scuppers on saltwater waves from the fire hose, moved all at once by Patrick's earlier example, I pick up the heart.

I am surprised, at first, to find that it is not warm. I hold it, beating, in my palm, in the thin bright light that lingers.

I hold it. And hold it. The heart does not stop beating. It is getting on toward midnight, but the light that's left won't fade. Gregg steaks what he has captured, working from tail to head. Translucent now, the cool flesh glows pale jade.

30 July. 66°N/54°W.

Last night I dreamed of Africa, the village where I once spent a year. Back then, on the night before the long rains came, I woke to find the termite mounds lit up by lightning, and was filled with a waking urge to make love to the earth, to see my own seed stain the rusty soil and bring forth frangipani, maize, cassava. It was a strange dream then, and stranger now, repeating, for the first time, in this world of salt water and ice and stone. I woke up feeling horny.

When we weighed the anchor at 0700 hours, the morning was already clear and warming. Near the mouth of the fjord, where its quiet water first received the ocean's waves, *Regina* started pitching gently. I had climbed out on the bowsprit, which I straddled, leaning back against the mainstay. Though I know that the sprit is fixed and it's the long wire stay that actually moves, I pretended that the opposite was true. I imagined that the upthrust, deep-veined wood was rooted in my own groin, lifting, holding for a moment, sinking down. Closing my eyes, I listened: Low waves licked the stem beneath me as I moved that sprit around inside the whole salt ocean, which moved with me, lapping and splashing as I rose and fell.

On helm at 0940, I am joined by the third mate, Patrick Wadden. Pat is a doctor's and teacher's son from Winona, Minnesota, and a former wide receiver on the high school football team. Though he looks like a dropout now, the truth is that he never dropped in, instead hanging out in a colony of shacks on stilts along the Mississippi, listening to old-timers and fishing for a living. For the three years before this voyage, he was chief mate of the Hudson River sloop *Clearwater,* which he calls "flagship of the People's Navy." He is also a puppeteer and a weaver. He likes poetry, especially the work of Robert Bly.

Patrick is barefoot, as usual. But he hasn't forgotten to wear his hat, a fantastic maroon concoction of earflaps, visor, turrets, escarpments, pom-pom, and tubular horn. A girlfriend knitted it several years ago; it now contains roughly equal quantities of wool, grease, and debris. Pat tosses a toothpick to leeward over his shoulder, thrusts his hands deep into well-patched pockets, and faces me across the binnacle. Spectra dance on his wire-rimmed glasses. He says, "You know, Harvey, yesterday was the first time I got a feel, a tiny feel, for Greenland. I mean Green-*land,* you know, the spirit that I kept missin' in the towns. Did you ever get up to that fishin' camp above the cove? Too bad. I think that's where it started.

"Just over the first ridge where we anchored there are two small freshwater lakes. I don't know how you pronounce them— Eqalgarrsuit was the easy one and— uh— yeah, well anyway, they were loaded with arctic char. On the shore there were piles of crude wooden boxes, each with a hole in one end. Fish traps. I went to look at 'em. There was a tent nearby, an old man lookin' out from it. He saw me and gestured to come on in.

"Inside there were seven people: the man, his wife, a few guys our age, and a couple of wives or daughters, granddaughters maybe. The old pair were like storybook Eskimos, straight from *Nanook of the North.* I felt a little weird 'cause we couldn't communicate. But the guy, all of them, were incredibly gleeful. Every few minutes his eyes'd wrinkle up, he'd pull his short pipe from between his lips, and just start laughin'. Uncontrollably. And the next thing you'd know, all of us—first them, then me—joined in.

"Around the third time this happened, the old man found a piece of paper, wrote down, '65,' and pointed at his stomach.

Then he wrote his name. I took the pencil and wrote, 'PATRICK, 28.' He took it back, addin' all of the children's names and ages. Finally, in big numbers, he wrote, '70.' He waited till he was sure I saw, then pointed at his wife and burst out laughin', twice as hard as before. She also thought it was a scream.

"After about five minutes, she calmed down and brought out dried fish and coffee. They had a little Primus stove and a tent that could have come from Sears. We ate and then, this was really nuts, the young girls pulled out a tape deck. They gestured for me to close my eyes. I did. I could hear the cassette going in. You know what came on? Neil Diamond! Really. When I opened my eyes, these three girls were all dancin' around the tent. And singin'. 'Song sung blue, everybody knows one. . . .' They had no idea what it meant, but they were fakin' it, lip-synchin', word for word.

"When they saw how amazed I looked, they decided to explain. The youngest girl traced circles in the air. Her older sister said, 'Taiwan.' "

"Taiwan?"

"No shit. And then they all joined in: 'Taiwan, Taiwan, Taiwan.'

"It took me a while to figure out. *DYE 1*. A radar dish. There's American Distant Early Warning people stationed on this coast. Maybe where those guys spend the winter. I bet that's where the tapes are from.

"The funny thing was that it all *felt* right, you know, traditional. They were so fuckin' happy with each other, camped in the middle of nowhere, catchin' and dryin' food for the winter, livin' off the land. And Harvey, those girls? They were really—I mean really—pretty."

I ask about the small cod in the jolly boat last night. Patrick grows quieter. It wasn't the killing, he says. After all, he has fished for a living. But somehow our time in the jolly boat, coming right after his visit ashore, let him finally "break through." Feeling the life in that fish, it seemed—he gropes for words—like it was "perfect," like the force in its small body was the concentrated spirit of the land. "Ships are such a *superficial* environment," he says. "They are always movin', passin' along the surface. But sometimes you have to go deeper. You've got to slow down, you know? To touch, I mean really touch, and feel."

"Whale ho!" Am I dreaming? I was. But now I'm up, the cry that woke me still sounding down the hatches. Curtain open, head out: Everyone making for companionways as if the ship's on fire. Even Don Patten is tripping it lightly. After them! On deck, half of our crew is flying up the rigging. People on the foretop and the maintop point in three directions, shouting "Humpbacks! Whales!"

Peter and Judy select a group whose path is parallel to ours, a thousand yards off the port beam. Noting their speed and direction, George decides to wear ship and approach them on our starboard side. A dozen hands leap to the braces. *Regina* feels them coaxing, considers for a minute or two, then agrees to fall off and begins her slow pivot to port.

Whales are not quiet animals. At two hundred yards, this group sounds like a bunch of old cars leaving rubber on a turn. As we pull abeam of them and listen, and the cameras click and whirr, I can visualize all the animals' respiratory gizmos, deep down, working—melon and goosebeak and nares—and can hear the water rich in plankton surge from their distended throats and lather through the long baleen.

I don't think I had admitted to myself, in the past few weeks, how lonely I'd become out here for something that wasn't us but was nevertheless *like* us, something quick, responsive. It wasn't just whales. Whatever draws them to this bank also brings other members of the sea community that they are part of. And today, encountering shearwaters, fulmars, terns—not particularly brainy animals—I still felt grateful for them, for the warm-blooded, finned, and feathered life that flies and swims to greet us: fellows, if not friends.

31 July. 66°N/54°W. Little Hellefiske Bank.

We are back on the fishing banks just north of Søndre Strømfjord, where we've found more humpback whales. A threesome was sighted at 0400 hours, four just after breakfast, two before lunch, and another pair this afternoon. The most recent pair were tolerant at first, then curious, then bold. One had a strange bent fluke and practically bumped our hull. This prompted tales of a time on Navidad Bank, in the Caribbean, when a cow rubbed up against *Regina*'s stern suggestively as if intent on mating.

Judy has spent years observing humpbacks off of Newfoundland; Toni and Peter have logged just as much time "in the field" with grays. George is a master at anticipating where a sounding whale may next appear and synchronizing our rhythm with the whales' own, that is, taking our cue from *them* so as not to intrude or scare them off. I am now getting the long looks at these animals that I couldn't get before.

For me, the most striking thing about humpbacks is their combination of size and power with grace. There is something so balletic about them: white flippers sequined with barnacles *en pointe,* waving or lolling out of the water, rising through a net of bubbles, breaching in a plume of spray. Occasionally they slap the water with their tails or churn it up in play. Usually, when they "up flukes" prior to sounding, even that is gentle. First comes the great curve of the slick black back, colossal, shining, arching more and more . . . then flukes high in the air, perpendicular to the water, the white flash of their underside like a salute or a signature, quivering one long moment. Then the tail slips straight down like a letter in a mail slot until all that's left are the two elongated little corners, crooked and poised like a pinkie over a teacup. At last, with a final languid flip, they too turn upright and slip into the water, leaving a glassy circle, a footprint on the surface of the sea.

Ten minutes later they are back and ready to repeat the sequence countless times. Today's final encounter was our longest yet. And the longer the animals stayed with us, the more obvious it became that they weren't seeking food or anything material at all. They were simply curious. The whales have found us as much as we've found them, and what's more, for identical motives. We are visiting because they want us to.

In fact, their curiosity exceeds our own. One scratches against the stern. Another swims along the rail; her hot spray lands on deck. Others play games, such as surfacing alternately on our port and starboard sides. Clearly, these animals like to keep us company. They circle *Regina Maris* for six hours.

1 August 65°N/54°W. Sukkertoppen Bank.

More whales. It's clear that we've found a significant population. As yet there have been no matches with animals sighted elsewhere, but it's still too soon to draw conclusions. How do you go about matching fluke shots? To start, you need a standard system to describe them. By laying a grid (two boxes high, five long) across the photo of each tail, you can then say, for example, that the ventral side is four-fifths white, that two parallel scars extend from box three down through box seven, that box ten shows telltale damage or deformity. Or you can group named whales by their fluke shapes (such as "deeply notched") and the pattern of their pigmentation. Judy and her former partners used this system to compile the first humpback whale catalog four years ago. Since then it has grown to include almost thirteen

hundred entries. Plans are afoot to computerize; the most likely
program would run a search by means of visual cues, with each
grid having a binary value corresponding to black or white. In the
meantime, however, the search and comparisons must be done by
eye. For the scientists, that means plenty of work to go around.

Their spirits have all improved. Judy spends hours aloft on
the foretop truck, looking positively beatific. When not sighting
whales in half-light at astounding distances or pointing out
Pomeranian jaegers, she is off in the darkroom developing film.
On the other side of the bulkhead, in the drylab, Toni pores over
black-and-white contact prints. She too has been getting up early
again, arriving on deck in a turtleneck inside a shirt under a
sweater inside a down vest stuffed into weather gear, rolled up and
trussed together like a bracciole.

Her good mood is not entirely because of whales. Two
nights ago, when cleaning the cabin she shares with Peter (opposite the captain's, with a private head and a single bed along each
wall), Toni tugged on a long drawer under her bunk and was
shocked to see the other half of a double bed pop up, on springs.
"Why didn't you tell us?" they both asked George, on their
thirty-third day at sea.

"Tell? . . . You mean you didn't *know?*"

Today they both skipped breakfast.

At eleven tonight the sun went down. On shore, the high crown
of the Sukkertop ice shone forth like burnished copper. We
switched on our running lights for the first time in twenty days.

Even though we are still far north, the quality of light is
changing once again, and the days are growing shorter for two
reasons. First, we have descended four degrees of latitude since
Disko, and as we head south, we leave the midnight sun astern.
Second, it is August; summer is about to turn, and its shrinking
daylight hints at the approach of arctic winter.

I have tried, here and there, to describe the quality of light
and space in this part of the world and something of their effect
on me. Within a week we will be leaving Greenland, to get clear
before the ice re-forms. Before we go, there is something related

I want to set down: the way in which the arctic sky and life at sea transform one's usual experience of time.

On shore, for the most part, time is what the clock says. It's mechanical, firm, a system everyone makes use of without thinking much about the physical reality to which it corresponds or the way it is derived. At sea, by contrast, you are constantly aware of this. Moreover, there seem to be different *types* of time, depending on how you define it.

One type is objective, *chronometric:* Time is distance, distance from Greenwich, longitude. A minute is a nautical mile, the measurable fragment of an arc. As you watch the sun and the moon describe that arc, uninterrupted, it is like riding a moving clock face past bright numerals fixed far off. Earth is a giant flywheel, and Time is the measure of its turning.

Ocean time is less remote and less predictable. Weather and wind respect no schedule; storms last as long as they please, and you respond to them on the terms they dictate. In this sense, they make a mockery of calculation and repeatedly dissolve the structures we impose. Time becomes fluid. Rhythms are broken down. In addition, this far north, the hours *look* less distinct from one another than they do "down south." Day and night, light and dark, overcast and clear—the categories run together. Every time starts to seem like any time, not only fluid but abstract too. Water and sky are not blue and green but a hundred subtle shades of tinted gray, and vision is neither occupied nor limited by mountains, buildings, trees. Unlike a landscape, the seascape doesn't block your sight; it extends beyond it. It exhausts your range.

A third type of time is exactly opposite. I call it *ship time,* meaning the rigid, immutable march of watches and the duties they entail. A construct, entirely artificial, this respects no occasion. Nothing affects its meshing gears, and it only reflects anything outside itself when things grow rough and the watches must be doubled. It is clear that we *need* routine, not just to run the ship but to sustain ourselves. In this sense one type of time counterbalances the other the way logic helps make meaning of experience; ship time provides a structure and the sense of pace that ocean time denies.

Finally, there is the type of time that I call *personal,* defined from within by one's own individual needs. On shore, time is private property. If you ask someone to work "overtime," you compensate for what you take away: "Time is money." But on *Regina,* time is collective property. Your hours off watch are not your own but on loan, as it were, from the common treasury, and you never know when this loan will be recalled. The moment that you begrudge it or try to own it, trouble starts.

If there is a lesson in all this, I suppose it's that no one definition represents the truth or that a full sense of time consists of all of them, the way white light contains all colors. To mediate among the various modes isn't easy. Between round-the-clock watches that limit our deep REM sleep and the midnight sun, which throws off our circadian rhythms, it is hard, even when the time allows, to think abstractly, hard to pursue a thought. The feeling is like chronic jet lag. It is always the morning after an all-night party.

And yet, because free time is so rare and so unpredictable, you are constantly forced to inhabit the present moment, and you learn not to squander it. You grow more accurate about and more responsive to your true desires. Not what you could or should do in the rare time that is yours alone. Not what is plausible, but what is necessary—what you need to do, most, now.

***

0000	Watch.
0400	Sleep.
0730	Breakfast.
0745	Sleep.
0830	Meeting.
0850	Sleep.
1000	Field day.
1110	Sleep.
1130	Lunch.
1200	Watch.
1600	Class.
1700	Sleep.
1730	Dinner.
1800	Sleep.
1915	Class.
2000	Watch.
2400	Sleep.

Root: "The part that's a bitch isn't missing sleep. It's putting yourself through waking up so many times."

2 August. 64°N/53°W.

Today we lost our steering. Shortly after breakfast, the cable that runs from the rudder to the helm succumbed to metal fatigue and parted. When I heard the loud pop and rushed on deck, the ship was faced bow to the wind, out of control, in irons. The mainsail luffed. The mizzen jerked against its vang. Four jibs crackled angrily as the huge blocks on their sheets, called *coconuts,* smacked against the forestay. All of the squares were backed. We were less than three miles from shore, adrift. What now?

On many a sleepy night, I have held up my head with both hands as George explained that sailing is largely physics—channeling natural energy, converting it to work, distributing the effort it supplies. In running through permutations of sixteen sails, the captain reckons factors such as *lift* and *chord* and *angles of attack,* moves the *center of effort* aft and forward of the *center of resistance.* He considers *aspect ratios.* He vectors the breeze and the current. Makes note of the broad hull's *lateral resistance* and the resulting leeway. Checks for *turbulence* along the foil of each sail.

Since my talent for physics rivals my skill with knots, I have understood at most half of this and retained perhaps a quarter. But I didn't need to understand the theory to appreciate what now took place.

Bill was amidships, Gregg on the foredeck, each with his watch on hand. Fran had shut down the main. As Lawrence, Pat, and Scott unrove the old cable and bent on another (a job that included splicing several ropes of steel), George issued a steady stream of orders to the mates. They in turn kept us backing and filling, bracing and hauling, constantly. Wherever you looked, sails rose and fell in unfamiliar patterns. For two hours, as *Regina* spread or flapped or folded back her wings, we held to course without a rudder, just by tending sail.

What an orchestration to be part of! What a show! For the whole time, George stood on the roof of the after deckhouse, a maestro in rehearsal clothes, demanding a little more of this, a little less of that, and feeling how the ship as a whole responded.

At last, a crank of the engine signaled that the new steering cable had been riven on. The plankton trawl could begin on time, as scheduled. As I went down the forward hatch for lunch, I heard, "Deborah, what is your course now?"

"One seven five."

"Let's see how she feels about one seven zero."

"One seven zero."

"That's good. Steady on."

At the foot of the aft companionway is a fuse box. It looks like Navy surplus—from the First World War. This afternoon there's a power cord plugged in. I follow it across the toes of two dozen boots lined up at the foot of the stairs, under mounds of weather gear hung on pegs, into Toni and Peter's cabin. There it disappears, like a rodent's tail, down an open hatch. A cup of tea sits untouched on the deck beside it. I can see the light from a safety lamp and hear scuffling sounds below. "Hello?" I call down.

The square of light grows brighter. A watch cap appears through the opening, clotted with something that resembles mud; then, under it, Gregg's face, the color of coal. What is he doing down there? I ask. (I remember him rushing eagerly from lunch as if bound for the Broadway stage.)

For weeks, he answers, Toni has complained of nauseating fumes. Gregg decided to inspect the fuel and sewage tanks. The only access is from in here, through the bilges, on all fours.

"I see," I reply, though sight is not the sense of which I am most aware. "Does anything *else* need doing?"

He grins wryly. "Check in the do book. Lawrence had it last."

Dank, cramped, a V-shaped wedge with inward-curving walls, *Regina*'s fo'c'sle has remained unaltered since the ship was launched and is saturated with the rough life it has seen. Up here the bunks are less than two feet wide, stacked up four high, and stepped outward, pyramid style, as they ascend. Five feet up, the forward wall is a door the size of a trash can lid. Each time the anchor is weighed, someone must wriggle through this door, fall down into slimy dark on the other side, and coil anchor chain as it comes on board. On rough days, those in the fo'c'sle hear it clank in time to the crowbars, reeving irons, and mallets hung beside their pillows. Tackles and harnesses swing from the roof; a doll from Puerto Plata plays a saxophone of straw though she is fixed to the wall by a brass tack through her tummy. There are wood clamps with jaws over two feet long, framed lithographs of seven-masted schooners, bins full of bull's-eyes and lizards of lignum vitae, and buckets hand-stitched out of worn sail and crammed full of maple fids.

And everywhere there is rope: twine, marline, fishnet, Manila—some of it tarred, some white as milk—on spools, in swinging coils. There is rope braid around the table's edge and handles of rope on the tool chest. Drawer after drawer holds grommets, brackets, brass tacks, and sheets of leather.

On the opposite bulkhead there's a bookshelf, varnished so many times that it's black. Scanning it now for the "do book," I find *Masting and Rigging, Refrigeration,* Yeats's and Neruda's poems, *Mycology, A Field Guide to Agaricus Bisporus, Teach Yourself Greenlandic, The Folklore of the Sea,* and *O Thou Improper, Thou Uncommon Noun.*

Well, that's Lawrence. And here, at last, is the do book, held open by a rubber band. The items on the left-hand page are all checked off and initialed. Moving down the right-hand page, I read:

- Secure all shackles
- Serve chafing gear to shrouds and pennants
- Seize the mizzen futtock shroud
- Mark chain shots
- Mount thole pins on the jolly boat
- Hang fire ax
- Adjust anchor windlass clutch tongues
- Redlead bobstay
- Mount foam nozzle, engine room

Now *there's* poetry: words to keep your tongue awake in your mouth!

The list continues for five pages. I have reached "inspect all steering gear for wear" (dated a week ago) when Lawrence comes in. He is cracking his fingers like a pianist. He has been using two pairs of pliers to unravel some hacksawed steering cable, saving its strands for future use as light-gauge wire.

"What can I do around here?" I ask. Lawrence's eyes twinkle.

"You know, Harvey, I've been wondering that myself. What *can* you do?"

He is cranking up the Laugh now, like a siren. It starts slow, then builds up to speed, and finally, after he shuts it off, winds down. It's an operatic laugh, with a funny blend of confidence and insecurity, as if he needs to prime the pump and get the audience started, playing Ed McMahon to his own Johnny Carson. It's the kind of thing that could get on your nerves in a hurry if you didn't like him.

But I do. And as soon as we're both done laughing, he says, "Let's see. You could grease the new cable and sew on a sleeve. How does that sound?"

Sounds fine.

Root had already done the greasing. So I cut out some canvas from our old course, threaded waxed hemp through the four-inch needle, strapped on a "sailor's palm," and started sewing. Soon Lawrence came by and suggested that I change from my simple lockstitch to a herringbone stitch, which is sewn by working two needles in tandem from opposing sides in order to butt the two edges in a flat seam rather than overlap them. He also taught me how to tie a water knot. This joins two lengths of thread so that under stress they will tighten up on each other rather than pull apart.

My next job was to prepare some steel cable that will be used to replace worn footropes. This is a three-stage process. After you've stretched the cable between two fixed points, you fill the groove between its twisted strands with line to make the surface level all around; that is called *worming*. Next you wrap it with burlap; that is *parceling*. Then, using a special mallet, you wind marline around the burlap tightly in the opposite direction; that is called *serving* a line. Once the served line has been brushed with pine tar, it will not be slippery, cut into any hemp lines that it rubs against, or corrode in the salty air.

Every task aboard a ship, no matter how small, has its own particular tradition, frequently passed on by means of rhymes or proverbs. When I became confused about which way to wrap the different fabrics on the line, I asked Lawrence how he remembers. "How do you think?" he asked, with the characteristic grin that appears when he plays word games, meaning, "I've got you now." "OK," I said, "let's have it."

Worm and parcel with the lay,
Turn and serve the other way.

The calluses in my finger joints have thickened painfully, and while I was busy parceling and serving, the one on my index finger split open down to the red flesh below. As I thought about stopping to tape it, I realized how completely focused on the work I had been for the past half hour. That has happened a few times lately, as smaller and smaller details hold my complete attention. And reward it. I derived as much pleasure from this simple, repetitive work as I have from many a complex paper that I wrote in graduate school.

I finished in time for dog watch. After supper and Judy's class, we hove to twelve miles out. Tomorrow it's back to Godthab.

3 August. Godthab.

The Hotel Grønland restaurant is out of reindeer. So Gregg and I decide to share a roasted breast of razorbill and a whale steak broiled with onions. Eat whale? Mostly, I'm just plain curious. But I'm also feeling very close, right now, to the people who live on—and with—whales, closer to them than to the animals' sometimes sanctimonious protectors, who never stray within a hundred miles of where their own food dies. Besides (I tell myself as the succulent, sizzling cube arrives), it's only a *minke* whale. . . .

Here goes. Jet black (from the myoglobin), just a little tough, with a little stronger taste than beef. But not fatty or fishy; in fact, very good. And no bones! We wonder how many fillets one whale provides. Five thousand? Ten? As for the seabird, it has the color of blood, the texture of liver, the taste of raw, day-old fish. Perhaps to disguise this, it has been slathered with hot honey. We stare at the all too generous helping silently. "Unusual," I volunteer.

"Not bad," says Swanzey of the Ever-Open Mind, reaching gingerly for more.

I say, "La Brea tar pits." We set the mess aside.

After lunch I went out walking. In the oldest part of town, I found the five-room national museum, where an exhibition poster caught my eye. At the center of its folk art painting stood a tall white man in clerical robes with his arms outstretched. One hand held a bottle of medicine, the other a long glass wand. With this he placed drops in the eyes of an Eskimo kneeling at his feet, hands clasped in supplication. The missionary was Hans Egede, who arrived here in 1721 with his brothers and their families, built the yellow house that stands across from the museum, and spent all his remaining days in Godthab.

By midcentury the town had been firmly established. A Romanized script for the Inupiaq tongue had been devised and used for a Greenland Bible. Next came colonial status, Danish officials, Lutheran ministers, and a state-run trade monopoly, the KBH.

But the colony's great days still lay ahead, with whaling. By the mid-nineteenth century, having fished out the stocks of right and Pacific sperm whales, the Yankee fleet turned northward, making Disko Bay the center of its operations. Along with Scottish whalers, they proceeded to wipe out most of the smaller whales on which traditional Inuit life depended.

Under the twin strains of intermarriage and economic change, the indigenous culture eroded. Greenlanders (as the new mixed race was called) gave up old hunting ways and moved into towns that could not support them. Their state of dependency and idleness continued, worsening during the Second World War.

When the Nazis occupied Denmark, Greenland was cut off. For the war's duration, it fell under American protection. After the war was over, Greenland did not wish to revert to colonial status. Under terms of a referendum held in 1952, it became a full department of the Danish kingdom. Over the next two decades, a wave of new Danish immigration brought renewal of a sort. But this meant different things to different people. For the Danes, with small families and professional skills, it meant high state salaries and good jobs. For the Greenlanders, it meant fishing camps turned into Scandinavian-style towns, housing projects, and the dole.

The political response to these events has been relatively recent, culminating in home rule in 1979. Greenland now has legislative power over its internal issues but defers to Denmark on defense and monetary matters and in foreign affairs. This arrangement is already being tested. "Why home rule?" the left wing asks. "Why not independence?"

To this there are two kinds of answers. One is simply that Greenland, with only fifty thousand inhabitants, couldn't constitute an independent nation or survive economically on its own. This rationale is based on local needs.

The other arguments, which are voiced less publicly, are based on more global concerns. Denmark belongs to the European Community, and one of its strongest chips in the EC's poker games is reciprocal fishing rights off Greenland. As periodic "cod wars" between England and Iceland have demonstrated, such rights are serious business; nobody wants to let them go, and if retaining them means pouring money into Greenland, even for roads thick enough to resist frost-heave, it's a price the Danes will gladly pay.

One final point. If you put away your old Mercator and instead consult a modern circumpolar map, you will suddenly see the world as military planners do. You will notice that the Denmark Strait and Greenland Sea flow awfully close to Moscow. You will think of the Arctic Ocean as a mediterranean sea between Us and Them, the main road for nuclear missiles, and you will view the entire Arctic as a "vital strategic arena." Vital, not as in life but as in annihilation of it. People who think in this way *need* Greenland; there will be no letting go. And so, ironically, Greenland's fate is still bound up inextricably with the sea. But now the terms of that relationship, which is at the culture's core, are being redefined from far away.

***

"You have a lot of infighting in this country—over local politics, home rule, whether to stay in the Common Market, and so on. But this plan is one of the few things that really rallies everybody. Everyone in Greenland opposes it because—because we are scared to death."

The speaker, Finn Lynge, does not look easily scared. A large man with mixed Inuit and Danish features, he combines the slow self-possession of a working man with the urgent eloquence of a natural leader. Born in Godthab when the town had six hundred residents, he was ordained a Lutheran minister in Denmark and served the church there (and twice in the United States) at various times. Later, having left the ministry, he worked for Radio Greenland and then entered politics. Now in his midforties, Finn is Greenland's representative to the European Community. He is someone with striking *presence,* an impressive and credible man.

After supper in the main salon, we are chatting over coffee. The talk has turned to Greenland's future, and in response to our questions, Finn is speaking of the Arctic Pilot Project.

Under terms awaiting Canadian government approval, a consortium led by Dome Petroleum and Petro-Canada plans to drill for natural gas on Melville Island, on Lancaster Sound in the high Canadian Arctic. Once liquefied, the gas would be taken 3200 miles in ice-breaking supertankers through the Northwest Passage, down the Davis Strait, and then on to plants in Quebec or Nova Scotia. Melville Sound is the spot where two Canadian ships were crushed by ice in 1969, spilling 400,000 gallons of oil. That same year, amid much fanfare, the *Manhattan* tried to sail a similar route. Despite the presence of support aircraft and three escort icebreakers, the supertanker wound up stuck in ice four times, once found itself in water only twelve feet deep, and suffered a ten-foot gash in its armored hull beneath the waterline. The *Manhattan* was a class 3 ship; by comparison, the new liquid natural gas tankers would be class 7 and then class 10—the largest vessels ever built. Double-hulled, thirteen hundred feet long, they are designed to break through ten feet of ice at a speed of twenty knots.

"The companies claim," says Finn, "that they will take all kinds of precautions and there will be no shipwrecks and so on. Well, *maybe*. I remember in nineteen sixty—no, fifty-eight, I believe, the Danes had built a ship that was supposed to be the finest polar vessel in the world. On its maiden voyage it was wrecked. More than a hundred people died.

"We know a thing or two about the sea up here. We have seen so many accidents in this part of the world that when Canadians come along and say they're absolutely *certain*, well . . ." His heavy shoulders shrug. He looks at his palms and then at his knuckles. Then he speaks again.

"A UN commission has declared the Lancaster Sound a 'world heritage area' because of its ecological sensitivity. Well, I'm no biologist, but I have been told by the Canadian Arctic Resources Commission that they consider it the most important ecological area in the entire Northern Hemisphere. The food chain that starts there supports the microorganisms, shrimp, fish, seals, and so on in the Davis Strait, on which our people depend for a living. Yet that is exactly the narrow passage a supertanker will go through—sixty times a year at first, and eventually, if successful, every ten hours the year round.

"You know, the Melville Bay and Davis Strait form a closed inlet, really, not open ocean. It takes only one wrecked super-tanker to upset the entire ecological balance. We subsist on codfish, shrimp, halibut, redfish, round-nosed grenadier, and then we have, as you know, the sealing and whaling. Even if there's no accident of any kind, there will be the underwater noise. Sea animals are very sensitive to noise. Last time you were here, Nikolaj Heinrich must have told you about the growing scarcity of whales in inlets, where the noise is felt more keenly. Did you look for them there? Then you found that out for yourselves. Well, this past February there was a workshop in Toronto. Scientists there calculated that if you have a 200,000-horsepower engine going full speed, then within a corridor of one hundred kilometers approximately on either side, all low-frequency communication between sea mammals will be destroyed. Which means they cannot—what's the word?—orient themselves, or communicate in order to migrate and to feed. Within fifteen kilometers, vibrations will be lethal, you know, like shock-fishing salmon from streams with hand grenades.

"It's a question of energy needs. So they say. But the Canadians already have plenty of natural gas, enough in Alberta to cover all imaginable needs through the turn of the century. They want the arctic gas for export to Western Europe, so they can sell Alberta gas to your country."

Up to this point, Finn's eloquence has been muted and restrained. Avoiding charged adjectives or personal asides, he has stuck mainly to the facts, in the manner of someone who has made the same case many times before. But when he starts to speak again, I detect raw suffering tinged with hopelessness, the end of the tape, so to speak, a dutiful recitation winding toward its close.

"So we're up against the shipping interests; oil companies; the world energy situation; Ottawa's desire to exploit resources on national, instead of provincial lands; the need of the Canadian government to prove its efficiency in the Arctic and to demonstrate to the United States that Canada can exercise sovereignty in the Northwest Passage. What has any of this got to do with Greenland?

"In past history, if a neighboring nation threatened the subsistence of ninety percent of your people, it was the same as a declaration of war. Should Greenland declare war on Canada? Sometimes I get very pessimistic." He stops talking.

I glance at the cabin's ceiling. Is it my imagination, or have the cracks in its timbers lengthened? *Regina* has her in-port smell again. All at once, she feels tired, beaten, old.

Don breaks the silence. "Does Greenland have legal jurisdiction in the strait?" he asks.

"Not past the twelve-mile zone. Under the Law of the Sea Treaty, we would have had the right to regulate activity within our two hundred–mile 'economic zone,' but that right would still not encompass 'normal peaceful transit.' Now the oil companies maintain that these supertankers would be in 'normal peaceful transit.' But it is not peaceful to the whales. It is not peaceful to the seals. And if some accident occurs, it will not be peaceful to the cod or shrimp—and surely not to us. But what can we do?"

"What about the new treaty?" Peter asks.

"For the past two years," says Finn, "many of us in Europe and this country, we had been optimistic. The UN seemed ready to rally all interested parties with practical effect to create some rational order where there was none. Now the way it looks to us here and in Europe—correct me if I'm wrong—this was sabotaged by your Mr. Reagan." He pauses. No one corrects him.

I have been listening with mixed pain and pity. This now turns to anger. It is one thing to debate the issues in centers of power, quite another to listen to those whose lives that power intrudes on and victimizes thousands of miles away.

Finn resumes, "As I mentioned when we started, there are some very hot debates in this country, especially about the EC. These matters are serious. Still, we can do something about that relationship, as well as our other ties and troubles. But if the Canadians and Americans decide to go ahead, we can do nothing."

His large hands curl to rest, upturned on our table. "I guess," he says quietly, so quietly I can hear his knuckles rub the varnished wood, "I guess, . . . well, . . . we're expendable."

I would not have believed you could fit so many working boats into one small harbor. This afternoon, because of crowding, we were asked to leave the dock. So we moored fifty feet off the end of the fishing pier and tied up rail to rail with the *Agpa*, a two-year-old patrol boat of the Royal Danish Navy.

After Finn Lynge's talk, a few of us went aboard for a party with the *Agpa*'s crew and their friends from shore. Before long there were twenty-five people in the enlisted mess, a room that measured ten feet on a side. All available space that wasn't filled with flesh was filled with beer—case after case of it—and vodka chasers. Some crew. Bombed-out bimbos in a haze of smoke and rock 'n roll, they drank with an astounding single-mindedness to get drunk, holding an open bottle in each hand.

Two hours later, 146 empty bottles stood on the cabin's floor, and I stood halfway between the *Agpa* and *Regina* with a foot on each vessel's rail while heeding nature's call. The sound of recycled Tuborg trickling into Godthab harbor struck me as particularly exquisite and emblematic. As I listened and reflected warmly on the music in all God's creation, I became aware of less divine sounds farther down the rail. Turning (without stopping the essential operation), I caught sight of two people in the shadows talking excitedly while passing something heavy from rail to rail. I decided to check it out.

Steady now. Easy. Thump, thump: back on board. I took two steps along the quarterdeck and then smelled smoke. I leapt down the aft companionway and saw the flames.

Gregg, Patrick, Dave, and Fran stood in the port-side passageway with axes and extinguishers. The walls were black with soot. The air was dense with chemical foam. Charred mattresses lay strewn about the deck. Gregg chopped at a bulkhead in Bill's cabin as Fran sprayed the base of the blaze inside.

After a couple of minutes it was over. The fire had started across from my bunk; apparently some salt water leaking onto wires under Patrick's mattress caused short-circuiting. When he noticed smoke, Pat tore off the mattress and chopped through the plywood it had rested on. But as soon as the smoldering wires got oxygen, they burst into open flame. Then the extinguisher that lives in the main salon failed to function properly. It wasn't until Gregg sped to the engine room and brought back the giant CO_2 extinguisher that they got things under control.

After we cleaned up, I lay on my acrid sheets and thought about several things. I thought of the wires I was sleeping on and the network of twelve-volt batteries hooked up in series under every bed, connecting us all like a sinister mirror image of the rig above. I thought of the *Agpa,* with her steel hull, fire walls in every cabin, watertight compartments and automatic sprinklers in the engine room—and by contrast, of this vessel, as authentic in the dangers she presents as in the pleasures she provides. And just before passing out, I remembered the old man in seaboots on the dock at Corner Brook: "You expect to cross the Davis Strait in *that?*"

4 August. Godthab.

At night on the foggy fish pier, dozens of lights on the masts of shrimpers and trawlers swayed in unison as their rigs tinkled gently in the breeze. A spanking new freighter, *Snowdrop,* had put in. Her decks were floodlit, but her high sides kept the pier below in shadow.

Lolling in that shadow for a while, I watched my shipmates come and go while I played the *flâneur* of Godthab, savoring the anonymity, the calm spectatorship, the fishy air. When someone came out for a smoke on the *Snowdrop*'s brow, I waved hello. The man waved back, introduced himself in English, and invited me aboard.

Einar was a short squat fellow in his forties with thinning flaxen hair. His cheekbones supported an astonishing expanse of flesh, with nary a trace of wrinkles, or of chin—in short, a perfect moon. We toured the ship. He was very kind and very out of shape; on the fifth step of a nine-step companionway, his breath came hard. In his cabin he mixed vodka into orange soda, and we sat down to talk.

My host was a Faroe Islander, like everyone else on board. His father had worked on a three-masted schooner that carried fishermen out to smaller boats on the Greenland banks until he was lost at sea. Einar has worked in the merchant navy for eighteen years.

He mixed another round. We were running low on soda, but had plenty of Stolichnaya. Because of the subject of my dissertation (Scottish literature), I happened to know a fair amount, tangentially, about the Faroe Islands and their nationalist cultural revival, including their ceremonial whale hunt called the *grinda-bod.* The Faroese still hunt pilot whales, he told me. When a large school is sighted, a call goes out for all available boats. These

173

converge, outflank the animals, and corral them into a selected cove. Then everyone on board the boats begins to slap the water with flat stones. This confuses the whales. Some mistake the sound for surf and swim away from it, toward the beaches. Others follow and start to ground themselves by the score. The people assigned to wait on shore approach the animals in the shallows and kill them "instantly" by thrusting a special knife behind the blowhole. Later, the meat is divided evenly and boiled in a stew.

It was strange to hear Einar describe the process so benignly. I was surprised (and secretly appalled) to hear that it still goes on. I had read that the spectacle of a hundred panicked whales who die by suffocation or lie gasping, paralyzed, with severed spinal chords is not nearly as "clean" as my kind host claimed. Now I didn't know how to connect it with his smiling face.

5 August. 64°N/53°W.

At 0600 hours we departed Godthab, and after a long day of sailing transects, hove to at 2300 hours in much the same place that we had started.

I have torn open the old jigging cut in the crease of my index finger again. Thanks to wet hemp and cold salt water, this keeps happening; after seven days I can still see down to the dermis, a livid shade of red. When I showed it to Patrick, he asked me if there are any plants on board. I replied that there is one, the little cactus in the pilothouse. "It's an aloe plant," he said. "Old sailor's remedy. Go put some on." In the pilothouse, just before slicing through the stem, I hesitated: It was the largest plant I had seen in thirty days.

We found eleven humpback whales today—and still not a single match with any in the catalog or with those we've previously sighted.

Toward dusk we found another whale, or rather, part of one, in an advanced stage of decomposition. It was a sperm whale, and when Don wanted a closer look at it, George was forced to come about and approach from upwind on account of the terrible odor. The huge face was riddled from the peckings of birds, discolored and badly bloated, and its eyes were gone. Worse still, the floating head was not connected to a body, for the animal had been sliced in half.

It seemed like there had been a rare and freakish accident, but when I asked about it, Don said no. Cetaceans nap on the surface, he explained, and it's not uncommon for oblivious ships to run them down. When a tanker recently arrived in California with a fin whale impaled on its bow, the crew didn't even know that it was there.

6 August. 62°N/52°W. Fyllas Bank.

Once again the day's log is a jumble of crisscrossed tracks and VMOs (various maneuvers ordered). This is because of our luck with finding whales; we have seen and chased another nine. It also reflects the reason for their abundance: We were back along the ice edge, where the ocean is most fertile and most dangerous, with a new pack drifting toward us. For the first time in nearly a month, the horizon showed a telltale glare and the absence of all color.

By midafternoon we were skirting the pack itself. This was fresh ice, more slush than solid, still forming. To pick our way through it in the mist, with the engine growling dully, and condensation dripping from the earrings on our spars, was to enter a maze whose walls were in constant motion. Whatever the opportunity in terms of our research, for the ship this situation represented danger. It warned that the season had begun to turn. The time had come to head for home.

Just before first dogwatch, George set a course for the west, with the sun skewered on *Regina*'s bowsprit. Greenland lay thirty-five miles astern, our landfall eight hundred miles before us. We were truly on our own again, alone with each other's rhythms, and the sea's.

1900 hours. Second dogwatch. This time of day is like promenade hour in little Spanish towns. The evening watch is waiting to go on at 2000 hours, the people who will have the midnight watch are taking a breather before they snatch a few hours' sleep, the idlers are relaxing after supper, and if the weather is halfway decent, all of them are likely to be taking a turn on deck.

Tonight the weather was more than fine. We were out of the coastal fog but still in the Greenland Current. The sky was pink, and finny, and the seas so dark they were almost black, except for the foam that slid along each crest like runny frosting. Astern, the pack ice was no longer visible, nor the shore itself, nor the sides of the grim volcanic mountains—only their chalky peaks, which caught the sunset like a rising moon, with a mottled glow of apricot and rose. The jumpiness of the first day out had given way to gentleness, a sense of "here we go again." Amidships, almost the entire crew had gathered.

In the middle of the group, on the port settee, sat Bill, with a concertina, and Root, with his guitar. At the break of the poop deck, George was belaboring his fiddle. Gregg had another guitar, Helene her recorders, Kathy a penny whistle. Judy and Toni sat on the paint locker. Rob and Jack leaned back on their elbows, letting their heads hang upside down across the windward rail. They were looking straight up at the maintop, feeling the wind through their hanging hair.

Then Peter launched into a song in dialect about a man who went out on Ilkly Moor without his hat, alas, and perished of the cold, alack, and was turned into food for ducks. This was set to the tune of a carol. Everyone joined in the chorus. Viewed from above, on the mainmast shroud, they seemed suddenly so small, this little circle, making music, clustered on a floating stage, with the ocean darkening all around and the land behind dissolving into memory. Most of the faces of the people below were in shadow, individual features fading, chins and hair and noses lit by the red glimmer like heads around a hearth.

As I started to swing down through the tangle of rope and ladders strung about me, I thought back to a conversation earlier today with Lawrence. Just after breakfast, I found him standing outboard on the channels, near the starboard mizzen shroud. He had found a fracture in the giant bottle screw into which a backstay fastened. This was serious, since the counterbalanced tension of the stays is what holds up the mast, like guy wires on a radio tower. Fran had constructed a steel splint, which Lawrence had then bolted onto the bottle screw. It would hold for a while. But it altered the tension on the backstay and made it necessary to adjust the opposing stays (four on each side) by backing off or tightening other bottle screws with a crowbar and a monkey wrench that weighed ten pounds.

Only when we had finished with the mizzen did I realize that we had just begun—that the mizzenmast, in turn, was connected by other stays to the mainmast, the mainmast to the foremast, the foremast to the jib boom, and so on. A single web distributed the tension over every inch of rig; no part, even the stoutest mast, stood on its own; the whole thing held together thanks to counterbalanced stress, so that a change in any single part affected every other.

As Lawrence eyeballed the fore topmast and hung by his hands from a stay to test its give, I asked how he'd learned to do that. "This? It's just—" he paused—"routine." He tightened a bottle screw one quarter turn.

"What do you call it?"

"Tuning the rig."

A long day later, as I stepped on deck to join in my shipmates' music, *Regina* indeed seemed like one great instrument, with her fretted shrouds, the chord of her sails, her belaying pins like tuning pegs, her hull the ocean's sounding board, her lignum vitae and mahogany, her oak and teak, her taut proud beauty and her lines that hum like harpstrings in the wind—an instrument that we, together, play.

When I first came on board, I thought that the whole world owed me. I was ready to make music, damn it. I was disappointed, angry that so little in my life would stay in tune. But tonight, as I barely heard the sounds we made before they were blown astern, I understood such disappointment to be arrogance.

It is arrogance to expect that our life always be music. It is false pride to demand to know the score. Harmony, like a following breeze at sea, is the exception. In a world where most things wind up broken or lost, our lot is to tack and tune.

7 August. 62°N/55°W. Davis Strait.

"What do they taste like?" Brenda asks.

"Not a lot," says Peter. "Crunchy."

Lisa puts her finger down her throat and giggles. Deborah says, "Oh, gross."

It is lunchtime, second seating.

"How do get them out?" Earle asks.

"You use your fingers. Hold 'em in one hand like this, right? Reach into the gill, like so. Push through the brain." They are talking about fish eyes. "A great source of fluid," Peter says.

"And vitamin C," adds George.

"So ya don't just snarf 'em down," Fran concludes, with a sidelong glance at Deborah. "Roll 'em around on yaw tongue a while. And chew before ya swallow."

They are into their favorite topics now, food and disaster, and it's clear that the conversation, such as it is, can only go downhill. But the truth is, this no longer bothers me the way it used to. Is it that I expect less, or am I myself less in need of "meaningful" or clever conversation? I have certainly stopped straining to initiate it. I talk less at meals than I used to, and if others ramble on, it's just white noise.

When I mentioned this to Judy yesterday, she had an explanation. "People need personal space," she said. "Because there is no physical privacy on board, it has to be created artificially. Remember how, in the first few days, everyone would say hello when they met in passageways? But pretty soon we began to ignore each other, right? You have to. It's the same thing with conversation, don't you think? People feel more vulnerable in groups; it's too scary to lay yourself open on a serious or controversial subject. Also, though you might get bored at times, you wouldn't *want* someone or other laying their trip on you at every meal. The endless small talk is a tacit way of respecting each other's space. It creates a sense of privacy in unbearably close surroundings."

In the pilothouse this evening, George agreed. When it comes to small talk, he believes that it helps to regard a crew not as friends but as family, the one group of people for whom one should not have to look good or be brilliant or amusing in order to *belong*. For a group like ours to function in that way, everyone must feel that they have a niche in its structure, their own role. When a crew first gets together, all members—especially the younger ones—need to place themselves in relation to each of the others. Stuck in close quarters with strangers, they do this by means of conversation. All of the small talk (and especially the dumb talk) is a declaration of self, George said. In a way that more meaningful conversation couldn't, it conveys the message, "This is who I am and *who I have a right to be*. For me to feel comfortable here and entrust my life to you, I must feel that you accept me, warts and all."

8 August. 61°N/57°W.

At 0030 hours, just off watch, I was half asleep when Canan woke me. "Come back on deck," she said with her face flushed, out of breath. "You've got to see this." Moments later I stepped from the aft companionway into the strangest light I had ever seen. With the moon now down, the sky was awash with stars. And over them—or underneath them, I should say—was a vast translucent tissue: the aurora borealis. I had seen the northern lights before from railroad cars in Canada—a few faint pillars half a world away—but nothing could have prepared me for this sight.

They arched straight overhead, extending upward from the east and west horizons. Sometimes there were broad green bands, extremely bright though pale. Then these would transform themselves to giant Vs, then diaphanous pink sheets of light that covered half the sky. They were not vivid like lightning or electric storms but gauzy, gentle, grand. Long ripples that resembled sea swells moved across their surface, making the edges wrinkle and then grow smooth. And just as a sheer silk negligee reveals the flesh it covers, so this pastel light let the stars prod up against it, and the brighter constellations glittered through.

According to his biography in the crew list, second mate Bill Cowan has worked as first mate on windjammers "including *Victory Chimes, Mattie, Mercantile,* and *Mary Day."* That list omits his most recent berth before *Regina,* on the schooner that went down, and today I found out why.

The *John F. Leavitt* was a topsail schooner built three years ago in Maine. Paid for largely by a single owner, she was launched to demonstrate the renewed commercial feasibility of sailing ships in an era of shrinking energy supplies. Her construction became a labor of love for the yard crew and future captain and was exhaustively documented. Work in the yards was was recorded on film from A to Z, and a film crew went along on the maiden voyage.

Because of unforeseen delays (few living people had ever built a wooden ship that size), the *Leavitt* wasn't launched until November. Bound for the south with a load of timber, she met a fierce storm in her second week at sea.

What happened next is a matter of some dispute. But basically, things went from bad to worse: Apparently, the ship took on water; she shifted ballast; her cargo booms broke loose. Her crew failed to control the situation—or were not allowed to do so. At the captain's order, they abandoned ship. The *Leavitt* was never seen again.

The crew spent two days and nights in their raft. No one was lost, however. And along with the radio beacons that attracted rescue planes, they had managed to take six steel cans, which contained their whole experience on film. Ironically, it was this record of the ordeal that led to still more trouble.

When the footage was finally screened (it was edited into a full-length movie), a variety of questions arose. Some concerned judgment: None of the crew had offshore experience, and one doesn't normally choose the North Atlantic in November for a shakedown cruise. Some concerned skill: Was the ship overloaded or ballasted wrong? Some concerned ethics: Many who viewed the film observed that standard precautions such as preventers weren't used, that the ship wasn't actually going down and should not have been abandoned, and that the captain had simply panicked. Old-timers were especially offended by the sight of him sitting in the deckhouse, speaking melodramatically into his radio, knowing that he was being filmed. Was he thinking of his ship or of the movie? Of saving lives or saving face, and perhaps recovering costs? Given the hope and pride that had been invested in the vessel and the consequences of her loss for the tall ship world, those who would normally be most sympathetic felt the most betrayed.

If there was a young Lord Jim in this affair, it was Bill Cowan. His experience up to that point had been limited to coastal waters. Since a first mate is responsible for proper stowage, if the ballast or cargo had indeed broken loose, the blame was partly his. Maybe that explains his iron hand with the main watch on *Regina* and the variation in his moods. He is proving himself to himself, I suppose. In his nightmares he must hear the joke that was told to me in a fake Maine drawl: "Ayuh. That boat was called the *Leave-it,* an' that's just what they did."

Except for some oozy squash and onions, we are now clean out of produce. Al does what he can with what's left and still claims that his grub "tastes as good on the way back up as it did goin' down."

This is true. Still, roasts and salads have been replaced by a series of nondescript stews over which a cold war has developed.

In the first stage, people refuse to eat them. Al refuses to thaw more food until what has been cooked gets finished.

George commends his thrift.

Then everyone else resorts to peanut butter.

Al hides the peanut butter.

Folks complain.

"I can't *look* at this anymore," says Earle one night. He is pointing at "vegetable broth," the remains of yesterday's vegetable soup, which was served for lunch, and the vegetable stew we had the day before that, for dinner. "Then you betta drink up," says Al, "or you'll see it again tomorrah."

Today he has promised something different. While I soak the hulls off lima beans, he searches for something everywhere, muttering, "This'll move it" and "They'll love this." He's a little bit manic, so I keep away. I pump the daytank. Develop an interest in the Danish 50-øre coin from 1919 screwed into the base of the foremast and a New York City subway token nailed below.

"Haavy, I can't find the pa— pa— hot stuff . . . red . . . Hungarian."

"Paprika?"

"That's it."

"What are you cooking?"

"Al-osh. Hey, you know what we do in Maine all summah? Fish and fuck. You know what happens in the wintah? It's too cold to fish! Don't go away."

He steps into his cabin. I can hear him dragging something heavy out of hiding. Tearing cardboard. *"God damn shit piss mothafuckin' bastuds—"* I rush inside.

Al is sitting on the edge of the lower berth with his head between his hands, a man who has been wounded in his spirit. On the floor between his feet is a box containing twenty-four brown bottles. "What the matter?" I ask.

"When we got off the *Agpa* the otha' night, I took away a little present."

"You mean they gave—"

"Come on. They was too drunk to find their own dicks. I took a case of beer. Two cases. All right, three. That's three times faw— twelve six-packs."

"So?"

Speech failed him. He just pointed to the carton.

Were they broken? Had the seals gone bad? I removed one. Ginger ale.

All was not lost, however. This being Saturday, George had broken out some rum for grog. To get the proportions right before others came down, the cook and galley slave performed exhaustive sampling.

During second dogwatch, we encountered a hundred pilot whales. "Logging" on the surface lazily, with only their friendly bulbous heads exposed, they all faced our way and looked mightily amused as we sailed closer. Pretty soon they were joined by a school of dolphins. While the whales were content to bob alongside, the dolphins leapt and tumbled, flashing their white flanks in the sunset, churning the viridian ocean into foam.

At 2200 hours there were northern lights again. This time the display was violent, emitting a white light that flared and trembled like a ribbon of magnesium on fire. As if that were not enough, they overlapped a meteor shower. The whole sky was exploding silently.

It was beautiful. And frightening. If the spectacle made me feel this way, I could only imagine what a Portuguese peasant might have felt as he gazed up through the rig five hundred years ago and "knew" that the edge of the earth was near. Five hundred years before *him,* Norse sailors "knew" that these lights were a sign of war back home: the Valkyries' armor flashing as they came to collect the slain. I "know" that they are electrical disturbances, the Van Allen belts. I have read that in a book. But is this information knowledge? It doesn't diminish the wonder or assuage the terror—not at all. What does it mean to "know" this way?

What does it mean to not know and admit it?

"You OK?" Helene asked, at the rail beside me.

"How about you?"

She glanced down at her dirty jumpsuit and held out her arms.

9 August. 59°N/57°W.

During the westward crossing, while our humpback research is on hold, the course in celestial navigation has begun. In classes twice each day, we learn about precession, Ptolemy, and Tycho Brahe. We do exercises and are quizzed on *Greenwich hour angles, Sumner lines,* and *local apparent noon.* Up on deck, there are audiovisual demonstrations, courtesy of the universe, and practice with the sextants. George is the professor; Patrick, Gregg, and Bill are his teaching assistants. The final exam will be a *three-body fix* using any combination of planets, moon, and stars, and to pass we will have to come within sixty miles of our true position.

From the sublime to the meticulous: What a thicket of words

and numbers! All are connected, every one is tricky, and each requires adjustments each step of the way. For example, it is not enough to shoot the moon or star you're looking for and "bring the body down." Having read its altitude from the sextant's scale, you must then begin to compensate for *index error* (particular to that sextant), *refraction* (light bends passing through the sky), *dip* (how high you are above the water), *horizontal parallax* (the angle from the surface versus the center of the body you are on), and *semidiameter* (the angle to the center, rather than the edges, of the body you are sighting). When you're finished with this, the observation stage, all that remains is to compute a triangle between Greenwich, Aries, and your navel, based on numerical readings combined with *chronometer error, watch difference,* daily increments for the sun and moon and planets (or *precession* if you're using stars), and the distance of your time zone from Greenwich, which must be adjusted for daylight savings, which must be adjusted for distance from the edge of your own zone.

I will not attempt to set down how one does all this. Suffice it to say that I am now as utterly ensnared in cosines as I was six weeks ago in leechlines and preventers. Still, after three days' practice, I am able to "swing the sextant" and work through the tables. Just this morning I confirmed beyond all doubt that we are in the Northern Hemisphere.

This morning's sunlines are likely to be our last for a while; by noon the sky had clouded over and the wind had turned northwesterly. So we braced up sharp on a starboard tack and continued to crawl along, making five knots or less. We are halfway across.

The afternoon was no less dismal, with everyone who was not on watch asleep. In the aft salon, George and I found each other in reflective moods. We started talking about writing and moved on to television, and then to 1940s politics and public figures in his father's circle whom George had met or known. I asked whether the leaders of that era—the Roosevelts and Churchills—seemed to him, as they do to me, of a different order from the leaders in my time. Yes, he replied, they had a certain quality—what Finn Lynge possessed, in fact, the other night at dinner. "Did you see," George asked, "the way the students responded, not just to his words, but to his presence? They were awestruck. They don't often see that in American politicians, that sense of *calling,* of politics as a duty, of real belief in one's country." George was required on deck. He stepped outside.

Five minutes later he was back, sitting down beside me, saying, "What does one do with all this? As one gets older, he has more information, more experiences—but, for instance, where does it fit that in 1942 I listened as Henry Stimson said, 'Watch this Colonel Eisenhower; he's a comer'?"

This was a way we hadn't talked before. Soon we moved on to marriages, to wives and lovers, fathers and sons. George said that what kept him sane through medical school in wartime were the Sunday visits to his parents' home: walks with his mother, sails with his father, their "shared interest in the sea."

As I listened, I thought, "So that's where a captain's confidence comes from." I was struck by the sense of entitlement, the entitlement of an aristocrat, unvoiced because it had always been assumed, from an early age. I was struck by the congruity of all that he described. Whatever challenges George took on, they all seemed of a piece; a sense of legacy and of continuity was involved. I feel no such congruity in my own life and never have.

Is it too late for that? In Godthab, I had purchased some tiny oilskins for a nephew. As George and I finished talking, I realized that they wouldn't go to my sister's child after all. I would put them in storage—just in case—for mine.

10 August. 57°N/57°W.

"All happy families resemble one another; but each unhappy family is unhappy in its own way." Tolstoy, of course. Within the extended family that is *Regina,* the nuclear families are the watches. By now there is no one on board who shrinks from any standard duty, and no watch is "better," or more reliable, than any other. Still, it's interesting to see how differently they accomplish the same work and how each has evolved its own particular style and ways of resolving trouble.

The members of the main watch are *Regina*'s solid soldiers, regular guys and gals. They are all about twenty years old, future biologists, serious, smart, a bit conventional perhaps, but uniformly pleasant. Of the three mates, Bill is the most inclined to give orders, and the people on his watch are the most inclined to receive them. Early on, he gave daily quizzes on the rigging. Similarly, with navigation, he doesn't try to make them understand the concepts the techniques are based on but simply leads them, over and over, through the tables. (In both cases, they have learned "how to" faster than the rest of us.) Bill has a temper. Work and duty stations are assigned without discussion, and if someone slacks off, Bill comes down hard. No one on his watch seems to mind this, perhaps because he is consistent. So is their deckhand, Scott, a wonderfully energetic guy whose spirits are as bright as his red hair. Lately he and Helene have spent a lot of private time commiserating about their sweethearts back home. If that keeps up, they may soon forget to miss them.

The mizzen watch, by contrast, are a motley crew. In experience and age, they range from Rob, seventeen, to Francis, who is studying for his ship master's license. They include the laziest student and the hardest-working, Earle, plus two other very moody types. This ragtag collection is perfectly suited to the leadership style that their mate Patrick acquired during three years on the *Clearwater*. Whereas Bill tends to be controlling, Pat is almost anarchic, leaning heavily on group process. Thus he doesn't even use a fixed rotation. At the start of each watch, the members decide what each of them feels like doing, and from then on they shuttle informally among duty stations, taking care to cover for one another fairly. There are frequent midnight meetings to discuss how things are going, and "picnics" in the lab at four A.M., when they come off watch and share the delicacies they bought in Godthab. If two people in the watch are quarreling, Pat will not intervene, so they have to work it out between them. This can get pretty crazy; for instance, their deckhand, Al Abend, has refused to speak to Brenda for three days or even to tell her why. But when things are going well, the mizzen watch is the most spontaneous and loosest of the three.

Loose is not the first word that comes to mind about the fore watch. We are the oldest watch on board, the quirkiest and most curmudgeonly. As a group, I think we bring more intellectually to the voyage and are somewhat more thoughtful about what it means, beyond the science and adventure. Perhaps because we are older, or in some ways less conventional, we were from the start more physically afraid and less receptive toward authority (I can see now why sailors must be drafted very young). Preoccupied with running the ship, Gregg has offered less specific step-by-step direction to our watch than the other mates gave theirs, and this left Joan a bit over her head. Faced with Gregg's reticence to boss us around, or even to broach unpleasant subjects, and Joan's uncertain bossiness, we were initially caught between them like children caught between a strict and a lenient parent. By now that's changed; we are, for better or for worse, a unit. How much I like or dislike a member of my watch doesn't matter so much. We are like siblings, with our own way of doing things. We even take pride in how difficult we are and poke fun at our goody-goody "cousins" in the other watches. It's impossible to think of the fore watch with any member of it missing.

This is not to say there aren't times when I wish each and

every one of them would disappear—and I'm sure that the reverse is also true.

David and Root are doing dishes. Root is washing. David is rinsing. Root wears a Walkman on his belt, with the earphones slung around his collar. It's been a dull day, and Dave, typically, is doing all he can to deny it. Sometimes you want him not to be quite so helpful and so understanding, so terribly, terribly *good*.

"I'm reading a marvelous book," he declares. "Do you know *Too Late the Phalarope* by Alan Paton?" Root bends, grunts, and starts to transfer dirty dishes to the sink from a plastic tub on the galley floor.

"It's set in South Africa, of course, and concerns . . ." He is off and running. As Root begins scrubbing, Dave lays out the major characters; by the time the soapy plates reach his half of the sink, he is into plot. Sometime around Chapter Three (and silverware), Root slips on his earphones. Halfway through Chapter Four, he turns up the volume.

David goes on talking. "So, when she finally makes it to Johannesburg—" There are no more saucers coming his way. He looks over at Root, who has put down his sponge and is swaying, with his eyes closed.

Dave yanks his arm. Root's eyes open. "Say what?" he asks, but does not take off the earphones.

David tears them off. He looks like he could cry. "I've been *talking* to you for ten minutes."

"No. That long?"

"I think it's incredibly rude for you to—"

"Listen man. It was you who was talkin'. No one axed you to. I don't give a flyin' fuck about your phalarope. It's cold out there. I'm tired. I got dishpan hands."

"Wilson Pickett," Toni says.

"No way."

"Al Green?"

"Earlier."

We've been trying for three weeks to recall who sang "When

a Man Loves a Woman." We're amidships. As we continue to rule out most of the Motown stable, we notice an antlike trickle of people flowing toward the bow and decide to follow them around the forward deckhouse to the cathead.

If you think of the bowsprit as the upright of a cross, with the foot its forward end, then its crosspiece is the cathead, a massive beam from which the anchors are hung, or "catted," on either end. It is one of the muted glories of *Regina,* a beautifully grained, foot-square oak timber with countless coats of varnish and a tawny glow. It is concave in the center from eight decades' wear and is capped by a bronze lion head on either end.

Mightier still is the Sampson post, a vertical beam that runs down from where the cathead and the jib boom intersect, straight into the stem and keel. It is here that the mizzen watch has gathered around Deborah. In the last two days she has apparently gone on too long—even for her—about real estate and hygiene. Her watchmates' response to this landlubberly behavior was to convince her that the Sampson post had grown dangerously loose and needed "tightening." Now, to the chorus of their collective praise, she is working up a most unhygienic sweat, landing blow after blow with the eight-pound mallet. Meanwhile, Scott lies on his back beside the post, with a yardstick: "One more," he encourages her. "And another . . ."

"How is it now?" she asks.

"*Real* good. Just give it a half dozen more." She labors on.

"Are you sure it's really moving?"

"Are you kidding?" Scott holds up the yardstick with an inch marked off between his fingers. "A little more would be great," he says. "Another inch and you're there."

Fran is stretched out on her back on the table in the aft salon. There is a pillow underneath her head, and her mouth is open. George shines a flashlight into it and holds up a small mirror over Fran's right cheek, which is swollen to the size of a peach. On her left side, Francis bends, staring into the mirror while wadding some surgical gauze.

"When is the last time you saw a dentist, Fran?" he asks.

"Too recently. I hate those guys."

He smiles. Glances at the peanut butter jar filled up with alcohol, and reaches toward it, for the pliers.

On lookout at 0420 hours, I am slipping into Major Dull-out mode when Root appears. "It's cold as shit out here," he says. "I broughtcha somethin'." Out comes the Walkman, which he drapes around my neck, and the headphones, which I pull on. Click:

> Wayl, ye gas 'er up, behind the wheel,
> With your arm around your sweet woman in your
>   Oldsmobile,
> Barrelin' down the boulevard,
> You're lookin' for the heart of Saturday night . . .

He keeps me company while I listen to the whole side of the tape. I'm flipping the cassette to let him listen to the other side when out of the dark a body hurtles toward us from the deck-house roof. It lands on deck. It's David, singing: "Doooo-wop," pause, "Doooo-wop." Clay's body follows, thudding down just in time for him to add, "Bow, bow. Hot town, summer in the city/Back of my neck gettin' burnt and gritty/Bend down, isn't it a pity/Doesn't seem to be a shadow in the city."

Dave: "All around people lookin' half dead/Walkin' on the sidewalk hotter than a match head . . ."

By now Root has recovered from the shock. He and Dave stare at each other for a second. Then Root joins in: "But at night it's a different world/Go out an' find a girl . . ." Another few lines and the four of us are dancing up and down the frozen foredeck, wailing, "Babe, don't ya know it's a pity/The days can't be like the nights/In the summer, in the city, in the summer, in the city."

Yeah.

11 August. 55°N/57°W.

For the past three days the wind has been westerly at ten to fifteen knots. Square-riggers can't sail as close to the wind as fore-and-aft-rigged ships, so we've been snuffling along straight south down the middle of the Labrador Sea. Today even the headwinds died. We began to motor-sail and headed east-southeast toward Labrador. It is worth remembering that the Norsemen also had "auxiliary power"—oars—and that given a choice, anyone in his right mind would choose twenty lusty Vikings over *Regina*'s engine.

That excuse for a main is another of our fearless leader's great economies. It has kept Fran up almost every night since Greenland, and at this point it's hard to say which one of them grumbles more. Fran has still never traded combat boots for sneakers or attempted to climb even one step above the deck. But in the past week she seems to have positively lived below it. When she emerged briefly tonight and took her usual place beside the serving dish at supper, she reminded me of a toadstool with its damp gills turning brown.

I suppose I didn't look too stunning either, and I was in a less than charitable mood to begin with, because no one had awakened me for first seating. When I confronted Craig, who was galley slave, he said it had never occurred to him that I was sleeping. Why not? I asked. Because, he said, three people had been hammering bungs into the deck a foot above my pillow.

More work on navigation. With skies remaining overcast, it has been hard to take sunlines or moonlines. Where possible, we have used stars instead, seeking likely candidates in the Sight Reduction Table and locating them through the gaps in clouds. But despite the cooperation of Rasalhague and Altair, I continue

192

having trouble. Apart from my struggle with math, I have found it hard to visualize the angles and spatial relationships that the numbers themselves describe. I kept overcomplicating, in the way beginners do before they learn how to be simple, and the complications kept on getting in my way. In particular, I could not understand why the declination of fixed stars doesn't vary drastically from different points on earth. Finally, in an effort to keep me (and themselves) from going crazy, Bill and Francis sat me down for some remedial cosmology.

Location, they began, is by definition relative to someplace else. The open ocean is unmappable, because it's all the same, so a map must be deduced and transferred onto it from some external source. That source is the sun and moon and stars.

Forget Copernicus, they said. In the Ptolemaic system, there are two concentric spheres—the starry one, and earth, which nests inside it like an orange inside its peel. What you are doing when you navigate is draw converging lines from "signposts" on the outer sphere to a known and unknown spot on the inner one, to triangulate (mark off) a section of its surface. On the cosmic scale, the whole earth is so small that it lacks meaningful dimension. In relative terms, it is a dot, a speck, a geometric point, so the measurements that one may use to navigate are merely angles, not physical distances. What Ptolemy intuitively grasped (and I could not) was that they don't *have* to be. You derive the necessary truth from a serviceable fiction. You can use a realm that you do not inhabit to measure the one you do.

12 August. 54°N/56°W.

"Land ho!" came the cry from the royal yard. The fore watch was on, and at 0954 hours, through patchy fog, Kathy had sighted Labrador.

Everyone poured on deck with great excitement and stood chattering in the rain. To celebrate, I appeared in my new sou'-wester hat. I had purchased it in Godthab, a marvelously grim black item, complete with earflaps and a chinstrap. The reaction this produced among the others was less than grim, alas. Among peels of laughter, it was suggested that I see how it felt with the front brim facing forward.

The last laugh, however, was on them. Leaving Greenland, we had agreed on a lottery to predict the time of our eastward landfall. I had predicted 0740 hours on August 12. That is the time, within an hour, that George identified Cape Harrison, and I became twenty-nine dollars richer for it. With my hat turned around so that the rain streamed off my back instead of down my collar, I gloated, faced the wind, and instructed my detractors: *Call me Oxenhorn!*

But that's not what they called me.

In reflecting on this journey, I have tried to make note of anything that a friend might need to know, or want to learn, about events, people, and places. I have tried to be accurate, and fair. What is harder than the details, however, and harder by far than the high and low points, is the time that is unremarkable in any way, yet comprises ninety percent of our life on board. This time is both ordinary and deeply affecting; it is hard to talk about directly without heightening—and therefore distorting. Perhaps the best approach is to describe the feeling associated with it. And for that, two very different images come to my mind.

One is a tupilak. This is an amulet, made by East Greenland Eskimos, that I purchased as a wedding gift in Godthab. It is freestanding, carved from a sperm whale's tooth, and like most tupilaks it is all of a piece but contains two different parts. The bottom half is an animal head (in this case an arctic fox), while the top is a semihuman face, skull-like, with flared nostrils, stylized geometric wrinkles, a macabre grin. Beneath its chin, above the fox's head, this *thing* holds its elbowless arms extended, with its webbed hands meeting at the fingertips.

The dual form is in keeping with its function, as a hunting charm to attract the prey and to ward off harm. Yet the roots of its design reach deeper. When an Inuit shaman was once asked what he believed in, he replied, "We do not believe. We fear." From the little that I have learned about old Inuit religion, I gather that the fear this shaman spoke of was not death—not even in a world where it is always close at hand—but that man would revert to the status of the beasts he hunted. That he himself could become what he strove to kill.

I keep that tupilak, for now, beside my pillow. I'm not sure exactly how I feel about it. But I know that its fusion of wonder and terror speaks to me. Why? It is impossible, I suppose, to live in this century and not fear a reversion to barbarism, on a scale never known before, or to deny the presence of the beast in one's own self. I do know that the shaman's words ring truer, to my ears, than more theistic and redemptive creeds.

The fear they instill is a wise fear: To fear nature leads one to respect it and to continue to receive what it provides, and to recognize the beast in oneself is already to transcend it. But as Montaigne wrote, "It needs courage to be afraid." That is why most people will do anything in order not to face the fear that my tupilak embodies. Above all, we dread the spaces where such fear slips in. And to avoid admitting it, we are trained to fill those spaces, to turn up the speed and volume. Wage war on the ordinary. Make it always *special;* make it go away. In constant, unacknowledged flight from tragic recognition, we equate pleasure with entertainment, and entertainment with distraction from our fear. What we seek to do is complicate, and thus obscure, the shaman's message. His fear finds expression as our fear of being bored.

Which leads me to my other image, of a drawing room on Beacon Hill, in Boston. It belongs to an elderly woman whom I call on every couple of months. Surrounded by plum-colored walls, impressionist art, and framed ancestral portraits, we talk more animatedly than I do with other friends one-third her age. By birth, she is as Brahmin as they come, the widow of a famous man of letters, and their home, when she was young, was filled with erudite and charming people. Yet recalling the four decades since he died (she told me recently), she is struck by how much her life falls into phases and, what's more, how discrete and discontinuous those eras are—not a single life at all, but many. Now approaching her tenth decade and still active (planning antinuke events and directing plays), she said that she no longer spends much time with "intellectuals."

"What sort of people *do* you see?" I asked.

"Interesting ones," I thought she said. But she had mumbled, so I checked again.

"Did you say 'interesting'?"

"Good God, no. Who could maintain that standard? Everyone is boring. All of us."

"What *did* you say?"

"Interest*ed.*"

"In you?" I asked. (She had touched a nerve.)

"In *life,*" she replied, with a wave of her palsied hand.

What brings the shaman and the dowager together, what brought them both to mind, was an experience I had last night. It was past eleven, in our twelfth hour on watch that day. Things were quiet. We were all dog tired. Lisa, Dave, and Joan were up on bow, and Kathy had the wheel. On deck it was so black that I could not make out her expression, and I tripped on the step up to the quarterdeck. But by now the ship is like a lover stretched beside you in the dark—so familiar that you visualize her every feature, recognize (by sound, smell, touch) what you cannot see.

Thus "feeling" my way aft, in the broadest sense, I stepped into the pilothouse with Gregg and Clay.

Both doors were open. Clay and I stood four feet apart and leaned against their frames. Between us, Gregg stood back against the after bulkhead. Out of the pocket of his canvas jacket he produced three cheap cigars. We lit all three from a single match and settled back in silence.

Except for a question here, a comment there, that silence went on, unbroken, for a long time. For a long time we just stood together, just—existing—in the lap of water, glow of gauges, mingled reek of the cheap cigars. Once in a while, Gregg watched up through the skylight, checking the trim of our sails. Clay stepped out, flicked his ash across the rail; its embers blew back, brightening, then disappeared. Inside again, he drew on his cigar to keep it going, and his face was lit up, orange, from below. When he exhaled, I felt the smoke I couldn't see against my ears.

That is all that happened. We were together. Working. Tired. We didn't have anything to say, or any need to say it.

At that that moment I felt very close to my friends, and to myself, and to the quiet, sad, persistent heart of things. I felt a peace that had eluded me in grander moments, on the ice cap, say, or in the gale. And I realized that they had not been the end to which all our quiet work and patience were the means but vice versa. That what we are educated to call "boredom" is perhaps better thought of as space or neutral emptiness. As possibility allowed to be just that. As grounding our faith in repetition. The journey out, I thought, is marked by danger. But persistence (Go on, say it: boredom) is the ticket home.

And so we stood there, smoking. Willing not to move.

At length the butts were flicked across the leeward rail, and each man spoke.

"I've got the bow."

"I'll take a turn on deck."

"I'll do the log."

HELM

13 August. 54°N/56°W. Eagle Cove, Labrador.

Juniper, tamarack, cloudberries, blueberries, sundews, milkwort: *land!*

I am sitting with Peter and Toni on orange sphagnum moss beside a pond the color of tea, overlooking a glassy cove. It is ten P.M., and the deep sponge of browns and greens that spreads out in all directions is made even more lush by the light of sunset. After twenty-one days off Greenland and another nine at sea, the fragrance is intense, the low growth a relative jungle.

Peter and I are naked. The pond (as we've just found out the hard way) contains two feet of water and one foot of silt; my shins look like they have been rolled in flour. Peter sits drying beatifically on a mound of caribou moss. With his stubby calves, his big flat feet, and his expression of patient wonder, he seems like a bearded toddler or a tenured elf.

Six hundred feet below, the ship swings on her anchor, trailing a long, slow arc of silver ripples. Slopes on the far side of the cove look exactly as they must have looked a thousand years ago, when the people of the Greenland saga completed this same crossing, fell on their knees to drink dew, and found it "the sweetest liquor they had ever known."

We are spending the night at anchor here for shelter. Yesterday, after sighting land and altering course for the south, we encountered dirty weather. By this morning we were taking long swells broadside, rolling ten degrees to port and eighteen to starboard. By this afternoon the wind had climbed to thirty-four knots; there were whitecaps and thick fog and approaching squall lines off our quarter. So we scandalized the main, bucked across a current toward the shore, and ducked behind Stony Island.

Then we continued inland into ever more protected coves, where the water grew still and we couldn't even hear the wind. We dropped the hook here during second dogwatch, and some of us lowered away for shore.

That was almost two hours ago. It is now getting dark. Peter and Toni are dressed and ready to return to the ship. I tell them to go ahead and watch them descend until they slip from view. Then it's just me, and the great, grim, shadowed landscape, and *Regina.*

This is the farthest I've been from the ship in weeks, and I've never looked down on her before from such a distance, in such isolation. Watching the gentle swing of the amber anchor light—the one bright spot in an all-too-total wilderness—I can't get over how little the vessel seems, which when I am on board is my home, my life, my world. Viewed from this outcrop, through encroaching darkness, she looks like a ship in a bottle—the message, in an unknown language, that the bottle, adrift, contains. We have taken her—she's taken us—from the Boston waterfront to Disko Bay, and now to here. The how is clear; the why is as mysterious, or more, than the migration of birds.

Nightfall. Green becomes purple and black. Down to the inlet. Flash my light. The putt-putt of the jolly boat. My name called over water. Climb up the channels. Anchor watch. Playing guitar on the foredeck. A big moon.

14 August. 52°N/55°W. Due East of Belle Isle.

After hoisting the anchor and sails at half past five this morning, we rounded Stony Island and rode south on the inshore stream of the Labrador Current. The water was frigid. Seas remained high from yesterday's storm. But the barometer had risen, bringing clearing, and a northwest breeze blew steady at fifteen knots.

We are approaching Newfoundland and beginning to meet a lot of humpbacks. As a group they seem more active than the ones that we encountered farther north. Yesterday morning several of them "flippered" and "lobtailed"—that is, slapped the water, making a noise we could hear from quite far off. Today a pair of juveniles breached repeatedly. As I lay in the bowsprit net, another whale relaxed almost directly underneath me; I could see the "stove bolts," or hair follicles on its head, and its snow-white flippers (twice the length of my whole body) sculling underwater. Climbing down a shroud ten minutes later, I turned to find that a full-grown whale had "spy-hopped"—that is, risen almost vertically—to get a better view of me.

To observe a forty-ton mass erupting through the surface, waterfalls trailing along its flanks and whirlpools eddying off its flippers, is to experience the engine of the natural world as frighteningly Other. But to have that engine turn and peer into your eyes, with a benign and speculative gaze, is to feel that perhaps the Otherness is not so other after all, to appreciate that you and it are looking at each other.

While my friends watch whales, I also watch the watchers, with their arms stretched out like wings across ratlines; legs spread-eagled, one boot two feet higher than the other; hanging off a windward shroud by one hand, sixty feet above the rail; sitting sidesaddle on the bowsprit snapping photographs, oblivious to its plunge. In silhouette especially, these positions are heroic, like figures in a landscape by Millet or a grand historic canvas by David.

Yet this is not the posturing I observed way back in Corner Brook; it's unself-conscious. Time spent aboard a small ship redistributes weight throughout one's body, lowering the center of gravity and focusing strength in the pelvis, belly, and thighs. And medical evidence is emerging from work with dyslexic students that the constant rocking from side to side promotes a physiological integration between right and left sides of the body and functions of the brain.

Call it body language if you will. Not the body saying, "This is me," but the body in a conversation with the forces that pass

through it—gravity, the energy of waves. As that dialogue continues, ceaselessly, the illusion of *stability* (as something we are
granted) gives way to the reality of *balance* (a process we achieve).

2300 hours. Alone, on helm. Because of the moon, it is very
bright, but because of the fog, that brightness is diffused, and
everything lacks edges.

Noises are also muffled. Fog blowing through the rig makes
a different sound from wind alone; there's a slushy feeling to it,
and I can hear it rubbing what it passes through. On either side
of the compass, long brass tubes called Flinders bars glow softly.
Inside the binnacle, compensating magnets hang like organ pipes
or clock chimes, or baleen.

On the helm at night you are not so alone as when on
lookout; you are with *Regina,* listening to what she has to say.
Darkness accentuates the vessel's speed and the force of water
rushing by. The sight of those mastheads circling is impossible to
get used to. Even harder to accept is the fact that they are under
your control. Grow careless, and you could tip her over, gybe her,
back the squares. It happens; tall ships do go down. Two dozen
people sleep below, your mates are somewhere aft, yet as you stare
at your two hands in the compass light's red glow, you could be
the last soul left on earth. You could be in outer space, among
the stars.

Ever since we came on deck, the moon (which is two days
short of full) has been rising slowly, as if climbing the port-side
mainmast shroud. On a hunch, I decide to try steering by it,
keeping the bright globe framed between two stays. Checking the
compass much less often, I can see that I don't need to be "glued"
to it. My method works; the course holds true.

We have given Belle Isle a wide berth tonight. At approximately 0400 hours we will round Cape Bauld. Tomorrow morning we will dock ten miles from where John Cabot landed back
in 1497, with the site of Leif Ericsson's landfall, 497 years before
that, five miles beyond.

Five hundred years ago, European mariners would sail north

to a point where the sun had the desired altitude and turn west, continuing until they reached this shore. This approach was called "latitude sailing." Earlier, the Vikings reached here by a similar technique, keeping Polaris at a fixed height on their right, or "star board" side. As I thought of them now and steered by the rising moon, I had to laugh. The idea that they perfected thirteen hundred years ago was the one I had just discovered on my own.

15 August. Docked, St. Anthony, Newfoundland.

St. Anthony is the main town of Newfoundland's northeast peninsula. We arrived here along with the rising sun—indeed, we seemed to ride in on its rays—and had all four lines on shore by 0700 hours. This is a brief stop to take on passengers and water; by sunrise tomorrow we'll be on our way. At morning meeting, George ran down the list of names of people who will join us for a five-day sail. These are potential backers; he is eager to create a good impression and urged all hands to make them welcome.

We will also be joined by his wife, Ann, and their children: Dominica, who is two, named for the island off of which she was conceived, and Pierce, age four and already a seasoned sailor. As George mentioned them, his eyes lit up, and his face grew almost boyish with anticipation.

Port or no port, it was Saturday, so we began by holding field day. Only when the ship was spotless did anyone set foot ashore. Anyone, that is, except the fore watch. For the sixth time in seven port calls, we had drawn the first anchor watch. Since there would be more work to do after lunch, when supplies arrived, this meant that after eleven days at sea, Gregg and a couple of others might not get off at all. In private, he asked

George to juggle the schedule just this once. George turned him down.

After lunch, with everything shipshape, I hitchhiked out of town to L'Anse-aux-Meadows. This was the spot where, on a hot summer day like this one, 980 years ago, Leif Ericsson set foot ashore. Having crossed the Davis Strait from Greenland, he had discovered a country with black spruce, clear streams, white beaches, and a sloping shore. This place was southern Labrador. Lief called it Markland—Land of Forests—and sailed on. Some 165 nautical miles south, he sailed between a wooded island and a cape jutting out to the north of the mainland.

A Norse saga, *Tale of the Greenlanders,* tells what happened next: "They steered a westerly course past the cape and found great shallows at ebb tide, so that their ship was beached and lay some distance from the sea. But they were so eager to go ashore that they could not wait until the tide rose under their ship. They ran up the shore to a place where a stream flows out of a lake, where they cast anchor." After the tide rose, they towed the ship to shore, "took their sleeping bags ashore and built themselves shelters. Later they decided to stay here during the winter and set up large houses. There was no lack of salmon either in the river or the lake, and it was bigger salmon than they had ever seen. Nature was so generous here that it seemed to them no cattle would need any winter fodder, but could graze outdoors. There was no frost in winter, and the grass hardly withered. The days and nights were more equal than in Greenland or Iceland. On the shortest day of winter the sun was up between breakfast time and late afternoon."

The cape that this passage describes was Cape Bauld; the island, Belle Isle; the shallows, Épaves Bay. As I stepped from the car this afternoon, I saw the long shallow beach and long grass moving in the breeze. On either side of the clear stream that still ran through it stood mysterious mounds overgrown with grass and some reconstructed Viking dwellings.

Like the colony at Red Bay, this site remained undiscovered, though long sought, until recent times. Only in 1960 did the

Norwegian Helge Ingstad undertake a systematic search for the true Vinland. When he reached L'Anse-aux-Meadows, the strange mounds were the tip-off. Excavations over the next eight years revealed what they concealed and made it possible to construct a facsimile of the village.

Inside the "great house," I lay back on a raised earth bench beside the firepit. I closed my eyes and imagined myself shut in for the duration of a gale, the wind making muffled thuds on the sod walls three feet thick, my knees drawn up under bearskin rugs among equally rough and shaggy faces with their eyes grown watery from peat smoke as they stared into the stone oil lamp, the only point of light within eight hundred miles.

From there I moved to the actual ruins. Foundations, anyway; there are eight in all. Beside the great hall had stood several smaller ones, with space for ninety people. There was a sauna paved with pebbles, a cooking pit lined with cobblestones, a chapel, and a forge.

Not all of this was built by Leif Ericsson. Two larger groups of colonists joined his original settlement later and stayed long enough to encounter aboriginal Americans. Whether those people were Indian or Eskimo isn't clear, but the Norsemen found them horribly ugly. Calling them Skrellings, a term of contempt meaning "scrawny ones" or "weaklings," they killed three kayaksfull without provocation in the year 1005. During this brief encounter, the Skrellings themselves were not too scrawny to kill the Norse leader, Leif's brother Thorvald.

Though peace was achieved and trading resumed, relations went awry again the following year when a certain Karlsnevi's bull came bellowing past this meadow toward the astonished Skrellings, who fled and did not return for twenty days. When they did come back, they brought with them a terrifying ballistic weapon that flew overhead with an almost supernatural sound. In his account of these events, from which I have borrowed freely, Samuel Eliot Morison suggests that this weapon was the inflated bladder of a moose. If so, the great Vikings were spared defeat by bladder only by the quick, fierce mind of Eric the Red's bastard daughter. Baring her breasts, she slapped them with a sword and screamed. The Skrellings ran away.

As a quick fix, this worked fine. But the colonists had had enough and packed for home. Perhaps to protect their reputation, they attributed Thorvald's death to a uniped (one-footed giant). And just before casting off, they murdered five innocent Skrellings they'd caught sleeping on the shore. Within a century, all they had built had burned, sunk, and been absorbed into the bog.

Strolling along Black Duck Creek, I discovered chunks of bog iron on its banks; these had supplied the Norsemen's slag. On the outside they resembled rabbit spoor; inside, they were vermilion. Farther on, where the stream became an inlet, I found northern coral. All of the chunks were small and rounded and did not appear broken off. Five minutes' work with a knife revealed why: They had fastened themselves around pebbles like ruffs on the necks of Elizabethan ladies and grown until the underlying stone was lost to view.

Climbing up to a sheltered niche, with ground cover rich as a Berber rug, I arranged a half dozen chunks of coral on the ground. The sun was going down and turning golden. In its polarizing rays, the waxy leaflets shone and trembled. The whiteness of white against such foliage, deep green and misted by the sea, bearing bunchberries, scarlet partridge berries, and blue iris, took my breath away.

I found myself kneeling, looking out to sea. Across Épaves Bay, in the Strait of Belle Isle, an archipelago lay scattered like my coral. Thunderheads were piled high above the Great and Little Sacred Isles, which were gathering pink fog like cotton candy. To the north, the coast of Labrador stretched out in sunlight. In the Strait a light chop sparkled. Wavelets piled up the long beach gently, seeming to walk past me, continuing onshore in one long unbroken motion that was then expressed as ripples in the grass.

My vantage point was an obvious choice, a kind of natural throne. Most likely some of the Norsemen, maybe Leif himself, had sat where I sat now. As I opened to the mildness of the breeze and the sweetness of the land, I tried to imagine what they would have wished for, felt, and seen.

In the chapel back at the dig site was an anteroom where the settlers left their shields on entering. Primitive boasters that they may have been, autocthonous to dark cold seas, they still knew what our culture is so busily forgetting: To worship, you must first take off your armor.

I lay back on the undergrowth. As the weight of my body crushed it, leaves and berries, the scent of juniper rose through my hair.

"Harvey, me by!" called Patrick. I had just stepped into the main salon, at seven. To welcome the guests on board there was wine, and everyone was present in one seating. At the starboard table alongside George sat his wife and children and their nanny; a large bald middle-aged man and a teenage boy who looked just like him, only on a smaller scale, with hair; Peter and Toni and Don Patten, with his daughter. Most of the crew had fled to the port-side table, where, from the look of things, they had done justice to the wine. With so many extra bodies wedged in, they were almost falling off the benches. Everyone was flushed. The whole scene looked like something out of Brueghel.

"Come here, by!" Pat shouted, and made space beside him. Others called out greetings. Once I had been wedged in, Patrick tried to pour me wine over his shoulder, holding the bottle like a flagon. As he missed my cup, I turned to get some food. But the serving dishes were all empty. When the others noticed, they began to pass scraps of meat and salad from their own plates down the table toward me. This sudden flow was funny—but not as funny as they seemed to think. It increased, and then accelerated, turning raucous and then finally erupting into a full-fledged food fight between Gregg and Judy.

When I'd first come in, I had sensed something slightly wrong. The crew were not just a little drunk; they were trying too hard to *act* it and ignoring the guests and children in the process. So no one on our side noticed when George excused himself from the other table, stood up, and left abruptly. A few minutes later he stalked back in with his thin lips quivering and barked across the cabin, "Put it down." The guests looked up. He had singled out Gregg.

Gregg froze, still smiling for a second, with his arm drawn back.

"You stop that. Stop that this instant."

Gregg had already stopped. He was also standing up, all eyes upon him, with a piece of lettuce dangling from his hand. He looked, and no doubt felt, absurd.

Still George went on: "What is wrong with you? You're supposed to show some leadership. Responsibility." George wheeled and took off down the aft port passageway.

It felt like a plug had been pulled. Dominica started crying, the nanny started fussing, and Peter reengaged our guests in talk. After the shortest possible proper pause, Ann rose and went aft. The crew got up in twos and threes, scraped their plates, and left by the forward hatch.

It was just before eight. I was off until four A.M. and planned to go into town. On the way past my bunk, I saw George standing by himself in his lower cabin, staring at the wall. I went to the head. A few minutes later, his door was shut. From behind it, I could hear a woman's voice, not Ann's: "How dare you speak to him that way?"

"Fuck him."

"Which one?"

"Fuck George."

We had been in the bar two hours.

"You know he fired Gregg once before."

"No shit? For what?"

"On another trip. George was having lunch down below and the ship changed course. Gregg was chasing whales."

"What's wrong with that?"

"He was doing it without orders. Under sail."

"George fired him for *that?*"

"That was part of it. You know Gregg thinks the crew should

have a say in science, like on *Westward.* He thinks there's too much emphasis on sailing. He wants more to do with education. George thinks his crew's job is to sail the boat."

"Typical."

"He's right, man. You can have only one captain."

"Who has to prove he's captain every second?"

"He doesn't have to prove it. That's what being captain means. If a crew is *used* to taking orders, they'll act right when they *have* to."

"It's the opposite. If a captain is normally laid back with his crew, then when he does have to give an order, it won't just be one more piece of bullshit. It'll stand out; everyone will recognize it for a real emergency. You think you couldn't tell the difference? I've been on plenty of other ships where the old man juggles watches when you get to port. George is just a tight-ass. The guy lines up his shoes before he goes to sleep! He loves standing up there on the deckhouse, ego-tripping. It's his personality."

Toni and Peter came in through the doors. They will be leaving us tomorrow, I'm very sad to say. They waved and sat down elsewhere to edit some reports.

More beer, more talk. "The trouble with George and Gregg is that they're so much alike."

"You gotta be kidding."

"Not what they think. Their attitude."

"Their latitude?"

"Their attitude. George lords it over people. Gregg, he just gets stiff. But old Gregg is also stubborn as a mule. He won't say nothin', but he just goes on doin' what he planned. And that holier-than-thou act gets old fast."

"It's not an act. He—"

"George trained half the mates on sailing ships today—"

"And fired the other half—"

"Now everyone shut up. OK? I want to tell a story. Two years ago, no, three, the ship was off Puerto Rico, late in the fall. We was tied up to the pier in San Juan harbor. There had been a hurricane, there was a heavy onshore swell, and to keep us off the dock, George set sea anchors out to windward. It was first dogwatch. There was this, like, cocktail party going on with lots of guests on board. Everyone had had a few—"

"Guests?"

"Gimme a break. OK. This Coast Guard cutter cruises up, they want to come in close to look us over. Morons. They approach us. George tries to wave 'em off. They just wave back; the assholes think he's only being friendly. So they keep on coming, right across our anchor lines.

"There's fifty people standing around amidships. None of 'em picks up on what is happening—only George. All of a sudden he yells, "Hit the deck!" and starts shoving everybody down. They all go flat—old guys, chicks in dresses—and a second later the cable shears. It was our bow-line, and it just *exploded*, man. It sounded like a fucking *cannon*. If anyone had been standing, they'd be dead."

"So what's the point?"

"The point is this, pal. You don't like his style, right? So what? You ever known a better sailor?"

No one had.

"Do you respect his judgment? Is there anybody anywhere that you'd trust more to get you home? That's all that matters. Period. That's what a captain's for."

16 August. 51°N/55°W.

At 0500 hours I was shaken awake by Joan. A nondrinker, she had kindly stood anchor watch alone for the rest of us since 0400. The night orders said to wake George at 0600 and cast off at 0630. But I had to get up at once, Joan said; she needed help. As I swung down from out of my bunk, I got dizzy and misjudged the distance, landing in a heap on the deck. My head felt like a melon. Anyone who needed help from me, I thought, must have real problems.

After I left the ship last night, Joan now explained, George had summoned Gregg to his cabin and lit into him again. Then Gregg and some others had gone to a bar and stayed off until two in the morning. Now it was his job as first mate to take *Regina* out of port in less than an hour. But he would not wake up for anything. Feeling less than terrific myself, I asked Joan to get me some coffee and hobbled toward the stench on the starboard side.

Gregg was lying on his stomach, with his shirt rolled up halfway, as if he had passed out in the act of trying to get out of it. His right arm was extended up beside his head, still holding on to an inverted coffee cup on the wet brown pillow. His left arm dangled off the bed, coated from wrist to forearm with dried vomit. Lifting his head with one hand, I poured hot coffee down his throat, two cups, and shook him. Then I separated his shirt from his skin, apologized for what was coming, and administered a bucketful of North Atlantic.

Ten minutes later, at 0550, the fore watch and first mate were standing by, amidships. Our guests were also up and about, their rosy-cheeked expectancy in contrast to our sour calm. George came forward from the aft salon. I wondered what he and Gregg would have to say to each other today.

George looked at Gregg. Gregg looked at George. George looked at Gregg some more.

Gregg nodded.

"Are you ready to cast off?" George asked.

"I'm ready," Gregg replied.

It was a glorious morning, with a perfect wind, and the order was to set all sail. We managed the job in twenty-five minutes, ungasketing, sheeting out, trimming, hauling "with a will," and even chanting as we hauled. The ship had never looked more beautiful. For the newcomers, it was quite a show. Clearing the headland, we filled away, making eight knots thanks to a following breeze with *Regina* rocking brightly.

I noticed that no one had overhauled the buntlines and started aloft for the fourth time that hour. As I swung out over the rail, Joan asked me, "Are you up to it?" Up to it? I *insisted*. And when my turn on lookout came, I asked Lisa to stand in for me there so that I could continue to brace and haul.

If you'd told me eight weeks ago that I would go up eighty feet in the air on ropes, in a blow, hung over, on three hours' sleep, I'd have called you crazy. If I'd known I would do it, I'd have called *me* crazy, too. Yet here I was, not only doing it but loving it. As I took a breather on the upper topsail yard, I felt unstoppable.

So did the others. You could see it in the free swing of their arms, which belied their bleary stares. David and Root were working side by side, David sweating the lines and Root tailing. They worked well together.

By 0800 hours all of the running rig was flemished, and the docking lines were flaked and stowed. By 0810 all members of the fore watch were asleep in their bunks again.

17 August. Fourché Harbour.

Yesterday afternoon brought plenty of sunshine and air temperatures in the fifties. We peeled off our long johns and gloves at last and continued south-southeast down White Bay, along Newfoundland's north peninsula. With the wind from the west at twenty-three knots, we sped along, and after a long beam reach tacked east at 1500 hours and headed in toward shore. At 0700 hours George found the break in the cliff face he'd been looking for. We sailed through its narrow mouth into a fjord with thousand-foot-high granite walls. Continuing along through growing stillness, we arrived at Williamsport, on Fourché Harbour.

Throughout Newfoundland's history, most of the island's population lived in villages like this one. There were at one time thirteen hundred of them, scattered along six hundred miles of coastline. Few had five hundred inhabitants. Most were inaccessible by land. Some did not have a cash economy until after the Second World War.

In a typical outport, everything sprawled helter-skelter. There were few if any streets, no town councils, and no town planning. Still, a certain uniformity was evident: Nearly every house had frontage on the water, with a dock, a boat, and a platform called a flake for drying cod.

What were the people's lives like? Quiet—a slow routine of fishing locally for cod and bringing it in to be salted. Of visits in homemade dorries to neighboring towns. Of austere worship in raw pews; of communal laundry days and country dances; of tea and turnips, and tobacco smoked in clay pipes called dudeens; of songs and stories told by lamplight late into the night in low-roofed parlors. Over generations, outport dwellers handed down a trove of ballads, jigs, reels, practical information, crafts, and legends. Along with its own traditions, each stretch of coast evolved its own dialect: that of St. John's touched by an Irish accent, the north shore's like the speech of seventeenth-century Devon and Cornwall. *That* is what I was hearing when we first reached Corner Brook, which made me think of Shakespeare's "rude mechanicals."

A saying of the old Newfoundlanders went, "Land is a place to cure fish." Their lives were closely tuned to the pitch of the sea and the rhythms of the natural world. But early in this century those rhythms were broken, and the balance they had provided was lost.

With the coming of the First World War, the sons of this Nursery for Seaman played a large role in the Allied merchant navy. When the war was over, many who had served chose not to return to the outports and moved on for good to Newfoundland's capital city, St. John's, or New York or Boston. Gravely depopulated, heavily dependent on one resource—cod—Newfoundland was devastated by the collapse of world markets for that resource after 1929. Over the following two decades, problems that had been chronic grew acute. In the outports, it was said, there was nothing but rum and poverty. Finally, in 1949, Newfoundlanders voted to renounce their dominion status in the

British Commonwealth, and Newfoundland became a Canadian province.

From then on, the decline of the outports was hastened by official policy. The new province's economic future was seen to lie with pulp and paper mills and massive hydroelectric projects. And it was argued that outports were no longer socially viable. Such small settlements, it seemed, were not moneymaking propositions; the harmony with nature—the almost unthinking maintenance of biological and social equilibrium that had sustained these communities for centuries—was gone. A vigorous "coastal resettlement program" drained the population into more accessible towns. Under pressure, people moved. What they found, in many cases, was a better livelihood. What they left behind was a way of life, and villages like the one where we were now moored: Williamsport.

We are in a ghost town. Near overgrown cottages, skeletal dories lie beached upside down in the tidal mud. At 1900 hours we tied up to the only dock still standing, alongside a ruined factory across from the ruined village on the fjord's east side. The moon had not yet risen. Under the cove's steep wall, the shadows were already deep. Vines emerged from the factory's rusting boilers. Frost-heaved slabs of concrete were stained a deep red; casks and machinery lay scattered among wind-curled sheets of corrugated roof. It could have been Conrad's Inner Station in *Heart of Darkness,* which was used to store ivory. In fact, it had been used to butcher whales.

It was not the sort of place you come upon by chance. Judy and George had been here before and had come back now for some particular reason. At suppertime a dory arrived; we were joined by Effie and Wesley Randall, two of the village's three current residents. Wesley was born in Williamsport some sixty-five years ago. He has seen it thrive and fade, revive and die, and now returns each summer for the fishing. Over coffee and pie, he told us the village's history.

Whaling operations in Newfoundland employed a method dating back to the early part of the century. Whales were killed at sea by catcher boats. In some operations, boats were then dispatched to bring in the floating carcasses; otherwise, the hunting boat would collect the catch itself and labor up the inlet to its station, trailing several giant corpses. Small cargo ships docked at the pier to onload the processed meat, bone meal (for fertilizer), oil, and baleen.

From 1905 to 1915 about a dozen companies vied for the five kinds of large whales that swam in Newfoundland waters: blue, fin, humpback, sei, and sperm. Catches soon declined. By the 1930s few onshore stations remained, and from then on the average take was small, around two hundred whales for the entire coastline. Whale populations started to recover.

Then, in 1939, the whaling station was opened here in Williamsport by the Olsen Whaling and Sealing Company, with equipment transferred from an older station in the south. A few years later two other nearby stations were reopened, and the changing nature of life on land began to disrupt life in the sea. Whaling without restrictions, the three operations took three thousand whales from 1947 to 1951 alone. The Williamsport station was shut down in 1951, only to be used again by a new firm in 1967. This time so many fin whales were slaughtered in so short a span that they were almost wiped out in local waters, yet the station kept on running until 1972.

I found this hard to believe; the place already has the timelessness of ruins. "Oh, yes," said Wesley, "it was all different then. With the jigging and the whaling, there was work, and some to spare, for fifty families. A hustle and a bustle. Surely."

In the evening I walked down the pier, stepping over missing planks, to the factory. The sky was still twilit, but the fjord was swaddled in gloom. Pale wads of mist were forming on the water. A full moon, rising, was not quite visible behind the rock walls along the near side of the fjord, but the far side was burnished by a colorless glow, half dusk, half moonlight. When we docked a few hours back, Al Stearns had jumped ashore to tie up the forward spring line. Then without a word he had lowered his head and just kept walking, like an animal tracking a scent. I hadn't seen him since. But now, as I turned a corner, he called to me softly, from above.

He was sitting with Fran on the corrugated roof of the factory, beside a hole through which blubber had been dropped into *cookers*. They weren't talking. There was something like an aura or magnetic charge around them. When Al did speak at last, he couldn't look at me. His voice was like damp black cloth. "I have the strangest feeling," he said. "Something in there keeps pulling me in."

Me too. When relieved from my watch on board at 0300 hours, I didn't lay below. I went ashore again, back to the factory.

In the past two months we have come to know so many humpback whales. In the bleakest seas we have seen them breach and blow and visit. How can I convey what it felt like to sit on the feeder ramp—gouged, crosshatched, and scarified by flensing knives? Below, the concrete held red puddles. Rust? Dissolved brick? How could I not imagine they were something else? Not see the great sad carcasses winched up, their blood cascading down the shoot between my feet, the weed-choked courtyard walled in by blocks of flesh?

The moon was now high overhead. Shinnying down the main shed's outer wall, I pried off a board with my marlinspike and stepped inside. Moonlight washed in through cracks in the roof and walls, fell here on a ten-foot-high cylinder, there on a circular valve, a trough. The factory was utterly quiet. Even my breathing seemed muffled by the dust, the heavy air. For a long time I felt nothing—and then I was intensely lonely. The space where I was standing gathered to itself, in sorrow, all that we have done to empty the world of our companions in it.

It is said that humpback songs are "ghostly." Well, this place was filled with ghosts: gigantic, innocent, unaccusing. Still, I imagined them saying, "Now that you've killed us, spoiled the water, denuded the land—*now* you decide it's time to listen to our songs, to find out what they mean!" I had listened to those songs a dozen times. I wanted to hear one now. Or any sound—a snake, a bat, even mosquitoes. But there was nothing.

***

At two o'clock this afternoon a quick torrential rain had come and gone. The sun was breaking through the clouds, and the woods along the shoreline glistened. Patrick, Brenda, Scott, Canan, and I set off exploring.

Across the fjord from the factory stood the remnants of Williamstown proper: a ring of twenty or thirty cottages in various stages of collapse around Fourché Harbour. The horseshoe-shaped inlet was shallow and clear. Fragments of timber and oarlocks, fishnets and floats, were embedded in its floor. At either end of the horseshoe, like stained molars in an otherwise toothless jaw, stood two homes in relatively good repair. The prim gray cottage with chintz curtains and a flat roof was the home of Wes and Effie; the one-room shack belonged to a solitary fisherman named Pierce Caravan. Maybe they had remained in their homes as others moved away, or maybe they had appropriated the houses closest to the harbor's mouth.

You would expect that the sole remaining people in a town might arrange to be neighbors. And so they had—Newfoundland style. To visit, they must get into a boat and arrive (is there any other way?) by water.

We arrived at Pierce's dock and found him working on his jigging boat, a trap skiff with a plywood housing built around the engine and inch-deep grooves cut in its cedar rail by fishing lines. On each compression stroke, the housing's walls puffed out like a lung, expelling blue smoke through their seams. "Yesterday," Pierce said by way of greeting, "it was lousy with fish. Some tick, I'll say. Four hunderd poun'." In the mud beneath the dock, fish heads, guts, and spines lay decomposing; in the open air, decay smelled almost sweet. Beside the dock, a flake was piled high with cod fillets that Pierce had salted down.

The man himself looked slightly salted too, with skin as rough as the surrounding cliffs and the ropelike arms and buttocks of a jockey. Horizontal wrinkles scored his face; even his nose had parallel creases across the bridge and an inch below, like the fathom lines on a chart. Staring openly at Brenda and Canan, like a puppy with a hard-on, he offered us tea, which we declined, and then directed us toward "the road."

Like many outports, Williamsport had been a village without streets: Where would they lead? But something was required to get from house to house, so residents built "the road," a board-walk on stilts that ran behind each house along the shore. We set off on it gingerly toward the back of the harbor, watching for dropped planks and rotten pilings, peering through caved-in roofs and buckled door frames from which wild brush sprouted like coral from a wreck.

Beyond an arched footbridge next to a cemetery overgrown with wild radish stood a frame church with its doors and windows gone. Its signboard lay face down, ingested by raspberry thickets. Inside the building, weatherbeaten pews encircled a central plat-form. Sunlight entered through the stovepipe's ceramic collar. There were no religious artifacts or other signs of worship. Noth-ing at all to turn over, poke at, stumble on. The building had been so austere, so modest when in use that now, abandoned, it scarcely seemed changed. Sumacs reached in through the win-dows. An alder poked up through the floor.

Outside again, the trace of a path led up and up, keeping close to a stream that could be heard but not seen. The recent rain was gurgling through the mulch and steaming off the foliage. The path rose on, past blooming fireweed and asters, speckled alders, black and yellow birches, rowan, scarlet mushrooms, shimmering ferns. High up, it ended suddenly, emerging at a pool between two waterfalls. We peeled off our sweaty weather gear and swam.

Back down at six P.M., we found that the tide had ebbed and the harbor was only a foot deep. Rather than hazard "the road" again, we pulled on our boots and waded toward the inlet's mouth, where Gregg, who was waiting for us in the Avon, waved and called across the water. We arrived back at *Regina* to find everyone on deck for a cocktail party. For dinner, Al served roast beef, done to perfection. Rare.

It all seems impossibly rich and full. I've begun to feel a little overwhelmed by the cumulative events of this voyage. On almost any day I have felt every kind of emotion with a purity and intensity I rarely knew before. It makes me realize that back home, if the environment is neutral—not too noisy, too filthy, too intrusive—then I think things are all right. But in fact a truce with our senses is not the same as an alliance. Though we may think so, we are not habituated to sensory deprivations. The absence of constant nourishment through the senses divorces us from nature's rhythms, traps us in ourselves and in each other, makes us brittle and subjective, thins the blood. In the city, sensuality is overemphasized and yet, paradoxically, is confined to certain types of relationships and situations. Here it is a ceaseless, wordless dialogue with patterns larger than oneself, a constant rinsing. Intimate, impersonal, this dialogue-sensation feeds the habit of perception, breeds deep feeling and clear thought.

Of course, the point is not really "here" or "there" at all but taking it with you, bringing it home. Is that still possible in a city, in our time? I don't know. All I know is that now, this moment, in this spot, what I can see is radiant, and fresh, and strange. I approach it as if beamed down on another planet called, perhaps, the Past.

After supper, as it grows dark, I find myself drawn to the factory once again. In its courtyard, Fran is puzzling over something that looks like a guillotine. As I approach, she fiddles with it, lifts her baseball cap, and scratches. If this were a cartoon, the next frame would show a light bulb over her cocked head: idea!

"Hi, Fran, how are you?"

"It's a saw. See? Runs on steam. These here—the cylindahs—are pistons. I bet there's a steam line undaground from that turbine." She points to a hut with one wall fallen down. "Yeah. This here carriage swings to the right. You adjust the blade angle with this arc. You haul the whale up here an' use a six-foot blade to section it, cut through the spine—"

"*What* blade?"

"The blade in the toolshed behind the cold room."

"Cold room?"

"Yeah. This here's the housing for a winch. You haul the pieces of blubbah up that ramp, cut 'em into chunks, and drop 'em through the roof, in there. Come on."

I follow her across a sunken threshold into a high-ceilinged, musty shed. Except for the scant light drizzling through the hole above, it's dark. "This thing's a mulling pot. There's two more on the pier that were nevah installed. The meat came down this shoot into the pots. These here are pumps. They sent the oil into these tanks, for different grades of purity. They run on current from the generating plant. Back here."

We step between joists into the building where I walked last night. Passing some boilers ("Very forties," says Fran), we reach the cold house ("Heat exchangahs, see?") and emerge through the adjacent office window into moonlight. Next door stands a three-walled shed.

The floor is covered with dry powder that resembles guano. Here and there I can see scraps of baleen, and discarded sacks stenciled

WHALE MEAL
NOT FOR HUMAN CONSUMPTION

There is no trace of bones.

"Look Fran," I volunteer, pointing at the ceiling. "Sifters."

"Uh huh. An' above them mounts for the cutting blades."

"They ground up everything—"

"That got here. Some of the bones didn't make it, though. Did you catch that field out in back of the cookers? This one here has nothin' growin' in it. But that one's full of weeds an' stuff. Know why? 'Cause it's been fertilized. No kiddin', poke around. There's whole jawbones underneath those bushes.

"Somebody really did a numbah on this place. I mean, check it out. All the fire walls on the boilahs are cracked. The blo-wahs've been taken out an' destroyed, so you can't use the parts from any one of 'em to rebuild the othahs. The generatah got run without lube oil, you can tell—the bearing metal is extruded through the casing. Somebody done it on purpose till they seized."

"What for?"

"Sabotage. 'If we're gettin' booted, we sure as hell ain't

leavin' it for the locals.' Kamikaze bullshit. Typical Japanese."

"What?"

"Part of the postwar reindustrialization crap."

"What?"

"Reparations."

"Who told you that?"

"Didn't have to tell me. Who do you *think* eats whale meat?"

"Yeah, but Fran—"

"You been to the workers' housing?"

"Housing? Where?"

"I was walkin' around in it, feelin' funny. I didn't know why. Then I says to myself, 'Christ, you're all bent ovah. The ceiling's way too low." Then I find these like hairnets in the back, the kind Jap women wear for cookin'. That reminded me of somethin' else, when I was workin for the Navy. Come here."

We walk back to the factory. Fran leads me to a small, square room and turns around in triumph. "Check it out: Clothes hooks, a sunken bath. Two benches undahneath the waterline. This here's the line in from the boilah room, steam ovahflow. This here's the drain line. Vents out to the fjord. No question"— finishing her summation to the jury: "Japanese!"

Some people operate in things; some people operate on things. Watching Fran poke through domestic refuse, I am struck by how much her approach resembles Jim Tuck's at Red Bay and Helge Ingstad's at L'Anse-aux-Meadows and, for that matter, how much the mind-set of all three shares with that of the Basques and the Vikings. They are all people of action, doers and makers, movers and shakers, finders-out of facts. How different my own responses are! Williamsport, for Fran, is a riddle to be cracked, a machine to be broken down and reassembled in the well-equipped tool shop of her mind, and in doing this she herself appears unmoved, in any fundamental way, by her own deductions. I, by contrast, have felt myself in a kind of dream state since the moment we arrived, an almost hallucinatory trance to which I surrendered whole, and willingly. I preferred to let the place's power work on *me*. What compelled me most about this place did not lend itself to being figured out, or "solved."

Six weeks ago I'd have called this contrast between Fran's way and mine a split between information and romance, between analysis (the craving for control) and self-surrender. But is that true? Observing Fran now, watching her mind perform *jetés* from fact to fact, I realize that her method has a romance all its own. Neither of us has the truth; each creates a version of the truth, and both my introspection and her practical deduction constitute, at most, a story line, a quest: the rage for order. The conclusions that she draws are plausible; they hang together. Whether or not they all are true, they are certainly, in Yeat's phrase, all "self-delighting." It's the game of tying them together that inspires her, and to think that the impulse behind this is merely practical, or fundamentally different from my own, is false.

I feel like I have been taken inside Fran's skull and allowed to look out through her eyes. And all at once I get it. I can feel how the world, for her, is a gigantic Tinkertoy, feel the pleasure she derives in doping out how it works.

I say so. Admiringly.

"Hey," Fran says. She is grinning ear to ear, and her snaggletoothed grin is almost beautiful. "Hey, babe," she says, "I'm an en-gi-*neer!*"

18 August. 50°N/55°W.

When I woke for breakfast, we were back at sea, heading east-southeast. All through our morning watch there was a cold steady downpour. Waves were at ten to twelve feet, and their motion was unorganized, erratic. This produced an unpleasant mix of pitching and rolling (my stomach was doing figure eights) and a serious heel. Because the twenty-six-knot wind kept backing, we were forced to change course frequently, which meant a lot of work aloft. At eleven the ship passed between the Horse Islands. It rounded Cape St. John in a squall at 1600 hours and proceeded east across the angry mouth of Notre Dame Bay.

By the time we came off duty after first dogwatch, my ears and nose were blocked, and I felt nauseous. I attributed that feeling to the heavy seas—and Screech. This is Newfoundland's native liquor, and it's aptly named. In the days of iron men and wooden ships (not vice versa, as today), Screech was produced by storing moonshine in empty rum casks so that it would absorb their flavor. The label on the bottle was simply a bright yellow map of Newfoundland with the letters S-C-R-E-E-C-H! heading east-northeast from Port-aux-Basques to Bonavista. According to legend, Newfie fishermen did not need sea charts; when the fog rolled in, they simply lifted up their bottles. Having lifted mine a bit too frequently last night, I spent this afternoon recovering in my bunk, watching water that we had shipped flow back and forth across the glass deck light.

Having skipped dinner, I felt steady enough to go up for second dogwatch and another two hours of nonstop rain. Our plan was to head east to clear Notre Dame Bay by morning. But when wave heights continued to increase, we sought shelter at Twillingate Harbor.

As *Regina* sailed in through the blackest night in weeks, we could barely see the town's lights through the fog. Just before midnight, a quarter mile off, both anchors were let fall. Concerned that the ship might drag, George ordered the mates to take anchor bearings every half hour through the night. Because I had developed an earache, I was allowed to sleep in until six A.M.

19 August. 49°N/53°W.

More rain; visibility four hundred yards. At 1100 hours we passed by Bacalhao Island and came to a starboard tack in order to ride the Labrador Current southward. I suppose that the contrast between water temperature (which remains in the midforties) and air temperature (which is up to fifty-four) is what produces all this fog.

Most of us have now stowed away our long johns and heavy jackets but are still forced to practically live in foul weather gear. In conditions that resemble standing under a faucet, the rubberized cloth grows clammy inside and sticks to your entire body. This is most unpleasant when you have to move around a lot aloft. The physical sensation, somewhere between suffocating and strangling, also multiplies any queasiness you feel. So you tend to peel off the oilskins ten times a day, only to struggle back into them as soon as you grow wet and cold again. As a result of this practice, and in spite of George's admonitions, foul weather gear lies scattered all over the ship, along with mildewed woolens.

Meanwhile, the heat stays on full blast, not for our sake but to help keep *Regina*'s timbers dry. Overheated below, underdressed when on deck, a crew that stayed healthy all through the ice is now getting ill. Two days ago only I had a cold. Yesterday two others had come down with it. Today, three more. "I *told* you to boil the rinse water," Joan intones. Oh, for the joys of life at sea, where everything is shared.

Rob is alone in the main salon. Leaning against an upper bunk, he lifts one foot, peels off his sock, shifts weight, and peels off the other. Reaching into a duffel bag, he extracts another pair. He raises these to his nose and grimaces. Tosses them back in the

226

bunk. Reaches into his bag once more and pulls out a second pair. Sniffs these. Rejects them too. Reaches down and retrieves the pair he had been wearing from the deck. Pulls them back on.

As Richard Henry Dana noted, "There are no umbrellas at sea." Yet despite the relentless rain, in the last two days we have acquired an umbrella of sorts: an umbrella of birds. Not content to follow astern, the way seagulls follow trawlers, they are everywhere—overhead, alongside, under the bowsprit, according to the habit of each species. Curiously, none of them actually land on the rail or yardarms. But they stay around us night and day, and it's a delight to observe their stylish ways.

For starters, there are the usual birds one sees at home: herring gulls, the occasional great blackbacked gull and common tern, and cormorants. There are the ever loyal fulmars, gazing down with amazed avuncular expressions from beside the flying jib. Sooty shearwaters, keeping their distance, zooming silently along at the waterline like missiles evading radar. And Wilson's petrels by the hundred. Sweet little birds, these hover at the surface, peeping softly, wings held over their backs in a butterfly-like motion as their limp feet skim the water.

The most aggressive species are the skuas and jaegers. Skuas are large, dark, heavy-bodied, and pugnacious birds that nest in Iceland. Making gutteral croaking sounds, they travel across midocean to this shore in midsummer and have the distinctive habit of harrying other species twice their size. The jaegers are swift black birds with long, forked antenna-like tails and white trim on bellies and wingtips, which are two feet apart. Their name is the German word for "hunter." Northern equivalents of the magnificent frigatebird, they wait until a gull or a tern has caught a fish and then swoop down on it in pairs from behind, from different heights and angles, like fighter planes attacking a bomber. The aerial combat is spectacular. I have watched a small fish get torn from a kittiwake's beak by one jaeger and be caught by the jaeger's partner, ten feet below, as all four creatures (jaegers, kittiwake, and codfish) hurtled by.

Still scarier, and much grander, is the gannet. Gannets are

huge birds. By the second week of life, the fledglings' bodies are so heavy relative to their wing strength that they can't fly; those that leap off cliffs fall to the water, where they are forced to float and are vulnerable to sharks. Those that reach adulthood become snow-white giants with black-tipped wings, a pointed tail, and an equally pointed, wedge-shaped beak like the nose of a Concorde. With their eyes set deep in a jet-black mask held on, as it were, by a black chinstrap and another black line down the side of their blue-gray bills, they look noble but discredited, like a heroic outlaw or a banished prince. This morning one bird with a five-foot wingspan overtook us to windward, cruising along with its head moving side to side. Then it plunged from a height of forty feet and disappeared beneath the water. When it emerged five seconds later, there was a four-pound fish between its jaws.

If bird life were an opera and the gannets its stars, then the chorus of three hundred would consist of murres. These homely, friendly, pigeon-sized pals are the penguins of the north. They have a similar tuxedo look (though to my eye less well tailored), and like all members of the alcid family, they use their stubby wings for swimming and diving. As they scoot by, those wings whir like propellers, and the birds seem to fly through water. Murres live in colonies on stony bluffs, where they stand upright, kibitzing loudly, by the tens of thousands. Males and females take turns brooding the single blue-green eggs, which are pear-shaped so that if pushed they will roll in circles rather than over the rock ledge.

We are seeing so many murres because a colony that may be the largest left in North America is several hours southeast of us, on an island ten miles out to sea. It is called Funk Island, as in "What a funk here is! Here's a damnèd funk, here's a grievous stink indeed!" Long before such English made it to the OED, the Frenchman Jacques Cartier landed on the "Isle of Birds" to re-provision his ship and declared the place "so exceedingly full of birds that one would think they had been stowed there." Nowadays some 200,000 murres remain on that guano-spattered granite slab thirty-five feet high and a half mile long. It is the smallest speck of land between Newfoundland and Greenland, and along with some even smaller specks to the west, is referred to as "the Funks" or "Stinking Islands." In two days we will reach the northern edge of the Grand Banks of Newfoundland, the richest fishing grounds on earth. It was fish that first brought Europeans here. It was fish, in a sense, that brought birds to Funk Island, and in one of nature's neat arrangements, it is potassium in the seabirds' droppings that sustains the plankton on which future fish will feed.

In the 1970s, the advent of stern trawlers and huge factory ships brought a frenzy of fishing to this area, and a horde of Russians, Portuguese, Spaniards, British, and Germans worked these grounds. They couldn't get down to St. John's very often, and the only place nearby to put ashore was Fogo Island, now as far to the west of us as the Funks are eastward. At first it was not considered one of the world's great liberty ports. But that opinion changed when the Fogo à Go-Go opened on the main street of Seldom-Come-By.

20 August. Trinity.

Our unsettled weather continues. In the past five consecutive watches, we have not had twenty minutes free. In the time between those watches I have been trying to shake off a cold, but from nine to twelve last night it was work just to stay in my bunk because of the heavy rolling. During midwatch, when I took the helm, we hit greasy ten-foot swells and powerful crosscurrents. The wheel began to jerk so hard that I thought it would break my arm. Several times I was forced to let go altogether and then fight it back to center, spoke by spoke. In four hours we hit three squalls.

At the moment I am almost like an animal; all I care about is eating, getting back to sleep, and staying warm. Everyone else looks dulled out too. At meals the chatter has died down; people

simply sit and stare. Looking at my shipmates' faces, I understand
a little more the expressions of people in Walker Evans photos of
the rural South or in old daguerrotypes of western miners. They
were not mean-spirited or mindless, bitter, or afraid—not anything but tired. They were just worn down.

At 0410 I had just lain down in bed when I heard a crash
in the passageway aft. I jumped out to find Clay sprawled flat
underneath the hanging oilskins. Coming off watch, he had let
his attention stray at last, missed a step on the slippery companionway, and fallen eleven steps to the deck below.

Ten minutes later I heard the same sound again. It was
Canan this time, coming down for a cup of coffee.

Ann Nichols and the children have been aboard for a week, and
their presence has created precisely the kind of distinctions that
George said it's wise to avoid. His attention is now divided, and
his happiness about being with them again is offset (from our
point of view) by a finicky impatience with, and distance from,
the crew.

It is really getting on our nerves to contend with a child's
tantrums and uncurbed demands at meals, where we ourselves are
increasingly restrained; to clean up after George's children while
he tells us to be neater; to come off watch and find the same five
seats reserved exclusively at every meal for members of the Nichols family cruise. When I woke today, or rather was awakened
by the children's screams, I found Kathy, Lisa, Clay, and Root
in the main salon. Root grimaced toward a message on the blackboard:

ALL HANDS NOTE:
ALL CLOTHING NOT REMOVED FROM DOO'S BAIT LOCKER
BY 09:30 WILL BE TOSSED OVERBOARD.

GN

It was ten-fifteen.

What's up? I asked. We all knew it was George who first
proposed that we dry clothes in that locker because he wouldn't

let us hang them in the rigging. Before they could answer, Himself walked in.

"You know," George remarked to the air (he was smiling, but his lips had disappeared), "I found a foul weather coat marked 'HOx' on my hook in the aft salon."

"HOx" is the mark on my belongings. No one spoke.

"I wonder what it means," he drawled. And scratched his head.

Oh, shit.

"You know what, George?" I said, "It was probably mine."

"Well, I'm glad you saw fit to use the past tense, Harvey."

Silence.

"George, if that coat is missing, I will bill you personally for a new one." Out of the corner of my eye, I caught sight of Lisa, whose mouth was hanging open in surprise. George stood still, looking down at me. His nose seemed to grow more aquiline. His cheeks went slack. He started to speak but then spun on his heel and, with shoulders up so high that they appeared to graze his earlobes, stalked back aft.

No one said anything when he was gone. I'd been way out of line. But so had he, goddammit. I had forgotten to take that coat in the aft salon because I was exhausted after watch. I worked my ass off last night. I didn't ask to be praised for that, but I certainly don't need to be insulted, either.

In fact, my foul weather coat had not been pitched across the rail, and for the first time in four days, I don't need it. During watch from noon to four, the skies at long last cleared. But the ocean grew still rougher; without that greasy heaviness that can keep seas low, we now have nine-foot swells. There is plenty of sea spray, dazzling in the glare, and heavy rolling; the water on deck amidships is knee deep.

Unlike a modern schooner with an open rail, *Regina* has hip-high bulwarks of solid oak. To allow the deckwash to run off, the bulwarks are pierced by square holes that resemble gunports or the crenellations on a fort. Called *freeing ports,* they are covered by doors as thick as a telephone book, hinged from above. Right

now they are making a fabulous racket, flapping open on each
leeward roll as the deckwash surges through, and slamming shut
with a bang on each roll to windward.

With Joan in the galley and Kathy ill, the fore watch is
shorthanded; those of us who can work are standing double duty
at the helm. During my first hour there I sing, as I often do, and
am joined, as I often am, by Lawrence and Helene. Together we
go down to the sea-o, catch the whales-o, huddle in the wee dark
hold by Archie's stove. Then many a hardy lad is lost, but after
a year and a day, we get the lady-o, though all our swains adore
her, when the heather is a bloomin', a-comin' through the rye.

For my second stint I am alone. I remember my clash with
George this morning, and my anger makes me tired. When I sing,
what comes out this time is Bob Dylan's song "Love Minus
Zero." Twice, George comes along and stands ten feet downwind. The first time, I go on singing (treat a person like a child
and he will act like one). The second time, we both are tense and
silent. It is clear that he's made himself available; he is offering
or waiting. But neither of us is willing to make the first move.

At 1600 hours there's a talk on navigation, on a shortcut that
compares the local hour angles (LHAs) for Aries and a choice of
seven precomputed stars. I have still not come within a hundred
miles of true position, even though today's class is the final formal
session before exams, which are one week away. The students are
winding down their individual research, too, and will present
their findings in the evenings that remain. For the first time
there's an intimation that we're entering the homestretch, that
this journey has an end.

The coast has started looking more like home. If in Greenland the earth seemed naked, then sailing south has been like
watching it get dressed. At Eagle Cove it pulled on some flimsy
underclothes of lichen; on Cape Bauld, a slip of grasses; along
White Bay, a fisherman's smock of underbrush and berries. And
in Trinity, where we let the anchor fall at 1830 hours, it has
swaddled itself at last in deciduous trees and gardens and mown
lawns.

This outport sits on a small peninsula in the lee of a rocky lookout, in a mirror-smooth, landlocked harbor. Seen after hundreds of miles of harsh escarpment, this inviting, drowsy shore reminds me of a woman fresh from her bath in the cool of evening who has slipped on a kimono of green velvet, and lain down.

Trinity was named by Gaspar Côrte-Real on Trinity Sunday, 1500. Established in 1558, the town claims to be the oldest European settlement in North America. It is also the site of the first court in the New World, held here in 1658, and the first vaccination in North America, performed in 1798. From the sixteenth to the nineteenth centuries, much of Newfoundland's fishing activity was based in three parallel bays named Trinity, Bonavista, and Conception. In 1837 a total of 206 sailing ships put out from Conception Bay alone, bearing over five thousand men to the seal hunt. At that time the annual catch in a decent year would be 400,000 pelts, and in its heyday Trinity was a wealthy town. Its prosperity was not without costs, however; in a bad year such as 1852, no fewer than forty ships were lost in storms, crushed in the ice, or set afire by overturned stoves. Such risks contributed to the decline of sail and to centralization of the hunt in larger sealing ships based in the capital, St. John's. But the bulk of their crews still hailed from Trinity and a score of neighboring villages with names like Happy Adventure, Heart's Content, Fair and False Bay, Turk's Cove, and Ireland's Eye.

I locate these on a map in the Trinity Museum, a converted Georgian-style captain's home. Though I am most interested in the museum's maps and documents, I find Patrick and Lawrence engrossed in a display of old fishing gear. Next to a quadruple-sheaved block that must weigh fifty pounds are some squares of split fir bark, labeled "rinds," used to cover the drying cod. For a week we've been singing a Newfie song with the chorus "Sods and rinds to cover your flake, cake and tea for supper" without having any idea what the line meant.

"A-ha," says Lawrence, winking. "A-*ha!* "You see that? See that?" His forehead wrinkles and his blue eyes flash. This is followed, sure as thunder follows lightning, by the Laugh.

***

Outside, it is nearly dark. The air is tinged with wood smoke and the smell of new-cut hay. A beacon light on the seaward side of the lookout has come on; its soft pulse is refracted through the fog, which beads up on the irridescent petals of geraniums in the flower beds we pass. Lawrence and Patrick are off to the Spouter Pub at the Village Inn. I decide to walk them there before returning to the ship to stand anchor watch.

A pair of humpack jawbones flank the inn's front walk, and the bootscrapers on its porch are vertebrae. Singing spills from an open doorway. Scott's favorite song, "Elvira," is blasting from a jukebox. Each time the Oak Ridge Boys get to the chorus, everybody pitches in: "A-loo, bow-ba-loo, bow-ba-loo, bow-ba-loo, El-vi-ra/My heart's on fire for Elvira." The sounds pulse out into the cool night air like heat from the mouth of a kiln.

It is nice to walk back alone. Halfway, the light from a cottage window casts long bars of shadow through a picket fence—the first fence I have seen in in fifty days. As I reach the dock, the Anglican church bell rings ten times, and the Catholic steeple answers, "Right you are." Clay's voice calls my name across the water, and a wet line jumps into my hand.

He and Joan step off the Avon and onto shore. I drive the boat back to the waiting ship at anchor, circling her bow for a look up at the sheerstrake, salt-caked dolphin striker, figurehead, and stem. For added strength, the frames in the prow were not sawed and bolted into shape, as in most vessels, but were cut out whole from special "compass timber"; that is, they are V-shaped slices taken out of living trees whose branches had grown naturally at the desired angle.

I pass around the ship's stern to the channels on the leeward side. Tying up there is like coming back under *Regina*'s wing. That odor! Diesel and dirt and hemp and bilge. Unmistakable. Hers—and mine.

21 August. Conception Bay.

A beautiful day: high cirrus clouds, blue sky, sun-spangled water.
During my lookout on morning watch, we crossed paths with ten
white-sided dolphins. Other than that, there was not much to do
except plant my rear end in the lookout chair, whose seat has
rotted out, and soak up sunshine.

After a good night's sleep, my perspective on the tiff with
George had changed. So the way he spoke to me was wrong. Big
deal. I'm not the only one who gets tired. And for Christ's sake,
he's twice my age. There's also the small fact that he's responsible
for the lives of everyone on board and in that sense is "on" every
minute of the day. I realized that I haven't been mindful enough
of the mental pressure he bears in addition to physical fatigue. It
was time to send my anger overboard. I resolved to apologize to
George and was thinking of what to say when I heard applause
in the deckhouse under me. Then the wetlab door flew open, and
an excited Sid emerged.

Sid's individual project has been fluke photography. Peter
and Toni trained him, and after they departed in St. Anthony, he
assumed an equal share in the work with Judy. In the darkroom
just now, he had matched a whale she photographed last week
outside Notre Dame Bay with a whale seen in 1975 on Navidad
Bank; it was Barnacle Bill. This was the first match Sid has made
and only the third between the two whale populations ever.

At eleven I ducked off watch to find a hat and was rooting
through my tangled sheets when I heard a voice behind me say,
"Oh, Haaavey." It was George. "Say, listen," he continued.
"There was a pair of gloves on the radiator in the aft salon. I
found them there this morning. Orange neoprene. Quite color-
ful. You know the kind I mean?"

I knew. They had "HOx" written on each wrist in Magic Marker.

"Well." Pause. "I decided to pitch them along with the others." Pause. "But I thought you'd be offended." Pause. "So I brought them down and put them on your pillow."

"Thank you, George."

"You're *welcome,* Harvey," he replied. We took each other's measure. Then he grinned, and his face dropped thirty years.

Back in the pilothouse at 1600 hours, George stood with a saw in his hand, above a length of pine. He had balanced it between the cabin's raised thresholds and was trying unsuccessfully to keep it in place as he sawed.

"How's things?" he asked as I bent down and held the wood steady.

"Terrific," I said. We laughed. He began to saw. "What will it be?" I asked, when the cut was done.

"Well, I noticed that one of the planks in the old girl's steering box is looking a little poky. So I thought I'd see what I could do. Now Harvey, my friend, have you got some questions for me?"

"I've had a thought or two since we spoke last time."

George set down the saw. "I thought you might," he said.

During our conversations lately, I have noticed a distinctive pattern. Faced with a question he regards as too direct, George more often than not evades it or answers with such reserve that what he says is no reply at all. But after we have moved on to something less overtly charged, he will bring the conversation back to the earlier point and respond with candor, even intimacy. Or a day or two later he will seek me out and offer a reply to the questions that earlier he seemed not to hear.

I began by repeating comments I have heard that the research content of the ORES program is thin, in fact almost a pretext for the sailing and adventure. How do the two goals fit together, I asked, and which is more important? If asked to rank his goals, George replied, he would place first-class research and good education together, as "1A" and "1B." The Outward Bound–type aspects of the experience would rank "a distant second."

"There is no question," he went on, "that in any undertaking, you create a lot of headaches for yourself by refusing to be just one thing. And you're subject to all sorts of criticism for it. But the good result—the result I'm aiming for—is a kind of *gestalt,* or mixture. It might help you to understand why we do things the way we do and how it got that way."

Fifteen years ago, George continued, the Sea Education Association program in Woods Hole was founded during the first big flush of the environmental movement, at the peak of interest in "experimental education." It was designed to get students excited about the ocean. Each course consisted of six weeks in the classroom on shore, followed by six weeks at sea in the topsail schooner *Westward.* In short, SEA was, and still is, an *educational* experience, designed primarily to transmit what is already known.

At roughly the same time, marine mammal research was burgeoning. But like other science research, it suffered from chauvinism and elitism—tendencies that George objected to quite strongly. He believed that relatively untrained people could provide data that are useful to science and that they could be trained in relatively little time. By going to where the animals were, a new program could stress original research over more structured education, and by spending most of her time at sea, an oceangoing ship would serve as a platform, a "crossroads," where all kinds of people doing all sorts of research could contribute and explore. Soon after George left SEA, he acquired *Regina Maris* with that goal in mind.

But if the science is what's primary, I asked, then why an old barkentine? A leaner operation would certainly cover more ground at less cost, and you could do the research a lot better with a fast ship, ample lab space, and modern hydraulics, just for starters.

"There's no question about it," George replied. "I guess I'd have to say it depends on what one means by 'teaching science.' If you're talking about handing down a body of information or a set of technical skills, there's no doubt that we could do it more efficiently. But we are more interested in science as a habit of mind that looks at all sorts of things and asks, 'How do they hold together? How can I make them work?' What *Regina* offers is the primary experience; it forces you to look at things as they are. It teaches you to *see.*"

I wondered what leads a man to give up his own research, and a deanship at Harvard Medical School, to spend so much time at sea aboard *Regina* in cramped quarters in the company of students. "What's the allure?" I asked.

"The allure of life at sea, I suppose, is its simplicity. On shore—especially in institutions—things are dependent on so many factors that the end results of what you do are nearly always out of your control. Nothing is ever quite completed. This life has its own discomforts and frustrations, to be sure. But the way things turn out here is a direct result of what *you* do, your own skill and judgment. And there's a way to gauge each day's success; you can mark it off with a pencil on a chart, as progress toward a goal."

"You mean there's objectivity."

"That"—he jabbed his finger at the sea—"is *real.* It's *there.* It will fascinate you. It can feed or kill you. But there's nothing *mean* about it, nothing wasteful."

"What about it translates to our life on shore?"

"Mortality."

Pat interrupted. We are back in commercial shipping lanes; he had the watch and was concerned about a freighter that seemed to be bearing down. "I've been keeping an eye on them," George said. "It's OK. They just want a closer view."

"Do you know the expression *nitchevo?*" he asked, once Pat had gone. "It's a Russian word. Means 'What the hell!'" I shot him a dubious look.

"Well, more or less. Anyhoo, it describes an attitude toward life. You've got it. So do most of the kids on board. I suspect it's what most of that bunch in Cambridge whom you run with—or sometimes think you want to run with—lack. They've got it all planned out: 'lifestyles,' careers. If they could, they would abolish weather. But they're missing something, Harvey. *Nitchevo!* They never learned how to go out on a limb. They're afraid to make mistakes."

A lighthouse loomed off the starboard bow. Cabot Island, Bonavista, Baccaliue . . . This one was Cape St. Francis. Every point's now labeled; we are nearing home.

"Are you talking about work or play?" I asked.

"It's interesting that you should say that. You remind me of something my father once said when I was about your age that made a big difference in my life as I got older. He said that a lot of folks spend most of their lives doing one thing in order to be able to do another. They are always trying to get through what they are doing to 'make time' for something else, and they wind up resenting both things.

"But life doesn't work like that. The only way not to resent the expenditure of time and effort is to devote yourself to the one activity you don't want to get *through*. You should choose as your life's work whatever feels most like play."

To get to the capital of Newfoundland, you sail south past mile after mile of unbroken sandstone cliffs until you reach Cape Spear. This is the easternmost point in North America, topped by a solitary lighthouse perched so high that it looks like a space-ship landing through the fog. A bit farther on, you reach Signal Hill, a 500-foot-high hump of stone on top of which sits a castle; here Marconi received the first transatlantic radio transmission. Then comes a chink in the wall. Sailing through, you find your-self in the Narrows, Signal Hill hanging over you to starboard, the Fort Amherst light just as close to port, its foghorn echoing. It's like a keyhole. All at once, you are through; the harbor opens up, and there, no more than a mile off, sits a city of 130,000 people.

St. John's is the only city I have seen whose entire downtown fronts on an active pier. We tied up at the promenade on Harbour Drive, one of several dozen ships moored bow to stern. To be suddenly set down beside buildings, crowds, and Friday night traffic was a shock; the speed at which everything moved felt strange. It was even stranger, furling sails, to glance out along the royal yard and see shop girls selling leotards in a seventh-story mall.

Ashore, the first order of business was the phones (we have not had news of home for fifty days). Here Lawrence led the charge. By now every corner of the fo'c'sle has been crammed with tiny reindeer vests and Inuit toys for his four-year-old, Teli-lah, and for the last week he has talked of little else. Tonight he finally reached her from a phone booth on the pier. It might have been a hot tub, from the way he looked when he returned.

Where I called, no one answered. I consoled myself with a cold freshwater shower. Back on deck, an equally well scrubbed George and Ann were heading out to dinner. He sported flannels and a navy blazer; Ann wore black and held him by the arm. He looked every inch the old whaling master, just returned to his young bride. Lawrence waved as they walked off. He had volunteered to stay on board tonight and put the kids to bed.

In the Lighthouse Bar, on Water Street, it was half past nine, a good-sized crowd on hand. Before our beer and burgers arrived, the manager stopped by. "You're the crew of that tall ship, aren't you?" he asked—and returned our cover charge.

As the night wore on and the place warmed up, everyone joined in the singing. Several times the folksinger on stage called attention to "our guests, the crew of *Regyna Maris,* just returned from Greenland." Later, having moved through "Jack Was Every Inch a Sailor" and "The Cliffs of Baccalieu," he called for quiet and announced that the next song was in our honor. It was "I'se the B'y":

Ohhhhhhhhhhhhhh . . .

I'se the b'y that builds the boat
And I'se the b'y that sails her!
I'se the b'y that catches the fish
And takes 'em home to Lizer.

(chorus)
Hip yer partner, Sally Tiboo!
Hip yer partner, Sally Brown!
Fogo, Twillingate, Moreton's Harbour,
All around the circle.

Sods and rinds to cover yer flake
Cake and tea for supper,
Codfish in the spring o' the year
Fried in maggoty butter.

I don't want your maggoty fish
That's no good for winter,
I could buy as good as that
Down in Bonavista.

I took Lizer to a dance
And faith but she could travel
And every step that she did take
Was up to her knees in gravel!

This is the quintessential Newfie song. Everyone there
joined in and walloped on through the whole thing several times.
As the pace picked up (and the variants on Lizer's knees moved
slowly toward her waistline), I leaned back in my chair, recalling:
Fogo, Twillingate, Baccalieu, the sods and rinds on Pierce's flake
. . . and *I*'se the b'y that sails her.

Looking up from the table, I found Judy watching me.
Her cheeks were mottled. "Harvey," she said, "I am a little bit
drunk, so there's is something I have to tell you." She was smiling, but her voice had the warble it gets when she is moved,
and when she spoke, the words came in a torrent: "I have been
watching you these past two months, and it has been a pleasure
to see the changes. For a while, I think, the life aboard ship
came harder to you than to some of the others. You seemed,
well, *rigid,* and you resisted, fought it tooth and nail every inch
of the way. But bit by bit you became more relaxed and involved and let it take hold of you and got into it and you grew
so—*helpful*—and, well, I just think, and others have noticed

too— and it's been a really important and wonderful part of *our* voyage—"

"Thank you," said the singer through his microphone. "Thank you all so very much. And to our friends who are heading out to sea again, safe journey. Long may your big jib draw!"

22 August. Docked, St. John's.

We woke up early to a perfect summer morning, with a hint of heat already in the air. It was Saturday; field day began right after breakfast. Except for a taxi dropping off three wobbly sailors, the promenade was empty. But on forty vessels up and down the pier there were people swabbing decks, hauling ice and trash out of open hatches, mending nets, and coiling down.

We were moored bow to stern with a Faroese side trawler and stern to bow with two Portuguese "pairs." As Lawrence explained, these boats always trawl in tandem, with their net stretched between them. Though there was empty space on the pier behind them, even here they were lashed side by side. On the *Ave Maria,* a man in a soccer shirt and a black beret with a mug in his hand chatted across two rails to a man in another beret, with a mug in *his* hand, on the stern of *Conceição Vilarinho.* The odor of espresso and the sound of Portuguese like birdsong wafted across *Regina*'s stern.

After morning meeting, as the watchbill was reviewed, I realized that we would be off until four P.M., back on from four to six, then off again until midnight (bedtime), and then off again until noon. A miracle! We piled into an air-conditioned van and drove off to meet John Lien.

John is a scientist at Memorial University, where he directs the Whale Research Group in the Extension Unit. An American, John came to Newfoundland thirteen years back, when involvement in Vietnam War resistance culminated in his being shot, which inspired him to flee. Now fortyish, he sounds younger but looks older around his brow and eyes. His manner of speech is strikingly direct and gentle, and his smile is a little wan; it makes his handsomeness seem incidental. When we were introduced in the vivarium today, a fledgling osprey clung to his right arm.

After a tour of the facility, we settled down in John's office, where he told us about the project's work with humpback whales. It's important to understand, he began, that whales come to Newfoundland for the exact same reason people did, and do—to catch fish. Since the different species are competing for the same resource, it is inevitable that whales will sometimes collide with fishing gear or get tangled in the gill nets. The animals can cause great damage, and if held beneath the surface, they will drown. Until 1977 the problem was not serious; only three to five whales were entrapped each year. But in 1978 that number jumped to 40, counting minke whales and basking sharks; in 1979 it swelled to 58; and by last year it had reached 150, more than half of them humpback whales.

There are several likely causes for this increase, John explained. First of all, the whales' numbers themselves may have increased after the Canadian ban on whaling took effect in 1972. There are anywhere from two thousand to four thousand humpbacks in the northwestern Atlantic, and estimated changes in the population range from a decrease of 14 percent to an increase of 8.5 percent per year.

A second explanation has to do with bait abundance. The late 1970s saw the demise of the great factory trawlers. Victims of their own efficiency, they had succeeded in doing what no fleets for five hundred years before them had accomplished—they depleted the fish stocks of the Grand Banks. Among the spawning concentrations overfished in the Banks' south area were the capelin, herringlike fish that form the main local diet of humpback whales. The loss of capelin may in turn have driven the humpback population in toward the northeast coast of Newfoundland. It certainly made them fish more competitively. Between 1974 and 1978, inshore sightings rose by 300 percent, and in Holyrood

Bay, whales were seen around the cod traps one hundred yards from shore.

Ironically, during the same period, technology was also expanding the humans' inshore fishing zone. Whereas in 1969 fully 28 percent of the vessels used had been rowboats, a decade later most of the boats were larger. From 1973 to 1978 alone, the amount of gear placed underwater tripled. And the gear itself changed too; where whales caught in cotton and hemp had been able to tear free, those now snared by synthetics couldn't: 42 percent of entrapped whales died.

There is no question, John reiterated, that the threat was real. We were talking here about small-scale fishing, often family operations. Trapped whales must be cut out of nets. The nets must then be brought ashore, repaired, and reset, and the downtime involved in doing all this can cost a small fisherman half of the very brief spawning season. Freeing the whales can itself be dangerous, especially since most Newfie fishermen live their lives on frigid waters and do not learn how to swim. And a village's entire beach and harbor can be fouled by a single rotting whale.

In the eyes of those whose gear was struck, they were being victimized, yet the rest of the world (which pontificated on preserving whales) didn't give a damn. On the one hand, the government refused to provide compensation for torn nets and lost income. On the other, radical conservation groups opposed any attempt to control the animals whom local folks regarded as a fish, like any other. Suspicious of outsiders, some of the villagers began taking things into their own hands.

After the 1978 season, the Upper Trinity South Development Association gathered 542 signatures for a plan to resume the banned whale hunt, and at least one whale was riddled with bullets in an atmosphere of gruesome carnival. Emotions were not calmed by six collisions between baffled whales and boats, nor when, in the village of Salvage the following year, a breaching humpback landed on a dory. Helplessness compounded anger and depression. Two populations, one human and the other cetacean, found themselves in conflict. Each was entrapped by their shared dilemma; both were suffering and confused.

This was the situation when John and his team arrived in 1979. Their immediate goal was to turn antagonism into cooperation. The first step in enlisting anyone's support, John believes, is to make yourself useful to them. He began by setting up a Whale Damage Report Card with the help of fishing unions and the local papers. By calling a twenty-four-hour toll-free number, fishermen could report entrapments. These reports made it possible to document damage and delineate a pattern. If a whale were alive, the research team could offer advice by phone or hop into cars at all hours of the night and go speeding off to distant outports. There, by observing entrapments in process, they started to develop a technique for rescue.

In 1979 the team received 328 calls from St. Mary's and Bonavista bays. In 1980 the number of calls rose to 813. As discussions with fishermen increased, John's group began to train them to report the incidents more carefully, to recognize humpback whales, and to distinguish them from basking sharks. "Is the animal longer or shorter than your boat?" they would ask. "What portion of the animal extends beyond the net?" Questioned in this way, the fishermen proved extremely accurate observers. By enlisting them in the process rather than telling them what they should do, John was able to develop trust in both directions.

This became important in establishing a major tenet, namely, that it was to the fishermen's own advantage to save trapped whales. Traditionally, whales had been allowed to die before being cut free, mainly because the men were afraid to get close to the living animals. But drowned whales often sank, and this multiplied the cost of losses. Using information that the fishermen themselves provided, the Memorial group realized that fewer than 15 percent of the humpbacks who became entrapped were adults; most were juveniles. By confronting these young animals, who were inexperienced and scared, the fishermen had been getting them even more riled up, leading them to thrash about and drag through additional gear.

The rescue team responded to such crisis situations with a blend of patience, goodwill, and guile. Upon arriving at the scene of an entrapment, they would first engage in a long, quiet talk with the fishermen, asking them which lines needed to be freed. In the course of explaining and advising, the local men would forget a little of their own fear and anger, and in the time that took, the trapped animal could habituate to the unfamiliar human presence. After an hour, when the whale was calm, the rescuers would slip into the water. Using special tools to maximize their distance from the whale, John's team (in the water) and the local people (in a boat) would work together to save both net *and* whale. Within two years their success rate had risen to 75 percent.

As far as releasing went, John had in effect motivated the fishermen to cooperate with the whales as a way to save fishing gear. When it came to *preventing* entrapments, he enlisted the cooperation of the whales themselves. Humpbacks, as our own encounters have made clear, are far from stupid; they can recognize and they can learn. Fishermen report that the chance of a collision decreases the longer a trap stays in the water. It stands to reason, therefore, that if you could set up a warning signal whales can understand but fish cannot, you'd be doing both the whales and fishermen a favor.

Various methods have been tried, all with the fishermen's advice and consultation. Visual cues seems less effective than aural signals such as "clangers" and "pingers." Someone has even tried replacing gill nets with nets of compressed air, like those the humpbacks use, but none works especially well. Happily, though, the need for such devices may become less urgent. The capelin stocks have been coming back strong, the humpies have been moving back offshore, and the whole intense experience can be filed, as it were, in the category of important lessons learned.

What are these lessons? First, suggested John, that the conflict between man and whale in Newfoundland was a conflict over food, reflecting a much larger competition worldwide. The question that it raises is, most simply, Are human beings willing to share what the earth provides with other species? Second, that a nonconfrontational mode of solving problems requires endless tact, ingenuity, and patience. In the face of the villagers' initial distrust, any kind of aggressive Greenpeace-like tactic would have been arrogant and counterproductive. For if the entrapments made clear just how interwoven ecological relationships can be, they also made clear that the villages depending on the sea had lost their social fabric. Under all sorts of external pressure, outport fishing was being reduced from a way of life to a business, judged solely by costs and benefits. In such a climate, the people didn't care about whales per se or the threats these animals face worldwide; they only saw their own livelihood threatened and were ready to go after the guilty parties. John cannot count, he remarked, the number of interviews, polls, and community meetings that took place—so many in fact, that he probably spent more time attending them than in the field.

That these meetings were not merely necessary but were the very heart of the enterprise is his final observation. For environmental and political values can't be separated, and a social fabric that's been torn must also be rewoven. This cannot be done by outsiders or by experts but must arise from the people involved at the local level. Thus the most important aspect of the Whale Watch operation was its work in training fishermen to do the work themselves, once the rescue teams had gone.

Have they succeeded? Here John smiled. He said that a fellow in Trinity Bay who had been their most vociferous opponent three years back now boasts that he has personally released seven healthy whales.

Our talk turned to other animals. Actually, John suggested, there may be other species whose ecological significance is much greater than that of whales, animals on whom it makes more sense to concentrate our studies. Because biology is regular (with modifications), we could learn as much, or even more, from humble creatures such as the field mouse. John would like to do more with common birds. His graduate work concerned the effects of food deprivation on creativity in swine—a topic, he said with a rueful smile, that has significance for feeding the Third World.

What struck me in these observations, even more than their inherent thoughtfulness, was the extent to which what John Lien thought was of a piece with the way he said it. The word *humble* cropped up several times, used in a way it is not used often: as a term of praise. I admired this and was moved to find out what inspired it in John.

Earlier, he had said that he wants to get out of the rescue program now, alluding to the stress of a job in which gasoline bills alone ran three thousand dollars a month. "And," he had volunteered laconically, "there are all sorts of costs for your private life." Judy had told me earlier that because of his "antiwar wound," John's lung occasionally collapses, and his wife must speed him to the hospital. With that in mind, I asked him why he undertook the rescue work in the first place.

"There was this problem that I'd heard of," John replied, "and nobody else was dealing with it. So I set out to find a solution. It was one of those things that life presents by accident, and you just can't refuse."

The staff had laid out some sandwiches. As we walked down the hall to eat lunch, a student pulled John aside: "You busy?"

"What's up?"

"If we can get hold of Andrew's boat, there's seven eagles on the cliff above White Cove, and . . ."

Eight P.M. The Agnes Pratt Home for the Aged, on Old Topsail Road. We are sitting in rows of bridge chairs, facing our hosts, in an opposite row. The accordionist is ready. We've been given nonalcoholic punch and copies of *Old Time Songs and Poetry of Newfoundland* and been asked to sing along. Ignatius Aloysius stands by the piano, leading. Five foot one and silver-haired, with his black suit buttoned to his breastbone and his vest buttoned up to his throat. " 'I'se the B'y'!" he cries, his small eyes twinkling. . . . 'A Great Big Sea Hove in Long Beach.' Now 'Lukey's Boat.' " After a rollicking version of "The Killigrew's Soiree," he decides on a change of pace and calls for "Let Me Fish Off Cape St. Mary's."

This is my favorite song of all, sung sweet and slow and plain. In an Irish tenor, Ignatius starts:

Take me back to my Western boat,
Let me fish off Cape St. Mary's,
Where the hag-downs sail and the foghorns wail
With my friends the Browns and the Clearys.
Let me fish off Cape St. Mary's.

Let me feel my dory lift
To the broad Atlantic combers,
Where the tide rips swirl and the wild ducks whirl,
Where Old Neptune calls the numbers
'Neath the broad Atlantic combers. . . .

By the time the second verse is over, there is something special, something intimate and unexpected, in the air. Pausing at his piano, the old choirmaster senses it and asks if one of us would like to take the lead. All heads turn instantly toward Lawrence. He puts down his book, and it is straight from the heart that the words now come, borne on the swells and eddies of his rich bass:

Let me sail up Golden Bay
With my oilskins all a-streamin'
From the thunder squall where I hauled my trawl
And my old Cape Ann a-gleamin'
With my oilskins all a-streamin' . . .

Let me view that rugged shore,
Where the beach is all a-glisten
With the capelin spawn where from dusk to dawn
You bait your trawl and listen
To the undertow a-hissin'.

When I reach that last big shoal
Where the ground swells break asunder,
Where the wild sands roll to the surges' toll
Let me be a man and take it
When my dory fails to make it.

As Lawrence sings these lines, his eyes close. I recall him standing in that spattered dory, pulling its plug at sunrise, eight long weeks ago. As he moves into the last verse, our hosts' bodies sag in the row of bridge chairs. They seem to be looking off into a distance, through eyes that are filling silently with tears.

> Take me back to that snug green cove
> Where the seas roll up their thunder.
> There let me rest in the earth's cool breast
> Where the stars shine out their wonder—
> And the seas roll up their thunder.

Back downtown, on Water Street, the Ship Inn. Over by the fire, Bill shares a table with a man of sixty-five with the long nose, upturned mouth, and close-set eyes of a Gallic peasant. Huge hands protrude from the cuffs of his frayed and tightly buttoned jacket. He is playing the fiddle while he talks, playing it so heedlessly that it seems like an extension of his body; so effortlessly that you get the feeling he could fiddle in his sleep. It's a crazy jig he's sawing out, full of sliding tempos and false codas. Bill has fetched the concertina from *Regina* and is struggling, vainly, to keep up. The old man smiles encouragement, like a kindly music teacher; each time Bill falls behind, the fiddle part improvises, loops back, gathers him up, and continues, making anything Bill plays sound like the lead. When Bill goes to the men's room, the old guy picks up the pace, like a parent setting off alone after strolling with a child. The last thing I hear as I head out for midnight watch is the fiddler's voice, saying, "Dat come to me in one night in a dream of water. I call it de 'Happiness Reel.' "

Our guests for a dinner on board had been a research group who had just arrived from Fogo Island for R&R, with whom we hooked up again at the Ship Inn. One was a woman with strawberry hair named Janet. When I left the bar, she said she would see me later. Now, at ten to one, she shows up at the dock. "Long watch," she says, and smiles, and steps across the rail.

We sit, leaning back on the break of the deck, and share the hard cider she has brought. It's a wonderful summer evening—

tranquil, warm. At one-thirty Joan comes aboard with a fellow named Dan. At two it's Bill, with a woman carrying his concertina. A deck lamp has been rigged and hung from the topping lift. In its dim orange light I can see Bill's arm around the woman, their two backs leaning on the binnacle—and sliding slowly down. From the far side of the forward deckhouse I hear whispers, then Joan's laugh. I'm reminded of the campfire scenes before a battle in old films about the Civil War. Any second a harmonica will play "Tenting Tonight" or "Battle Cry of Freedom."

"Does this feel natural to you?" Janet asks.

"It feels nice."

"I mean, do you get used to it?"

It's a funny sort of life, I think to myself. At night you're magic; in the morning, you are gone.

"I can't tell you," she says, "how overwhelming this is for an outsider. What it was like to come below and step into that scene at dinner—the energy, the feeling of accomplishment and warmth. This ship, you people, all together. It's like the way a couple seem to strangers, only there are thirty of you. Like there's something secret going on between you. Like you've all been dipped in something, and it glows."

23 August. St. John's.

In 1527 an English trader named John Rutt sailed into St. John's harbor to explore it for his sovereign, Henry VIII. On arrival, he was surprised to find no less than fourteen ships already there. Eleven were Norman; one, Breton; two, Portuguese. Two centuries later, the French alone had five hundred ships in Atlantic Canada, manned by more than 27,000 sailors. At the peak of sealing, a hundred years after that, the number had swelled still further. Even today St. John's is the busiest fishing port in North America.

This morning, because of a hurricane watch, no fewer than forty-nine ships have put in to port. There are draggers and long-liners. Ten-dory bankers. Old-fashioned side trawlers shingled with rust. And a U.S. Navy vessel called the *Range Sentinel,* which Fran says is a submarine guidance ship. It bristles with spikes and domes and grids; hit the wrong control by accident, and you'd probably microwave the city. There's a Russian fishing boat close by—coincidence? Two scallopers. A green-and-red stern-trawler with seaweed dangling from its paravanes. An ocean-going tugboat. A couple of old schooners. And towering over all the rest, a barkentine, bright banners fluttering on all three masts.

On our last night in the final port of call, where I wanted to be most of all was alone aboard *Regina.* So I offered to sit in for someone else and split the evening watch with Earle. At ten, when he relieved me, I stepped off and placed some calls.

This time I caught everyone at home. One friend was stoned in his Greenwich Village studio and hadn't been out all day. "Too hot," he said. "Too hot to cook. Too hot to do anything. No, everyone's away." As he described, in great detail, the *Leave It to Beaver* rerun he was watching, I tried to stay with him, managed for a while, but then failed. "Are you OK?" he said at length. "You don't sound like you. Are you on Valium or something?"

A second friend was in her new living room, near Boston. She could not decide between butcher block and oak. The move had been a real bitch, two hours late, and seven rooms turned out to be not so large for a single person, once all the furniture arrived.

Last call: to my parents, so excited they could hardly talk. When would I visit them? my father asked. I should take the bus, he advised (and be sure to read the schedule very carefully); it would mean "less strain" than having to drive three hours. They were so relieved, my mother added; she had feared that the trip would be too tough for me.

It's a common experience, I suppose, to return from some momentous time and be surprised to find that nothing has changed, that the people you left behind are not prepared to recognize the change in you, and keep speaking to the former self that you've outgrown. It is hard to express the deflation that I felt as I stepped from that phone booth and looked at the suddenly foreign pier. As I thought of my first friend, and the raw, relentless, solitary pain that his sarcasm could not conceal, I wished I could give him a little of what had been given me, that I could let him sit for just one hour on the foretop and be healed by the clean, cold freedom of a polar sky. But I knew now that I couldn't; that was his life, and this was mine.

Or *was* it? Back there, among the people I had phoned, is where I really live, not out at sea or in port among Cape Verde sailors. What in all this experience would translate, when I reached home? What was most *me?*

I set off down the pier. Past the *Joy of Salem,* the *Aida Peixoto,* and the *Polar Explorer.* The *Étoile de St. Pierre,* the *Maria de Ramos Pascoal,* the *Sea Hunter,* and the *Seafed Margaree.*

I walked. And walked. Because of the storm, most boats had run extra lines to shore and also to one another, bow to stern, in one long chain the whole length of the waterfront. By the time I had reached its end, these ropes seemed everywhere. I began to walk slower and slower, stooping to touch each one as I stepped over it, and the sensation that this produced in me was so intense that I finally just sat down.

What had struck me about the ropes was how they were made. None of them, from the slightest jibsheets to the three-inch-thick bow-line on the *Range Sentinel,* was a single, unitary line. Each was composed of interwoven strands, themselves composed of up to a dozen more. Nor were these lesser fibers wrapped around a central core. There was none. If you separated each rope's equal parts, wound only around each other, you would have no rope at all.

This voyage, nearly over, has opened my eyes to many new things: science, sailing, history, the different cultures we have seen. I have found myself touched by each and, most of all, perhaps, by an attitude toward work, toward living, that is grounded centrally and simply in necessity.

In the company of people whose purposes appear more practical and single-minded, I have been led to ask what is necessary in my own being. And to admit that I still don't know. Though I care about whales, I am not a scientist; though I handle sails, I will never be a sailor; and the culture of this area, for all that I admire it, is not my own. In fact, in some ways the example of men like Gregg and George only heightens my personal sense of dispossession and of scatter. Faced with their example, I have often felt both envious and wistful. I have longed to find in myself an equivalent, single, central strand.

And that, tonight, is where the ropes come in. Could it be that my whole approach, this quest for "unity," is an illusion, not to be projected on oneself, or others, or the world? In a healthy ecosystem, for example, stability increases with diversity of species. The sweetness of an old guitar lies in its overtones. And a rope's strength under stress is born of many strands.

Maybe, then, the problem isn't knowing "who you really are" but thinking that you ever can know. In an age when experience is so far-ranging and the demands of daily life are so complex, perhaps integrity resides not in one "true" strand of endeavor or desire but in the intelligence and love and dignity with which each person's crazily conflicting strands are parceled, wormed, and served. That kind of strength is filamental—flexible, though prone to fray. It binds against itself, and holds.

I started back. Halfway, a Nova Scotia boat had apparently docked at high water. The lead on its after spring line wasn't clean, and now that the tide was out, there was too much strain on the bits and rail. I called down below. The captain emerged and together we slacked the after spring and stern lines. In the minute or two that this took, he seemed to be sizing me up. When we finished, he asked point-blank, "Would you be wanting a position?"

"A position?" I thought to myself. "Yes, more than anything in the world." But I had no idea what that might be or how long the next one I assumed might last.

24 August. 47°N/52°W.

Forty miles out to sea, I sit with Judy and Canan on the forward deckhouse, watching puffins. If the gannet is princely and the jaeger a dark knight-errant, then in the court of pelagic birds, the puffin is the jester. It is a dumpy bird with a black head and body, bright red feet, and fat white cheeks like moons. Above those cheeks are yellow eyes rimmed with red. Worried eyes, under quizzical, nearly vertical lids, the eyes of a harried bureaucrat. And well might the puffin worry. For stuck on the front of its face is the most preposterous beak I have ever seen: a triangular wedge half the size of its head with black and white stripes, a bright yellow spot, and a tip colored tropical orange.

Like their relatives the murres and the penguins, puffins burrow in crevices on rocky coasts and eat small fish and shellfish. Their colonies are not as large as those of murres, however, and between 1978 and 1980 their numbers plummeted. During that time, the overfishing of capelin that drove humpback whales inshore toward Trinity's cod nets also deprived the puffins of their food. By the end of the great stern-trawling boom of the seventies, infant puffins by the tens of thousands starved to death and were found mummified, their bellies filled with gravel. Moreover, without the guano they would have produced, the surrounding waters were in turn depleted of the nutrients required by diatoms, on which new spawns of capelin would have fed. It's a typical story, one that illustrates, again, that where the ocean is concerned, there are no isolated acts. Any change in human habits is invariably felt across the whole web of relationships that comprise an ecosystem.

Happily, there are signs that the capelin are recovering. If they are not fished out again, there may yet be long-term hope for puffins. They will never approach their former numbers, but the species may at least survive.

One of the last great puffin rookeries in North America is on Great Island, in Tors Cove, now slipping by on *Regina*'s starboard side. Through binoculars I can see thousands of birds perched upright along the cliffs like crowds at an avian Woodstock. Many of them are literally hopping up and down. "You know the Newfoundlanders' word for puffin?" Judy asks, as a particularly chubby one torpedoes by. "Hatchetface." It's the perfectly goofy name, I think, for a perfectly Newfie bird.

25 August. 46°N/55°W. Grand Banks of Newfoundland.

Between midnight and four A.M., *Regina* passed Cape Race and tacked to eastward. As I dressed for dawn-watch, I could feel that the motion of the ship had changed. In rounding the cape, we had emerged from the lee of Newfoundland and were now exposed to swells that had crossed several thousand miles of ocean. On her new course south-southeast, *Regina* caught them four points off her bow, which was simultaneously tipped and lifted, like the corner of a label being peeled.

The result was a seesaw motion, pivoting on the fulcrum of each wave crest. When the stern plunged down, the bowsprit angled skyward. When the ship seesawed the other way, her stern rose into the air. Because *Regina* has an old-fashioned cutaway transom, the rudder was repeatedly lifted clear out of the water, and we would lose steerageway. During my stint from four to five, there were times when I'd turn the wheel and wait, and nothing at all would happen. Then the bow would pull to windward, like a wayward horse against its bridle. Or the wheel would go slack in my hands, then reverse and deliver a vicious kick. The ship felt unhappy.

At 0500 hours I rotated to the bow. No matter how much time you spend up there, there is always more to notice, more to learn. It's not the sights that change but the quality of your attention, your capacity to take interest in ever smaller levels of detail. Distinctions grow more subtle through repeated observation, in the way that rural dialects develop twenty different words for types of hills or rainbows.

For example, take *Regina*'s motion when she's meeting seas head on. When you stand atop the Logan's Locker (clear of the waves that break on board), your eyes are roughly fourteen feet above the sea. The tip of the bowsprit, sharply steeved, is four or five feet higher. When the ship is pitched all the way forward (down), its sprit (about twenty feet long) lies parallel to the surface and may even touch it. Great flumes rise on either side like inverse waterfalls and rush past at the level of your eyes, along both rails. More water pours aboard—across the catheads, through the chain brake, swirling around the bits and padeyes, crashing against the locker at your feet, where it parts, and roars around the deckhouse in two glittering streams. Then, as the ship continues to tilt backward, the bowsprit soars, until it is pointing heavenward at an angle of forty-five degrees, with its tip twenty-five feet high. The whole change happens in two seconds.

I have gauged these numbers carefully to convey the force involved. What numbers can't convey is the quality of the motion. Here conventional, extrapolated words can be misleading. *Regina Maris* most surely does not "smack" the waves. She does not "slice through" them, nor could her progress be called, by any stretch of the imagination, "bounding." Clinging to the deckhouse like a barnacle on the rostrum of a whale, what you sense above all is gravity as a great weight pushes down. What you feel is the irresistible force of wind brought to bear on an immeasurable weight of water. Your ship is the intermediary in this elemental struggle, her prow the point at which what is invisible acquires cutting form.

Coming off bow watch at 0600, I found Gregg in the aft salon, hunched over charts. He wasn't looking at them, though, and an untouched cup of tea stood by his elbow. In the dim light, with his heavy-lidded eyes, he reminded me of a fish that hovers near the bottom, resting. When this fish at length bestirred itself to step on deck, I followed.

When we pitch this hard, I asked, what keeps the ship's hull rigid? Why doesn't it bend back and forth upon itself like a piece of wire and weaken in the middle? Gregg replied that it does, over time. The process, called *hogging*, is the opposite of sagging and describes a ship whose bow and stern have fallen, like an old behind. *Regina,* he said, is "extremely hogged." I could see it if I sighted forward down the rail.

It was just before sunrise, damp, and the colorless light seemed absorbed in the mist like water in a sponge. Though I tried to recognize what Gregg described, I couldn't. "Well, look at the backstays," he suggested, arching his upraised hand. "George has them screwed down so tight that the masts are bowed." I was still at a loss, having no grounds for comparison.

"OK." He tried again. "Have you noticed the rail by the break of the deck?" We moved to the spot he had described. Between the balusters was a joint I hadn't noticed, where two sections of the rail were joined. I watched it but saw nothing.

"Feel it. Put your hand on there."

I did. The rail was flexing, open and closed, as *Regina* struggled to meet each swell and cambered over.

For the rest of the afternoon, long twelve-foot seas rolled up from the south, and *Regina* labored through them. The barometer stayed low as a "back door" front, the tail of the past days' storm, spiraled slowly out to sea. The air was heavy, suffocating. Below decks it was like the second before an elevator stops, repeated several thousand times.

In the early afternoon we altered course for the southwest, and the heaves gave way to heavy rolling. If you have ever been seasick, you know the power of suggestion in the process; once it occurs to you that you *might* be ill, it's incredibly hard to get the possibility off your mind. No matter how mild it is, the sloshing feeling in your ears and stomach grows harder to ignore the longer it goes on. By suppertime today, it had gone on for eleven hours.

On deck for the second dogwatch, we lay to as a third squall passed, followed by a pink sky and a soaring rainbow. By sunset there were clearing signs to westward. But at 2100 hours, when I turned in, the sea was still running high.

26 August. 45°N/57°W. Two Hundred Miles East of Cape Breton Island.

By the time the sun had crossed the sky again, the sea had calmed and the weather had turned ideal. Shortly before sunset, I climbed aloft to watch for the "green flash." This is the visual effect that can occur when the horizon is unbroken and the sky is free of clouds. The instant after the sun goes down, the place where it has been flares and turns green. The phenomenon is frequently talked about at sea but witnessed much less often. To increase my chances, I decided to go up to the very top yard, the royal.

The last few steps to the royal yard are very hard to manage. As it nears the the top of the third (topgallant) mast, the shroud becomes so narrow that your foot cannot fit into it. To ascend this last stretch (known as Jacob's Ladder), you essentially walk up the steeply angled wire on your toes with your chest against the mast (the friction helps) and your arms as far as they will reach around it. I still had not done this. Each time that I arrived at the critical point, I would take a step up, then hesitate and back down.

Tonight I finally did it. Standing on the footrope of the royal yard, I observed the ocean stretched before me like a sheet of gold lamé. I had spent the early morning seasick, on my knees, looking upward at the undersides of waves. Now I was gazing down on the backs of flying birds.

"Anotha' lousy day in paradise!" said a voice behind me. Bill, of course. As I turned, my hat blew off. Both of us reached for it. Both caught it, and we wound up holding it between our hands.

"Whatchya thinkin' about?" Bill asked, once he had sat down. We both faced forward, legs hanging over the front of the yard, on opposite sides of the mast.

"This trip," I replied.

"Regrets?"

"Not really. You?"

"I didn't get to tee off of an iceberg."

"Maybe next time."

"Yeah." The squinty grin. The display of teeth.

"What else?" I asked.

"About getting home. About the *Leavitt.*" I waited. When he didn't say more, I asked whether he still thinks about it often.

"Haahvey, there's a joke in my hometown, now. My hometown. You know how it goes? 'They called that boat the *Leave-it,* and—'"

"I've heard it, Bill."

He paused, then spoke more quietly: "Do you know what that boat meant to me? We built her. And we lost her. A big part of me is still down there on board that boat, and it always will be."

The sun had become a red ball close to the horizon. A bright band stretched between it and our bow, like a river through the sea. "I'm on at twelve," Bill said, as he stood and turned. "Betta' snag some Zs." As he descended Jacob's Ladder, sunset turned the crown of his blond head scarlet. I could see it shining through the shrouds.

Still hoping to catch a glimpse of the green flash, I stayed where I was until my watch began. But the sun did not oblige me. It just flattened, and then went down.

27 August. 44°N/59°W.

The expedition's research report, *An Ecological Study of Whales, Seabirds and the Marine Environment off West Greenland and Eastern Canada,* has now been drafted. Altogether, there were twenty-two "hydrographic stations" at which we conducted sampling. We observed ten species of cetaceans and sixty-two different humpback whales.

Of the thirty-seven sighted off Newfoundland and Labrador, sixteen percent had been previously photographed; of the twenty-five off Greenland, not one. This means that the Greenland whales are probably a discrete population. Extrapolating from the number seen in the area searched to the total area they are thought to occupy, it appears that the number of Greenland humpbacks is quite small—only one or two hundred. If this is true, even the annual take of ten that is currently allowed may reduce the breeding pool to beneath required numbers and cause that population to decline.

Some facts and figures:

- Until men began to kill them, whales were the dominant animal presence in all seas. At the start of the eighteenth century, in the Gulf of St. Lawrence, they were in such abundance and came so close to the land that they could be harpooned from shore.
- At that century's close, the density of sperm whales in all southern oceans averaged one for every twenty-five square miles.
- Between 1868 and 1911, Scottish whalers killed more than twenty thousand beluga whales in the Davis Strait alone.

261

- In one year, 1956, ten thousand pilot whales were killed on three beaches in Trinity Bay.
- Approximately four thousand whales were butchered in Williamsport and two nearby towns between 1947 and 1972. This number equals or exceeds the number of humpbacks now alive in the entire North Atlantic. There were once more than a hundred thousand.

Every time that I have seen a whale, its beauty, power, and intelligence have been self-evident. When I look at these animals close up, when they look back at me, I am therefore moved to ask: Did our forebears in their own tall ships not see what we admire? If not, why not? And if they did, how could they so heedlessly destroy it? To pose these questions is to ask how different we are from those who came before us in our perceptions of and assumptions about the natural world.

The simplest answer is, of course, historical: Our forebears killed on such a scale because they had to. So long as animal populations were incalculably great and the human population was comparatively small, no one considered that any part of nature could be seriously depleted, let alone destroyed.

But even if ignorance explains the scale of the various slaughters waged on birds and mammals, it can't account for the savagery with which their decimation was pursued or the rage that was as thorough as it was wanton. It can't account for the clubbings by the hundred thousand or the burnings and skinnings alive or the attitudes of Victorian gents who regarded such activities as sport.

Nor can ignorance explain why the killing of many species continued after its practical payoff had passed and its long-term effects were known. As the profit went out of whale oil, for example, whalers might kill a humpback and keep only its baleen. Or they might strike a sperm whale and cut out just the melon. In the last days of the Hudson Bay whale fishery, ships would fire on more bowheads than they could possibly pursue, knowing full well that some of the wounded whales would simply bleed to death or try to hide under the ice, get trapped, and drown.

In this kind of hunt there was no sense of reciprocity or gratitude to what one killed, no sense of cycle or of season, such as Inuit hunters had. This approach, to the extent it was thought through at all, was linear, exploitative, sequential. Is one species in decline? Find another to destroy. Has technology made the kill unnecessary? Invent a new need to perpetuate it. The reasons for which whales are killed now have outstripped not only necessity but also decency and common sense. The ten thousand pilot whales alluded to were used to fatten minks for furriers. The whales that were butchered in Williamsport became pet food in Japan. There is only one remaining use for sperm whale oil—as a lubricant in the guidance systems of ICBMs.

It is a strange coincidence but, the more one thinks about it, apt. Perhaps the kind of mind that could still countenance the killing of a sperm whale and the sort that can produce and contemplate the use of nuclear arms have something critical in common. To try and name it is to move beyond what we *should* do to what in ourselves prevents us, as a group, from doing it, from instrumentality to motivation. Unless we can figure this out, all the rational planning of the biologists—their calculation of takes and yields—will be in vain.

In his parable of Moby Dick and Ahab, Melville saw the hunt as emblematic of something in our culture. He intuited the spiritual void that "drove" it and envisioned where its private, grim obsessions and rapacity might lead. Much as I revere that book, however, there is little in its underlying Calvinist milieu that allows a way out from its centripetal dark core toward a different kind of relationship to the earth and nature. Perhaps we must seek that way out in alternative traditions.

Early on in the Jewish Passover seder comes the story of four sons. They are identified as "wise," "simple," "foolish," and "wicked," depending on the questions that they ask. The wicked son is the one who asks his father, "What is the meaning of this service to you?" Why is this wicked? Because, it is explained, by saying *you* instead of *us,* he excludes himself from the group and denies his obligations to it. What is "wicked," in other words, is not the conscious commission of an evil deed but the capacity for separation and denial of connections, which Ahab represents in the extreme.

The concept of group loyalty, and of renewal grounded in the legacy each member willingly takes on, is terribly important. For it shifts the emphasis from an individual in relation to his God to the individual as member of a group—from *conscience,* expressed as private thought, to *conduct* toward all of God's creation.

That suggests some possible answers to my earlier questions. First of all, it provides a way of understanding how the various holocausts on wildlife occurred. In order to conduct such slaughter, our forebears had to have assumed an implicit separation between themselves and the objects of their slaughter, between their own well-being and that of what they killed. This fundamental lack of respect for the other extended across the board, from whales to spearbills to Beothuk Indians to Skrellings.

Second, it reminds us not to assume that we are better than they or inclined to inflict less harm. Because the current threats to ocean life are environmental and diffuse, they are easier to deny. Since people don't live in the ocean, it has no constituency, no local representatives. To change our behavior for the sake of results we won't immediately see, to take steps that may not bear fruit until after we ourselves are gone, requires a motive.

That motive can't be altruism. Most of what people claim to do for the sake of others has more to do with themselves than with the actual deed, and in any case, arguments derived from "should" do not change minds.

What might the motive be? For early Jews, the emphasis on loyalty to tribe derived from a sense of threat; group cohesion was a means of survival. Given how close we have brought one another to extinction, maybe our only hope as a species is to expand that sense of the threatened tribe to encompass other species and extend our use of the pronoun *we* considerably further than was previously dared. Having so long exercised dominion as permission to destroy, we must reimagine it as *stewardship;* we must shepherd on a global scale.

The Creation is at our mercy. We have made ourselves responsible for the life that ours depends on, from copepods to whales. To think differently about these animals is to think differently about ourselves as well. From now on, we must all stand watch. One tribe. One family. One crew.

28 August. 43°N/63°W.

It's becoming hard to tell who has the watch and who's off duty. Nobody wants to stay below. Last night we passed Sable Island far to starboard. Today we are fifty miles south of Nova Scotia and less than three hundred east of Maine. It is time to prepare *Regina* for arrival.

Patrick lies face up in the bowsprit netting, painting the ship's figurehead; though he wiggles the paintbrush deep inside her bodice, she continues to stare seaward with her usual fierce gaze. Back aft, wherever you look, someone is sanding and goobering, scraping and slushing. Serving the ratlines. Scouring brightwork. Oiling teak lizards and lignum vitae bull's-eyes. Shining the bell, and the little collars of brass around each hole in the pinrail. Pounding the chains and anchors. "Rust never sleeps!" warns Joan.

It is traditional for sailors to honor their homebound ship this way. And as every captain knew and ours knows, it is cheaper to make your crew perform such work at sea than pay to have it done on shore. Be that as it may, *Regina*'s looking better now than on the morning we left Boston.

"Sailing was a gift my father gave me," George says, reminiscing. It's a dream of an afternoon: high cumulus, blue skies, light wind. The ship is scarcely moving. We are over the Sable Island Bank, with only ninety fathoms under keel, on the lookout for bottlenose whales.

On the fantail Root is playing his guitar. When I pulled back the curtain of his bunk to wake him, I saw his two feet pointing up—and a third, between them, pointing down. Now even his Tom Waits croon sounds happy. Nearby, Rob and Jack are sprawled across the steering box like seals on a harbor rock. "A wake off the stern," Jack exclaims, "a wake off the stern!" Better that than asleep on the bow.

We are standing, George and I, near the break of the poop deck. What has brought forth the mention of his father is the sight of his own children at play. Pierce is being typically fearless as he walks along the fife rail. "Pierce-o," George reminds him, "you be careful." Pierce-o crinkles his nose and glances at his little sister.

Dominica, not yet three, stands fifteen feet above him on the mainmast shroud, wearing overalls, a life preserver, and a tiny harness. Her mother stands on the shroud two steps below, with the harness tethered to her waist and an arm on either side of her daughter. But Ann isn't helping Dominica; she is letting her climb on her own. As they toddle toward the seventh batten, George squints upward, smiling proudly. "Hey, Dominica-nica, whatcha' doin' up there?" he calls.

But she's all business, can't be bothered, so he turns back to me. "Now *tell* me, Harvey. I've been mulling over something that you said last week, and it strikes *me* that . . ." There is something very nice, these days, in the way he offers his opinions. Phrases I hadn't heard before creep in: "as you well know"; "you've seen enough to understand"; "as you yourself can vouch for." Or, in response to a comment of mine about *Regina,* "There is something about the old girl, no question. I can see you've caught it. Yup. She's got you too." Then Dominica starts to howl.

Her mother and she are back on deck. Dominica is staring up at where they've been. Big tears pool in her wide eyes and roll down her upturned face.

"Domi*nica,* " George says, "what's the *matter?*"

"Did she get frightened?" I ask Ann.

"Hardly. She's upset with me. She didn't want to come down."

＊＊＊

When I asked to join this expedition last winter, my pitch to George was twofold. In addition to the writing I would do to help obtain future grants, I'd provide an "elective course" on the literature of the sea, "to help fill up free time." How he managed to keep a straight face I do not know.

In the past few weeks, however, he has encouraged me several times to offer a class or a reading. After fishing around for topics, I realized that what I really wanted to present was something more personal, a way to help the students in particular reflect on what they've done and seen. We have scheduled a time for tomorrow, after supper.

Toward the end of second dogwatch, I'm on lookout. I decide to do my watching from aloft, in case a green flash occurs. All squares are set. As I reach the topgallant yard, we tack and brace. I get a free ride when the yard swings around. Then it's back off the footrope and on up Jacob's Ladder to the royal.

Something about it is different today. Because the sail is now set, the yard has been hauled upward. It is not at the level of my chest, as it was last night, but above my head—and well above where the top shroud fastens to the mast and ends. How the hell do you get to the yard when it's hauled up so high?

There is no need to, I remind myself. And before I even know that I'm going to do it, I have grabbed hold overhead, stepped off the shrouds into thin air, done a chin-up over the royal yard, and sat down, facing forward.

Nitchevo! I say it again as I catch my breath and decide to go still higher.

Question: What do you do when there's nothing to hold on to?

Answer: You stop trying to hold on.

I am standing on the royal yard. Not the footrope, but the yard itself, above *Regina*'s highest sail. A hundred feet below, I see white Vs form, vanish, and re-form around the prow. From this height, they are silent.

There will be no flash tonight. The western sky has a dusty

look from distant cirrostratus. The ocean looks like honey. I have never seen it quite so gentle, never felt such neither-wet-nor-dry, neither hot-nor-cold, translucent, ancient air.

On the level of my eyes in all directions, there is nothing. I am standing in the middle of the sky.

This week I passed the navigation test; my final fix was forty miles off. Coming down from the rig tonight, at dusk, I saw others taking theirs. There were seven people on the stern. They ranged in age from eighteen to sixty. Each one held a sextant, pointed toward a different star.

"What a piece of work is man, how noble in reason, how infinite in faculties . . . in action, how like an angel, in apprehension, how like a god. . . ." In my bunk, looking up through the deadlight now, I can visualize the stars that they were sighting, growing brighter on this long, soft evening. And the semicircle of encroaching darkness sliding east to west across the sky as if it were God's eyelid, closing. As my own lids grow heavy, I can still see seven shipmates standing on the fantail, as still as runic stones. Borne forward. Shooting stars.

At 0230 hours Gregg hears a familiar voice on the radio. He gets on and after a few minutes raises the R/V *Westward,* SEA's ship, heading out from Woods Hole. Gregg's last position on board her was second mate. When they hear that it's him, aboard *Regina Maris,* we exchange positions. Twenty minutes later, *Westward* comes into view with all sails set and her worklights blazing. We turn on our spreader lights, and the ships sail side by side.

Gregg is one big smile. When the "gam" is over, and they are back on course, I ask about the *Westward.* She's modern, Gregg says, "not *Regina.* " But that program changed his life. The chief mate, he continues, was amazing. Never lectured, never raised his voice. But the guy was always working. He just loved to fix things. Any time you came on deck, just to see him made you feel real good inside, made you want to do something useful too.

As Gregg tells me this, his face grows softer—tranquil, radiant, incredibly alive. He is describing all that is most worthy in himself and doesn't even know it.

Clay comes in, a stopwatch in his hand; our speed is down to four knots. I check the chart. It's still a good long way to Boston. We are due in on the thirty-first, and it is ORES policy that every expedition be back home on time.

That's George.

Does it mean we will have to motor in?

"Depends on when the fair wind comes."

Not if the fair wind comes, but *when*. That's Gregg.

29 August. Georges Bank.

In the talk tonight, I began with my own experience. We had a good laugh as I recalled my romantic expectations before coming on and my indignation and frustration once I was aboard. When I mentioned how everyone else seemed to have it more together, it emerged that each one of us had thought that about all the others. Everyone felt scared and stupid. Angry, too, when asked to do things that we clearly weren't ready for. What sticks in my mind most of all, I said, was the longing for something—anything—to just *stay put*. For the deck to stop moving, for the food to sit still in the plate and the plate to sit still on the table, for the compass to stop swinging every time I took the wheel.

Looking back, it seems clear that the mates did not *expect* us to be competent. What we were meant to learn in those first few days—what mattered most—was not a particular set of skills but a new way of thinking. Being mindful. We were being trained to notice everything, to make that level of awareness so habitual that it became unconscious, to pay attention in the same way that one pays out line.

"How fast is the helm responding?" "Should it be so quiet if the generator's on?" "Why is the sky to the east that peculiar color?" "Is there always condensation in the daytank gauge?" "Why is the life ring light stored upside down?" To get in the habit of asking questions was to get in the habit of answering them yourself. What you gained in the process, when allowed to make your own mistakes, was self-reliance, the ability and the desire to follow through.

Along with such independence, learned alone, came a second lesson: interdependence. All those rules! The way dishes were done. (Here Joan guffawed.) Being woken up for morning meeting, even when there was nothing to discuss. Having everybody drink the same-strength coffee.

But again, the main point wasn't the rules themselves. Nor was it to demonstrate someone's authority. ("Someone's?" Lawrence asked.) Rather, it was to break down the habit of mind that makes exceptions and desires special treatment. To replace it with a habit of heart called unity.

People around the cabin nodded. Bit by bit, I added, we began to accept, without having it defined, a code of service: of doing whatever you are doing well. Not because someone will check up or will reward you, but because the ship's very functioning assumes that individual commitments be sustained in private for the public good. So much of the pressure on land is toward seeking loopholes in order to excel; at sea it is toward refusing them in order to belong.

It all comes out so stilted when I write it down this way! Having shared a few selections from my journal and feeling the warmth that filled the room, I wanted to give something different, something I had still held back so far that was not the ship or thoughts about the voyage, not *about* anything at all, but something that was—me.

I put down the rest of my notes and instead recited two new poems.

ON PESCADERO BEACH

At first it was the puppy with blue eyes
And fur like foam, stalking the seagulls
Twice his size until he could have caught
One, but got scared, lay down, played dead, and barked
Back at the undertow— he made us laugh
And led us round the bend to some new game:

A dead whale. Was it then the stiff, split skin,
The rotten fin and stinking vertebrae
That made us whoop and rush the cliff, and scale
Its hieroglyphic clay face, grabbing
At exposed roots, ice plants, stunted pines,
Assuming, on a bluff, that they would hold?

Was it the hawk we startled from its ledge
Or the three crab legs it left behind
Which broke our contemplation of the slow
Pacific swell, provoking you to dance
That lunatic kazatsky? Cantilevered
On the brink, you made yourself the balance,

Laughing when I cried out, "Don't kick, you'll fall!"
Later, I found a monarch butterfly's
One wing stuck to the pelvis of our whale,
Detached, fluttering still, as it compelled
Whatever sun oozed through the acrid haze
To rise in quivering colors from decay.

IBIS

The drought persisted. Mornings he would stand
Among the hogs on one leg, balancing
Half sunk in that rich filth he had to probe,
To peck at curd, extending his thin neck

As if for slaughter: Bird, who having not
Invented justice, charged no violation,
Claimed no dignity his need could shame—
Just bird alone, who came at dawn, cried out

(continued)

And went on feeding. By late afternoon
The offal in his feathers dried. He preened,
Puffed his warm breast out wide, then circled off
Across the cow kraal, raising a harsh cry

From dung to heaven. Sought no witness, made
A job of drift between baked laterite
And fertile sty; flew fast, as if his wings
Could scrape the bright rust from an arid sky.

In writing these poems, I had tried to capture something of the ship's and ocean's rhythms; while reciting them, I could feel the actual rocking that seemed to accompany each line. When I finished, there was absolute silence in the cabin. It went on for thirty seconds, broken only by the creaking of *Regina*'s bones. Finally, someone said, "This is the nicest moment of the voyage."

A discussion began and went on for a half hour. It might have lasted longer, but the fore watch was due on deck. A short while later I noticed that the rest of the crew had joined us there. People were standing alone or in twos and threes along the rail, facing outward.

Curiously, no one joined me. As I stood amidships, I felt drained, like a battery that had been on charge for a very long time and then discharged totally. As if something enormous had passed through me, as if I'd been filled up only to be emptied, like, well, like a *vessel*.

Into that hollow feeling flowed another, as I realized that none of the full-time crew had said a word. My heart sank. I'd been kidding myself. Again. Gabbing on like a schoolboy about unity. To them it must have seemed ridiculous.

"Hey, buddy."

It was Al, with Bill and Fran.

"That," he said, "was what we could of used on my otha' trips."

"No foolin'," Fran said warmly. "You're all right, man. That was really in-ter-es-ting. Fuckin' A-one!" Then Al said "Look!" and pointed.

Dead ahead, over Massachusetts Bay, the sun was going down. As it sank past the horizon, it dwindled from an oblong to a point of flame. And in the moment of its vanishing, it turned from red to green.

30 August. Massachusetts Bay.

Rolling home, rolling home,
Rolling home across the sea.
Rolling home to old New England,
Rolling home, dear land, to thee.

The ship having made good speed all night, our position at morning meeting was twenty miles off of Provincetown. "Now, folks, what I propose to do," said George, "is swing over to Stellwagen Bank and find some humpback whales."

At 0800 hours the fore watch went back on. We were all well rested, having slept since twelve, and with the air so light, we decided to squeeze everything we could out of the sails. So we played with a dozen different combinations. "Stand by the main topgallant staysail. . . . Hands to your upper topsail gear. . . . Ready to port? (Yo!) Ready to starboard? (Ready!) Let go your bunts and clewlines. . . . Hawwwwl on your sheets. Good to starboard. Good to port. . . ." We luffed on toward Cape Cod.

After a lunch of two-bean salad, I sat down amidships, working on the rope mat I've been making from an old jib sheet. Weaving rope from a pattern that was serpentine, like old Celtic animal art, I had gotten stuck. Then Bill sat down to help. "Let's stop for a second," he said, "and figyah it out." We did, and I began again. Soon it was time to "whip" the bitter ends and bind them. Bill went to get some seizing line, and I stretched out athwartships, with my shirt off, on my stomach.

While soaking up the deck's warmth, I stared at the few square inches in between my face and my arm. I had personally replaced the oakum there three times. I had seen blood flow across that spot, and diesel fuel, and vomit; I had seen it under frigid, roiled water. Now it was warm and as smooth as drift-wood. I had never, I thought, felt anything so clean.

31 August. Boston. Aquarium Wharf.

On deck at 0600 hours, the only sound was the squeak of Manila in the blocks as the main watch braced the yards. A hazy calm, not of open ocean but of summer morning in the city: traffic lights changing unnoticed, newsstands opening, a million souls about to emerge and swarm.

Having spent the night near Peddock's Island, we weighed anchor at eight and entered the channel of Boston Harbor, quiet except for those who work it, to whom it truly belongs. A tug passed by; Fran shouted to her friends aboard. A police boat signaled; Fran knew them too. She swung her binoculars toward Lewis Wharf, where her tugboat *Luna* is moored, and hollered, "George, she floats!"

Aloft, alone, I straddled the topgallant yard, sipping peace and ease. I felt as if I'd been born there, a creature of light and sky. As we passed Logan Airport to starboard, an incoming plane screamed by, eighty feet over my head. From below I heard whistles and laughter: "Harvey, what are you *doing* there?!"

What I was doing was crying. I did not want to come down.

We passed Castle Island. The last time I had been there, ashore, looking out to sea felt like freedom. It was Boston's 350th birthday, the Tall Ships parade. I and a few hundred thousand others had watched them sail in, *Regina* among them, the faceless figures on their upper spars alert, unreachable as gods. And here I was, here, now, that shore deserted save for one man, walking one dog, staring at us silently . . . and me in equal silence, ninety-seven feet above the water, sailing home.

All the way to heaven is heaven, all of it a kiss. Some kisses are for love, some for commiseration; open your mouth or close your eyes—each by itself means something, and will someday mean something different; each is a wave in the sea.

Whoever loves that sea, wrote Conrad, loves the ship's routine. "*Routine:* derived from 'route,' a line of pilgrimage or travel." How widely must one travel, and how far afield, to discover the value of that word? No matter. To believe in the journey is to have already arrived. And to surrender to the long haul, willingly, is to take it and make it your own.

This was a gift.

I took it, and came down. I closed my eyes, and felt the ship I stood on bearing me through other dawns to other harbors. I thanked her. Thanked all who had ever sailed her. Then opened my heart to friends on a sunlit pier, to spring lines whizzing through the air, to shouts and laughter, names called over water, and to waves.

HOME

Five years have passed since the trip to Greenland. I would like to be able to report that I have since found the security I sought and resolved all the doubts expressed five years ago.

I can't. But if that journey didn't prove to be a turning point, it remains an enduring reference point for the way I view my own life, and the greater life it is part of, and how I would like to live.

I am of a generation often faulted for preoccupation with the self and an inability to make or keep commitments. From childhood we were relentlessly exhorted to make ourselves *special*—to achieve, achieve, achieve. Beneath that impulse (and the style of education it inspired) lay the assumption that the way to be a complete and successful human being is to cast your own net ever wider, to leave your individual mark upon more and more.

What many of us are coming to understand is that this way of living has enormous costs. We are perpetually spread too thin, fragmented, scattered. As we strain to hold together more and more, we bring less and less of ourselves to each spinning moment. In the manic pursuit of gaining and becoming, what is lost is the capacity for simply *being:* with each other, with nature, with ourselves. Not surprisingly, when we think of freedom, we locate it outside our daily round. We define it as escape.

What I discovered aboard *Regina* is that we have it backward. Freedom, Hegel said, is recognition of necessity. In exercising self-restraint, in accepting the kinds of limits that I had previously squandered so much energy evading, I experienced a sense of purpose and a kind of solidarity I'd never known before. I had gone far off to bring what mattered closer—gone to sea and come back feeling grounded—relieved of the burden of specialness, reprieved from the lonely ego, released but also reengaged.

In the past five years I have worked aboard other ships, sailed on *Regina* a few more times, and remained close with a number of

279

the crew. Judy went on to design a conservation plan for Belize and spent last summer sailing through the Northwest Passage. Bill Cowan became captain of the *Bowdoin,* Peary's schooner on his journey to the North Pole. Bill and Al at long last *did* tee off from an arctic glacier.

Patrick went back to his crowd along the Hudson River. He and his wife produce puppet theater now, and when police banned banners from a No Nukes march at the United Nations building in New York, the *Clearwater* sailed up and down along the East River with a thirty-foot dove designed by Patrick fluttering from its mast.

Gregg Swanzey has commanded half a dozen ships, including Bartlett's famous *Effie Morrison,* now called the *Ernestina.* We have sailed together many times.

Root is an engineer, now building a suspension bridge in Sicily.

Brenda was proposed to (and accepted) on the ship's topgallant yard.

Forsaking plans to find two tugboats filled with gold that she claims went down during World War II, Fran operates the *Luna* as a school in Boston Harbor. When I last dropped by, I encountered two cowed "interns" grilling her steak dinner while she lathed a miniature cannon that will be a gift for George.

At sixty-five, George Nichols finally retired as president of ORES. Newly honored with the title of master mariner, he was setting out to circumnavigate the globe. As of now, he, Ann, Pierce, Dominica, first mate Lawrence, deckhand Canan, and the crew of the schooner *Rambler* are in mid-Pacific. Passing Brazil, they lost all power. Rounding the Horn, they hit fifty-foot waves that stove in the portholes. Anchored off Pitcairn Island, Canan and her boyfriend married. George performed the service. They are all due back next year.

ORES will not be here when they return. Despite the efforts of new management, the organization could not stay afloat financially. Enrollments had been falling; a new generation of students viewed such "offbeat" programs as an interruption of careers. And government grants had been mercilessly slashed;

there were more important things to spend science money on (like Star Wars) than on knowledge gathered from the sea.

Regina Maris will be missing too. She sank last night. She was at her dock in Boston Harbor. The temperature was six below zero, the wind chill minus fifty. Shortly after four A.M., the boat-yard watchman heard a long loud crack and arrived to find everything except the mastheads underwater.

No longer seaworthy, the ship had recently been sold off to developers who would rebuild her, tastefully, they said, as a restaurant in Quincy. As of yesterday, her future seemed assured.

Today the papers blame her sinking on the freakish cold; maybe a plank sprung, or she spewed her oakum. The hull was never exactly tight. But somehow I can't help believing that she didn't *want* to end up a trendy nightspot. Maybe, after forty-two expeditions and eighty years at sea from the South Pacific to the Baltic, she had served enough and was ready. I like to think of her waiting until everyone was safe ashore, and no one was there to see, when she lowered her beautiful bulwarks to the waves at last, and said goodbye.